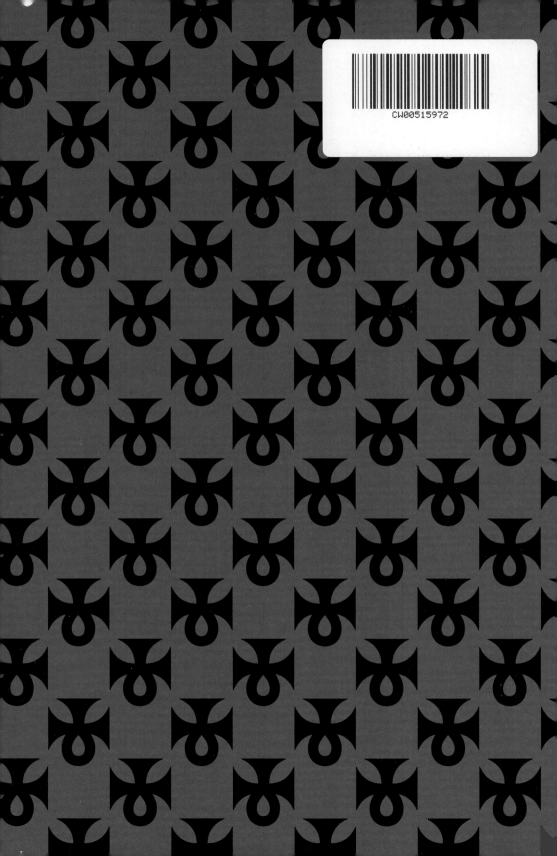

Come My Fanatics

Also by Dan Franklin

Heavy: How Metal Changes the Way We See the World

Come My Fanatics

A Journey into the World of
Electric Wizard

DAN FRANKLIN

WHITE
RABBIT

First published in Great Britain in 2023 by White Rabbit,
an imprint of The Orion Publishing Group Ltd
Carmelite House, 50 Victoria Embankment
London EC4Y 0DZ

An Hachette UK Company

1 3 5 7 9 10 8 6 4 2

A CIP catalogue record for this book is
available from the British Library.

ISBN (Hardback) 978 1 4746 2540 1
ISBN (eBook) 978 1 4746 2542 5
ISBN (Audio) 978 1 4746 2543 2

Typeset by Input Data Services Ltd, Bridgwater, Somerset

Printed in Great Britain by Clays Ltd, Elcograf S.p.A

www.whiterabbitbooks.co.uk
www.orionbooks.co.uk

For Bea

'[. . .] We know what happened to those who chanced to meet the Great God Pan, and those who are wise know that all symbols are symbols of something, not of nothing. It was, indeed, an exquisite symbol beneath which men long ago veiled their knowledge of the most awful, most secret forces which lie at the heart of all things; forces before which the souls of men must wither and die and blacken, as their bodies blacken under the electric current. Such forces cannot be named, cannot be spoken, cannot be imagined except under a veil and symbol, a symbol to the most of us appearing a quaint, poetic fancy, to some a foolish, silly tale. But you and I, at all events, have known something of the terror that may dwell in the secret place of life, manifested under human flesh; that which is without form taking to itself a form. Oh, Austin, how can it be? How is it that the very sunlight does not turn to blackness before this thing, the hard earth melt and boil beneath such a burden?'

– Arthur Machen, *The Great God Pan*

Contents

The Chosen Few

Jus Oborn – guitar, vocals (1993–present)
Liz Buckingham – guitar (2003–present)
Simon Poole – drums (2012, 2014–present)
Haz Wheaton – bass (2018–present)
Clayton Burgess – bass (2014–2018)
Mark Greening – drums (1993–2003, 2012–2014)
Glenn Charman – bass (2012–2014)
Tas Danazoglou – bass (2008–2012)
Shaun Rutter – drums (2006–2012)
Rob Al-Issa – bass (2003–2008)
Justin Greaves – drums (2003–2006)
Tim Bagshaw – bass (1993–2003)

Foreword

By Nick Ruskell

'They're the heaviest band on Earth. They're from Dorset, of all places, and the rumble they come out with could shake the fucking planet apart.'

This is how I learned of the existence of Electric Wizard, in the winter of 1998, via a feature on stoner rock and doom bands in the pages of *Kerrang!*. It would be a long time before this Sabbath-obsessed, fifteen-year-old schoolboy would actually hear what that sounded like, but my imagination was already running wild. The vibe was already there – the accompanying picture showed three burnouts in leather jackets photographed in front of a wall with the word 'Dope' sprayed on it; the recommended record had the alluring title *Come My Fanatics . . .*; I already knew how witchy bits of Dorset were, I'd been there on Scout camp.

Next to their stoner rock peers, Electric Wizard felt genuinely dangerous. From that small picture and the few comments I could find on them – bottomless pockets of drugs, almost impossible to contact, a band who often wouldn't turn up to gigs, and the ones where they did they'd spend the time jamming at dangerous volumes on ancient amps – in my mind grew visions of a world of weed smoked in rural churchyards, witches, crucifixes and headstones everywhere you looked, with endless Iommi riffs playing in the background.

When, six or seven months later, I eventually found a copy of the album in a record shop, I had to buy it immediately, worried that it would disappear and I'd never see it again. What I had in my mind, and how they'd been described to me, were both proven inexorably correct as soon as the first apocalyptic chord of 'Return Trip' fuzzed from the stereo. But whatever bad vibes I thought there would be, I didn't imagine anything like that song's 'I hope this fucking world fucking burns away/And I'd kill you all if I had my way' howl, or the 'Drugs, sex, every sort of filth' sample at the start of 'Wizard In Black'. I also hadn't anticipated that a record was *actually* able to tear a stereo speaker apart, but that's how my girlfriend's father's woofer bit the dust. A noble death.

I can't be the only one to have such a clear and memorable origin story for when the Wizard first cast a spell on them. For many, that first hit will have been a profound one, where you're left altered by it. And though the entry points will be different, the allure will still be the same: there's a powerful magic to Electric Wizard unlike any other band on earth.

Two decades and change since that first discovery, I am still an acolyte of the witchcult. I have seen Electric Wizard live more times than I can count, to ever-larger audiences, all as obsessed with the riffs and the vibes as me. I have interviewed them many times, and visited Jus Oborn and Liz Buckingham at home, where the latter has shown me the human skull a friend gifted to her, and the former told stories about teenage forays into the occult that almost killed people, and intentionally trying to have nightmarish bad trips on LSD because 'it's awesome, like a ghost train'. They are one of the few bands who have managed to keep such an atmosphere, such a mystique, about them as they grow, and only expanded their power as they've done so. There is still that irresistible black magic to them that is now so embedded in their bones, it's there forever.

In some ways, this would have been unthinkable back then. You don't grow out of something so powerful easily as a listener, but the idea of Electric Wizard's name at the top of the bill at Camden Roundhouse, or headlining a stage at Donington, was a fanciful one. They were too heavy, too apart from everything else going on, one of those frustratingly great bands who other people didn't want to concern themselves with. They were also just too chaotic.

Not that they were chasing much bigger, anyway. Half the time they seemed like they were about to split up. The first time I saw them live – at the Camden Underworld in April 2002 just as *Let Us Prey* had been released, having to drunkenly support myself with my face against a pillar, not noticing someone being sick down my back when they played – much of the gig was spent arguing and walking off, only to be pushed back onstage by staff from their then-record label. *Kerrang!* had reported a similar thing during an interview in America, when then-drummer Mark Greening apparently drank a load of bleach, and Jus smashed a bottle of beer by throwing it against the wall of a New York venue, declaring that they should go both their separate ways, and also home. Enjoy this while it lasts, I thought.

But here we are. The enduring power of the Wizard comes not from an indomitable spirit and heroic determination to push through and succeed *a la* Ronnie James Dio or Judas Priest's Rob Halford, but from being Electric Wizard. Even now, there is in a way a similar underground, word-of-mouth quality to them like there was in the day. You have to *know*. And when you do, it's almost impossible to turn away.

And Electric Wizard do indeed encompass, as my mind conjured up as a teenager, an entire world. The impact they've had on doom and the metal underground can't really be expressed as an either-or thing. It's like saying you're a fan of sunlight, or breathing oxygen, or Black Sabbath. How many bands are there trying to match the horrible, bloody-knuckled fuzz of *Come My Fanatics* . . . or *Dopethrone*? And how many, for all

3

their searching for ancient amps and pedals, manage to? How many obscure and forgotten 60s and 70s horror and exploitation movies are the underground now conversant with? How much biker iconography and occult art has become part of the fabric of doom? It's impossible to imagine the scale of it without the hand of the Wizard in there somewhere. Just as one can't imagine the band's world without it.

The difference is that for Electric Wizard, this is life. In or out of the band, Electric Wizard means to be an outsider, to live in that world, away from the normal one. As with Lemmy, this isn't simply an outfit one wears to a gig, but a deep-seated lifestyle that's only for a chosen few. Fanatics only. This goes a good way to explaining why they remain such a unique band: few others have the personality and lifer's stomach for it.

As I look back on my own memories of the Wizard to welcome you to this book, one that says much about them is a gig in the Devon seaside town of Seaton. Returning from a not entirely unheard-of period of inactivity, they had quietly been added to the bill of HawkEaster, the springtime festival run and headlined by Hawkwind, held that year in the town hall; I'd only spotted it when looking at Hawkwind's website. Arriving, we were greeted by the sight of a beer barrel on a pasting table, a painting of the Queen, a faded Union Flag, and nice, normal families with children doing egg hunts and having their faces painted as rabbits. When they came onstage at dinner time, few – that is to say, quite literally three people – seemed to know who the Wizard were. As the traditional projections of violence and nudity from vintage exploitation films rolled behind them, I remember parents leading their kids out with their hands over their eyes, their own horrified features silently asking what the world was coming to.

Eventually, after being told more than once to turn down, the lights came up and the plug was pulled. As an officious council type with their own microphone came onstage to announce that if this carried on the gig would be over and there would be no Hawkwind for anybody, I remember Jus continuing to scream into the air before eventually admitting the jig was up. The band packed up their gear while visibly laughing their heads off. As someone who seemed to know who these apparent criminals were, I was suddenly surrounded by folk half horrified, half intrigued as to what it was they'd just seen. According to Jus afterwards, the band had been told, with almost comic perfection, to leave town.

This is, to me, instructive of what Electric Wizard are about. Jus once told me, 'I hope that we stand for what everyone perceives as wrong about heavy metal,' that they were 'rebellion against normality and boredom.' On this day, when normals had to experience the band first hand, achievement achieved.

It was here that I definitively stopped thinking of Electric Wizard as a doom band, and as something more in tune with Hawkwind. Outsiders, explorers of space, wanting to blow your mind, and keeping on at it in their own world to great success away from the glare of more normal reality. Members have come and gone, but they remain as much as an idea as they are a band.

As their witchcult continues to grow, and the band mark their thirtieth year — albeit in different form than they started — there is much left to uncover about this most shadowy of collectives. This book will illuminate, but not so much that it will rob the Wizard of their mystique.

Come, fanatics. Let us prey . . .

Nick Ruskell, February 2023

Prologue
The Mirrors of Tuzun Thune

If you gaze into the mirror, what do you see?

Is it your true self, or a shadow?

How do you know the reflection vanishes into the void when you step away?

Are you reality's servant, or have you created it?

'The Mirrors of Tuzun Thune' is a story about Kull, King of Valusia, by Robert E. Howard. It was one of only three stories about the king that were published in Howard's lifetime. It appeared in *Weird Tales* magazine in September 1929.

Howard, a Texan, shouted his tales out loud as he wrote, sending them out onto the night wind.[1] He forged vivid stories of a mythic tenor. He created another world of blood, fire and ice. In time he decided that *our* world was not for him. He shot himself in 1936, when he was only thirty years old. Like the protagonists of his stories – most notably Conan the Barbarian – he became a legend after his lifetime.

In 'The Mirrors of Tuzun Thune', Kull the Atlantean is weary of the world. He is advised to see a wizard of the Elder Race who lives in the House of a Thousand Mirrors.

'Mirrors are the world, Kull,' the wizard tells him when they meet. 'Gaze into my mirrors and be wise.'[2]

Kull stares into the mirrors. In one he sees the past; in another, the future. In the mirror of the deepest magic he contemplates his own reflection and is thrown into an existential crisis: 'Which of us is the ghost of the other?' he asks. 'Mayhap these mirrors are but windows through which we look into another world. Does he think the same of me? Am I no more than a shadow, a reflection of himself – to him, as he to me?'[3]

From then on, Kull returns to the House of a Thousand Mirrors every day. He spends hours in front of the mirror that perturbs him. The business of his palace is neglected. Kull speculates that the image in the mirror has an individuality apart from his own. He starts to doubt if he has summoned the reflection, and whether instead it has summoned him. Is his reality merely the shadow of a world beyond the mirror after all?

He begins to wish he could step into that mirror and enter the personality beyond it. But he delays. If he goes beyond the mirror, will he ever return? Will he find an identical world or one far richer than his own? He is so beset by these thoughts that they destabilise his notions of what is reality and what is illusion.

The wizard Tuzun Thune lurks behind him.

'Man must believe to accomplish,' Tuzun Thune tells Kull. 'Form is shadow, substance is illusion, materiality is dream; man is because he believes he is; what is man but a dream of the gods? Yet man can be that which he wishes to be; form and substance, they are but shadows. The mind, the ego, the essence of the god-dream – that is real, that is immortal.'[4]

Kull continues to brood. Soon, he begins to dissolve into the mirror . . .

This is a book about a band called Electric Wizard. The band was formed in an old market town in Dorset. Over the course of thirty years, they have created some of the heaviest music ever. Their music expresses an intuition – a belief – that there is a world beyond this one, pressing against it. That there is a parallel reality hidden from view which their music tears into and reveals.

Electric Wizard are both well known and also shrouded in mystery. They are a cult in the true sense of the word – music tailored for a subsection of society with its own code, aesthetic and archetypes: an acquired taste. But once you step into the band's realm, it is almost impossible to leave. Their music is the sound of cosmic fear as well as the hidden horrors lying around us all the time. And their cult is always growing.

Electric Wizard are a band of fanatics. They are fanatical about their music and the things it contains: from the black mass ritual to the biker gang to the mind-melding acid trip. They demand allegiance to a set of principles that the average person is completely ignorant about. They want to be misunderstood. They want to be feared. They want to be hated.

Electric Wizard is a doom metal band – a stratum of metal music which concerns itself with the concept of judgement. The most uncomfortable truth that the band represents is that the universe does not care enough about us to judge us. We are alone. We are unlikely to be remembered. In despair, there is liberation. Electric Wizard wants you to be free.

They are a conduit for an energy that all metal bands attempt to tame. They let it flow through them more freely than most. In this way they go above and beyond metal music to that other realm. They join the ranks of artists working in other forms who have dealt with the blood consciousness of this land – an English mindset stripped of the authority of law, the tyranny of religion and obligations of society. They use isolation as a weapon against conforming to the mainstream. This book is an exploration of their attempts to reach that other intuited and transcendent realm, and the consequences it has wrought on themselves and those around them.

PROLOGUE

In Electric Wizard's struggle to reach beyond our day-to-day
to express themselves they were almost destroyed by material
reality. But then they resolved to create their own shadow world
and established themselves as one of England's greatest-ever
bands.

Theirs is a tale of transgression: how a band violates norms
and defies the rules that govern our lives – the limits imposed
upon our behaviour and our perception. More than that, it is
about transgression in the sense of crossing a boundary. This
is the story of how the Wizard stepped through the mirror –
and the chosen few of its members who were fit, and unfit,
for the task.

Chapter One

In Wimborne

We met in the shadow of the Minster. It was my first time in the Dorset town of Wimborne. I was meeting Jus Oborn, founding guitarist and singer of Electric Wizard, and Liz Buckingham, guitarist since 2003. They hadn't been in the town for a decade. We were here because this was where Jus (née Justin, but I'll refer to him as Jus) grew up and where Electric Wizard began as a three-piece in 1993, with Tim Bagshaw on bass and Mark Greening on drums.

Looking at the quaint green in front of us in the bright, early June sunshine, it was hard to imagine that Electric Wizard used to drop acid here, then party and vomit into the night.

Wimborne is important because it is where Electric Wizard began. The experiences the band had in the town were formative. Electric Wizard might have sounded as colossal if they had grown up in another part of the British Isles. But they didn't. They grew up in Dorset. The landscape, the history (recent and ancient), the drugs, the gangs, the pubs, the strange encounters and practices, the hidden networks and secret social currents of this place all fed into the early incarnation of the band and have remained, a residue, ever since.

Wimborne is first mentioned in the *Anglo-Saxon Chronicle* in 718, when the monastery was founded by Cuthburga, the sister of Ine, king of the West Saxons. The settlement is not mentioned

again until 871 when it says that King Aethelred's body 'lies
in the monastery of Wimborne'.[5] For Jus, tripping on acid here
next to the edifice containing Aethelred's tomb, the Minster
was square and solid – it was something he clung to. Here, he
communed with the bones of Aethelred, the king of Wessex (and
older brother of Alfred the Great), who died in a battle against
the Danes. His reign foreshadowed the unification of England in
the late ninth and early tenth centuries.

When they formed Electric Wizard, the members shared
stoned ideas about rising up to overthrow the Norman invasion
of 1066 and the occupation they felt *was still ongoing*. Only by
headlining a giant festival and unleashing seismic doom from
hundreds of amps could they generate the necessary power for
the English to finally throw off the Norman yoke.

The Minster houses a rare, mediaeval astronomical clock
in its west tower. It has a chained library – one of the earliest
public libraries and the second-largest chained library in
Britain. When Jus was young, the library used to be maintained
by a stooped, Quasimodo-like librarian. The building also
boasts the 'Man in the Wall', the body of eccentric barrister
Anthony Ettrick. Because he had fallen out with the church,
Etrrick vowed not to be buried inside or outside of the building,
nor above ground, nor below it. But he had a change of heart,
and his way of rowing back his proclamation without exactly
reneging on his vow was to be buried in the wall. He even
commissioned his own coffin with the year he thought he would
die inscribed on it – 1693. He lived another ten years beyond
that. His coffin resides in an inlet of the masonry.

In 1600, a woman called Mary Brewer believed she saw
the devil appear behind the priest in the pulpit of the church.
She returned later to shit on the spot where she had seen the
devil standing. A young witness, Elizabeth Sandell, thought
Brewer was acting suspiciously and approached the spot,

finding 'excrement newly done'. No punishment was handed down by the Peculiar Court that heard the case. Perhaps they sympathised with this extreme act of godly solidarity. That same year, the central spire and steeple of the church collapsed. Miraculously, no-one was hurt.

As we talked, the 'Quarter Jack' chimed for 2.15 p.m. This striking jack in the form of a soldier stands in the north window of the west tower of the church and swings his hammers to ring out each quarter of the hour. It dates back to 1662 when it was carved by a carpenter from nearby Blandford and was gowned in lead so it looked like a monk. Its current appearance – in a Grenadier uniform – dates from the early nineteenth century when it was repainted as a sign of loyalty during the Napoleonic Wars. Jus recounted the local legend of a French soldier who was taken in and protected by the local people during the war. Supposedly, the soldier hid up in the west tower when the English came hunting for him, and perhaps was even trapped in the form of the Quarter Jack.

Jus was born in 1971 and grew up in Wimborne. In the seventies and eighties, the town was rougher around the edges than the cleaned-up market town of today, in which a Waitrose now stands on the site of the old cricket pitch. Farrow & Ball, the upmarket paint manufacturer, has its head office nearby. Jus's dad, Mike Oborn, used to work at the slaughterhouse at Uddens Cross – a huge factory of death just outside of town. He came home reeking of its strange, creamy smell. Jus and friends snuck out to explore the factory, glimpsing the stains on the walls and inhaling the unmistakable odour. Working there was a traumatic experience. Mike is a vegetarian now.

The abattoir employed bikers. They used to gather in a pub called The Three Lions (now The Minster Arms on West Street). You could get a drink underage in there if you had enough of a rat 'tache. The bikers brought heroin into town to generate some more income. The Oddfellows Arms around the corner on Church Street was another intimidating establishment. It was fierce and local, and frequented by the bell ringers from the church.

Jus's mother's family is from Wimborne. Scrivens, the optician in the town centre, still bears the family name, though Rosemary was born a war baby in Colorado. Jus's father was from Weymouth. His parents sold their dairy farm and bought a house in Corfe Mullen – a dormitory village for the south-east Dorset conurbation of which Wimborne is a part, along with coastal Poole (about six miles due south) as well as Bournemouth and some other satellite towns.

Mike was a trickster figure with a high-pitched laugh, knocking about with troublemakers; participant in (but rarely the instigator of) nefarious goings-on. In the early sixties, he dressed like a barbarian, in a fur coat gilet or a leather jacket with his name written in studs on the back. He was known to wear a cutlass by his side. He also owned a shotgun. He rode a motorbike and ran with a gang of other teenage hard-nuts and imbeciles. When Jus was still a kid, Mike was a member of a four-wheel drive club down near the tank museum in Bovington, alongside Jon Lord, Hammond organ player of Deep Purple.

Jus was in a gang himself at school when he was thirteen. The members modelled themselves on the New York gangs from Walter Hill's 1979 film *The Warriors*. They drank, fought and were vicious little shits, terrorising their fellow pupils. Each member wore a denim jacket with a Hawkwind patch. Their peers mistook the hawk for an eagle, so they were known as the Eagle Gang.

We walked into the old Cornmarket plaza, past the dentist where Jus and his friends stole mercury. Mercury is a useful ingredient for black magic ceremonies. It is supposed to have supernatural powers and participants have been known to inhale its vapour from burning candles or even to drink it. (Do I need to tell you that this is a very bad idea?)

On the western side of the plaza, next to The White Hart pub, is Wimborne Masonic Hall – a former Methodist Church until 1883. Here the masons used to gather in their cloaks, sold by a jewellery shop in the town square. Where the upper windows are now bricked up, Jus's friends reported seeing people being hung up and whipped. This was not the only part of town where children glimpsed the strange and depraved. It is rumoured that the building has an entrance to a sequence of tunnels beneath the town. Jus knew a girl whose grandparents lived in Gordon House, on Wimborne's main thoroughfare of West Borough, which also had an entrance to this subterranean tunnel network. He went down there once, got about a hundred yards along and found it bricked off. There is a network of tunnels in the writer H.P. Lovecraft's Innsmouth from his 1932 story 'The Shadow Over Innsmouth', where the fictional town's Masonic Hall came to be the headquarters of a cult called The Esoteric Order of Dagon. The tunnels beneath Wimborne give the town a Lovecraftian air.

They were also useful for smugglers. Wimborne's proximity to the towns of Christchurch and Poole on the south coast of Dorset made the landing and sale of contraband a town-wide activity, with numerous gangs operating well into the nineteeth century, including the notorious eighteenth-century Isaac Gulliver. When they brought goods ashore the smugglers wore white sheets coated in phosphorus, so they glowed in the dark and spooked the locals. It was like a scene from the 1898 novel *Moonfleet* by J. Meade Falkner, or something out of *Scooby-Doo*.

From his base in the Kinson area, Gulliver operated along the coast, from Christchurch in the east to Lyme Regis in the west. The nooks and crannies of the coastline made ideal landing spots for the 'moonrakers', as did the Dorset heathland for smuggling the goods out into the county's settlements. Gulliver's cut-price, black-market goods and ready employment for local

14

men in his gangs were vital in lifting the town's citizens out of poverty – supplementing their wages when they were being kept poor by wealthy landowners. He was notorious, very popular and cultivated great loyalty with the inhabitants of Wimborne.

One popular legend about Gulliver is that he was pardoned in 1782 for revealing a plot to murder the mad king, George III. He had already amassed his own land and property near Wimborne and he went on the straight and narrow after his pardon. He started a legitimate business on West Borough in the town in 1817 when he was seventy-two years old. He even became a churchwarden. When he died in 1822, he was buried in the nave aisle of the Minster. He remains a folk hero in Wimborne – a figurehead for giving the people what they wanted, subverting the law and then ascending to an undeniable position of power and influence.

In the 1980s and 1990s, after the town's annual folk festival – four days of debauchery, music and Morris dancers – the Cornmarket more than once saw British Bulldog-type confrontations between drinkers at The White Hart pub and the police. The White Hart was a gathering place for the freaks of the town – drawn from different social (and musical) tribes but driven together by their outsider status. During one stand-off, the Wizard's former drummer, Mark, was captured by the police. They forcibly shaved his head. The folk festival connected with Jus – particularly the pre-Christian rituals evidenced in the Morris dancing. When he began finding success with his music, he felt he was similarly documenting another kind of ritual for future generations.

West Borough, heading northwards towards the Tivoli cinema, was the location of the tuck shop. The owner traded video nasties under the counter and eventually went to prison for it. Jus's mum used to rent legitimate videos but rental mistakes were made as illicit VHS tapes were mixed up with the legal ones.

For all she knew, she had brought home *Zombie Flesh-Eaters* for her kids to watch. Opposite the tuck shop was the labyrinthine doctor's surgery – the kind of place where the sadistic doctors prodded your balls when you came in complaining of a sore throat. It's now a Wetherspoons pub.

A little further up the road, the Tivoli cinema conceals a Georgian facade – inside it looks like a mini Grande Ballroom (the famous Detroit live music venue). It was designed and constructed as a cinema and theatre in 1936 by the architect Edward de Wilde Holding. The edifice was originally part of the rebuilding of the town in the eighteenth century that replaced the irregular, timber-framed buildings of wattle and daub with airy, spacious townhouses. 'Society' was established, with coaches transporting the wealthy families between their respective country piles: the Hanhams, Bankes, Fitches, Sturts and Glyns.

Jus used to sneak in through the back door of the cinema to watch horror movies with his dad. He also remembers that the queue for the original *Watership Down* stretched some four hundred feet back down to The King's Head hotel. Jus once walked past the cinema on the way to school and was astonished to see the lobby cards blazoned with naked women. They were showing a porno film in the cinema's dying days – though it might easily have been *Come Play with Me* or a similar, low-budget seventies sex comedy.

By the 1990s, the Tivoli was a rundown hellhole full of junkies – there was a hole in the roof, the place was full of rot and there was a pond in the orchestra pit. A collective of bands and other societies, groups, businesses and powerful individuals known as The Friends of the Tivoli, under the aegis of an ageing punk-rocker mayor, resolved to bring it back from the brink. At that time, there were between twenty and thirty active bands in the town, some of them signed to development contracts at major labels, though they didn't do much with them. It was in the restored venue that Electric Wizard headlined the Wimborne Festival in 1998, their final gig in the town. Electric Wizard were the shit band who everyone hated – but they ended up touring the world.

Before our trip to Wimborne, Jus sent me a documentary about the musician Robert Fripp made in 1985 as part of the BBC series *Late Night in Concert*. It's called *Robert Fripp: New York – Wimborne*. Jus's dad was in the same class as Fripp in primary school. Robert was a nerdy child and Mike and his mates used to call him 'Fripper'. He is (arguably) Wimborne's most famous son. The introduction of the TV programme bills him as the 'legendary guitarist' of King Crimson. It follows him in and around Wimborne, which the narrator says 'he considers, rather eccentrically, to be the centre of the universe'.

Made a good fifteen years after King Crimson's first album, Fripp, verging on forty years old, is full of it here. In one scene in the town's record shop, Square Records, he dispenses advice to a young musician from a band called Social Science while he signs copies of the latest King Crimson album, *Three of a Perfect Pair*: 'If you want to be successful in music in England, you have to live in London. I'm very sorry to say you can't do it from Wimborne. You have to go and live in London for seven years. Resign yourself to it. The industry in this country are [sic] in London and they are not going to come to you. *They are not going to come to you.* Even trips on the river, even tea in the Yew Tree cafe, will not seduce the industry to come down here. You have to go to them. For a period of time. And then, if you're good enough, ambitious enough, and really, really want it, maybe you'll be successful.'

Why seven years in particular? Only Fripp knows.

Around the corner from the Tivoli, we arrived at Jus's primary school. It was an authoritarian establishment where they sent pupils to a shack for corporal punishment. It was the seventies: the golden age of institutional abuse. One of the teachers was a real-life war hero from the destruction of the German *Bismarck* battleship – he was even depicted in the 1960 film, *Sink the Bismarck!* The park next to the school contained a slide which was purportedly the biggest in England – now gone. It also contained a gazebo where teenage Jus and his friends used to get stoned – still standing.

Nearby was the cemetery containing the grave of Montague John Druitt, one of the men suspected to be Jack the Ripper. Originally from Bournemouth, he drowned himself in the Thames after he had been mysteriously dismissed from the school in Blackheath that employed him as an assistant teacher to supplement his income as a barrister. His suicide shortly followed the Miller's Court murder of Mary Kelly in November 1888. Melville Macnaghten, the Met police chief who named Druitt as a suspect, stated that his family suspected Druitt of being the Ripper and that he had a reputation for being 'sexually insane'. Jus's dad and his friend – an armed robber called 'Mad Joycey' – orchestrated a black mass at Druitt's grave for the *News of the World* in the late sixties.

Down a passageway back into the centre of town we came to the old Scout hut with its flaking green paint. On Wednesdays, Nazi enthusiasts would gather inside to socialise and display their wares. The local children glimpsed swastikas through the windows. One of Jus's childhood neighbours was a member of this secret society. He invited Jus around to inspect the giant picture of Hitler on his wall and his collection of SS uniforms. He ended up being the manager of one of the town's supermarkets.

In the late eighties and early nineties, the alleyways
behind West Borough were strewn with drug addicts and the
homeless. Heroin had grown into a huge problem, catalysed by
its importation by the local biker gangs. Jus, Mark and Tim all
had friends who died of their addictions. The more enterprising
addicts made their way to Bournemouth to be nearer its source.
It affected a lot of people close to Electric Wizard and set them
against the 'black drug' forever.

Threading our way back through the town in the direction of
the Minster again, we came across the Albion pub. Jus used to
date the landlord's daughter back when there were lines of coke
on the bar and topless girls for entertainment. The landlord shot
himself in the head in the pub garden one day.

Nearby was the post office, which was always well stocked
with American horror comics to feed Jus's childhood imagination. As kids, they shot rats with air rifles around the back.
Gullivers Bookshop is still here too, which, if you didn't know
better, you might think was named after Jonathan Swift's
fictional character. Down one of the back streets was a beautiful
herbal garden tended by an old woman who the town's children
suspected was a witch.

Along the Crown Mead pedestrian route heading east away
from the centre, we passed the library with its shallow sloping
roof which often proved too tempting for the Friday-night drunks
who frequently tumbled off it. We took the footbridge over the
mill stream and came to the pedestrian shopping precinct which
was built in the mid-seventies. When Jus was very young there
was nothing here but an island bounded by the River Allen. It
was good for catching pike – one kid had his finger bitten off by
a pike next to The Rising Sun pub downstream.

This islet is believed to be one of the oldest inhabited parts of
the British Isles, though it can only be dated with any certainty
from the Saxon settlements in Wessex from the fifth century

onwards. The name Wimborne is derived from the Saxon
'*Win-burnan*'. The River Allen was known to the Saxons as the
Win(n), meaning 'meadow'. The '*burnan*' part is the origin of
what we call a 'borne', meaning stream or brook. This would
make Wimborne the 'meadow-stream'. 'Win' can also mean wine,
and Rudolf of Fulda, a Benedictine monk and chronicler, wrote
in the 800s that Wimborne meant 'wine-stream' because of 'the
clearness and sweetness of the water there, which was better
than any other in the land'.

As the settlement grew over the centuries, alluvial loams
around the town proved good for pasture and growing crops.
There was evidence of a market since 1200, when a market
and fair were held on St Cuthburga's Day (31 August). Sheep
farming provided wool, meat, milk, bone and horn. Cloth and
wool dominated the mediaeval export trade and the proximity
to the southern ports contributed to the settlement's growth.
After the Reformation in the seventeenth century, the trades
practised in the town expanded significantly: there were butch-
ers, tailors, carpenters, tanners, curriers, cutlers, collar makers
and braziers. By 1824, there were bakers, boot and shoemakers,
chair makers, linen drapers and tailors, through to surgeons
and pawnbrokers, auctioneers and tallow chandlers. And then
there was the brewery supplying the fourteen inns and four
beer shops. Wimborne still retains its reputation for its hostel-
ries and pub crawls. All town life was here by the late twentieth
century too: the butcher, the baker, the candlestick maker, the
mason, the Nazi memorabilia collector, the paedophile and the
heroin addict.

In the middle of the island's shopping precinct is a Co-op
supermarket, which used to be a Safeway. There are entrances
at both ends of the building. These gave the local kids the
perfect opportunity to 'do a *Psychomania*'. This involved cycling
through one set of automatic doors, straight through the

supermarket, and then out of the doors at the other end, causing as much mayhem as they could on the way.

Psychomania is a 1973 English film about a biker gang called The Living Dead. It was a regular late-night feature on television when Jus was growing up. In the film, the gang's leader, Tom, gains immortality by killing himself riding his motorcycle off a bridge into a river, by way of a hard-to-fathom black magic ceremony involving a toad and an amulet. As they bury their assumed-dead leader, mounted on his bike in a too-shallow grave at a stone circle called The Seven Witches (erected by the film crew next to the M3, near the village of Littleton in Surrey), one of the gang serenades him on his acoustic guitar with a song called 'Riding Free':

And the world never knew his name
But the chosen few knew of his fame

Roaring like a bat out of hell from beyond the grave, and now the living dead, Tom encourages the other members of the gang to commit suicide too. But the spell only works if the subject really wants to kill themselves. Any hesitation and they die for good.

In one sequence, the gang tear through a town centre in the brutalist surroundings of the Hepworth Way shopping centre in Walton-on-Thames, Surrey. They knock a workman off a ladder inexplicably erected in the middle of the pavement and joust on their motorbikes with umbrellas. They are 'long-haired git[s]' in the eyes of the police – a hippy nuisance that isn't missed when they snuff themselves out.

It's a peculiar vision of an English biker gang. The bikes, terrain, weather and the gang themselves were simply shitter than their larger-than-life American equivalents. There are no Harley Davidsons or desert sunsets in sight. But it conjures a strangely intense atmosphere – and the premise, though risible, has grown more disturbing over time. The glorification of suicide in the film teeters on the irresponsible.

Towards the end of the film, The Living Dead roar into a supermarket, get their bikes caught on the stacks of tins which they scatter across the floor and even send an occupied baby's pram flying. This scene was the inspiration for the Wimborne bicycle jaunt through Safeway. Jus worked in the Safeway for a period. That didn't stop him from pursuing the *Psychomania* antics. His boss was a pushover and tended to back away from confronting him about it. The absurdity of *Psychomania* appealed to the sense of humour of Wimborne's young people. They loved the notion of living for ever if they killed themselves. When asked at school what he wanted to do for a career, Jus replied that he wanted to get a chopper motorbike, ride to Afghanistan and score loads of heroin.

Then there was heavy music. In the eighties, bike and metal culture were intertwined. Bikers and metalheads were both regarded with suspicion, if not disdain, by wider society. The older brother of one of Jus's school friends was in a biker gang and his bedroom was full of posters of arena-straddling rock freaks: Deep Purple, Rainbow and Status Quo. But as Jus got old enough to seriously consider getting involved in motorbikes, the biker gang in Wimborne quickly deteriorated and became a pitiful sight. The leaders were clearly twats, their bikes were shit, and the upcoming generation wore one-piece leather suits with Yamaha written on the back. Jus started to think he had missed the boat.

Mike Oborn was set against the idea in any case. He bought Jus a guitar to steer him away from the whole bike thing. Jus soon saw the upside as he transferred the notion of the true biker's death-drive to heavy rock music. How about suicide by way of guitar? Or a premature end as a guarantee of rock immortality? Years later, Electric Wizard's fascination with *Psychomania* became a self-fulfilling prophecy.

We walked down to the bridge at East Street. The hump of
the bridge was good for a *Dukes of Hazzard*-type jump if you
could get the momentum up from the traffic lights. Jus once
snuck out with a couple of his parents' lodgers to attempt the
jump in their souped-up Cortina.

Here on East Street, at the bottom end of the shopping
precinct – opposite The Rising Sun pub and above what is now
a beauty salon – was a nightclub and snooker hall called Cartoons. It was here Electric Wizard played their first gig in 1993.
They crammed onto a small stage in the corner and played very
loudly for about forty-five minutes, to a handful of old hippies.
Long before they settled on playing actual songs in their sets,
they jammed on a load of Cream and Sabbath-sounding riffs.
The hippies loved it and the Wizard were convinced they were
the best band ever.

Cartoons is now a venue called The Club, with a faux-neon
logo. It looked very closed when we were there and it was hard
to tell whether it was just a crap small-town nightclub, a strip
club, or both. The place has not transmuted into anything of
splendour since its time as Cartoons. Electric Wizard were
popular with the long-hairs at their first gig, but as the nineties
progressed and their reputation grew outside of Wimborne, they
talked incessantly about their copious drug use and how fucked
up the town was – to the dismay of the locals. But being in a
band was never about being popular. It was the way to solidify
their *unpopularity*.

Jus's childhood home was a three-storey Victorian terraced
house on New Borough Road, a short walk south of the town
centre. It looked unremarkable when we stood outside, but then
its normality took on a more sinister edge as Jus told stories

about the poltergeist in its basement that enjoyed chasing him up the stairs and once smashed a load of plant pots out of spite.

There wasn't a telephone in the family home until Jus was fifteen. Dorset evolved slowly – certain parts of the county didn't get electricity until the 1960s. Going to Bournemouth was like flying to the moon. One childhood visit became the stuff of family legend: 'The Day We Went to Bournemouth'.[6]

From 1847 until 1977 there was a station in this part of town that served the Southampton and Dorchester railway. Recently closed by the time that Jus was a child, the local kids smashed windows and got up to no good on the derelict site. Around the station was a collection of shops, including a bookshop. Like the local Safeway, it was full of pulp novels from the seventies released by the New English Library imprint – carousels of biker and skinhead novels, as well as out-there science fiction featuring gigantic crabs and slugs. Jus spent hours as a child in the bookshop poring over the books.

As well as fiction such as *The Devil's Rider* by Alex R. Stuart (another English biker story), NEL published the book *Freewheelin Frank* by Hells Angel Frank Reynolds. As told to Michael McClure, a writer from the San Francisco counterculture of the 1960s, the book reads like a beat prose-poem. In an early scene, Frank takes a cap of acid and climbs an oak tree in a desert location called Squaw's Rock where the Hells Angels have gathered on a 'run'. Frank wraps himself around a branch of the tree and imagines himself as the serpent in the Garden of Eden (one with feelings of kindness), among his brothers and their 'old ladies'.[7] He believes that LSD has jerked the rug out from under the Hells Angels who have taken it, in the best way possible.

By contrast, in a 1973 BBC documentary about an English chapter of the Hells Angels, the narrator describes a run as 'a moment of glamour snatched from lives hollow with monotony.'

On their filmed run, the English Angels take charge of a derelict canal boat just outside Berkhamsted and watch *Doctor Who* on a small, portable, solid-state transistor television as the rain pours outside.[8]

In Frank's book, he states that love will win out over fortune and fame. He has a theory of one sex that dictates 'there will be no reproduction when mankind reaches its climax and is fully developed'.[9] The narrative is an uncomfortable melange of acid-fried advanced consciousness and lawless, primitive violence. In the second half of the book, Frank describes in a matter-of-fact voice the mass rape, filth, fire and brutality of the 1966 Fourth of July gathering at Lake Bass in California – an event of sup- posed unity and brotherhood cut off from the rules and morals of wider society. The Angels lure in, taunt and torture members of biker pretenders The Gypsy Jokers, and sexually assault their girlfriends ('If they would not stand up and defend their women then the deviates led them away'[10]).

Frank states that 'the earth is a Hell and on it are Hell's [sic] Angels'.[11] Unlike some of his brothers who fought the peace and love movement in violent skirmishes at Berkeley and elsewhere, he opts to hang out with Ken Kesey at Kesey's house in La Honda. The Hells Angels' long hair and stripped-down bikes really mean something to them. But Frank is looking further. Frank paints and he stargazes. He looks down at Satan's Slaves, another biker gang from the San Fernando Valley, as sexual deviants – even though he admits to raping four women at Lake Bass (or was it five? He can't remember). In his twisted logic, acts of violence are the necessary flare-ups and release valves of a life of brotherly love.

'A Hell's Angel [sic] is supposed to be a person of hatred against his time which he lives in,' he states. 'He likes no one, furthermore loves no one, and furthermore only depends upon his brothers. I talk this to my people, what I just said here, and they listen and add on. And yet burst out in violence and hatred from day to day. But the Hell's Angels' true instincts are of love. If they are not they'll go down the drain with all the millions of other phony [sic] men on the earth.'[12]

Frank has tears of joy in his eyes when he rides his bike on acid for the first time, leaving La Honda. This was different to Jus's approach to LSD in his teens in Wimborne, when he purposely listened to death metal bands like Autopsy to trigger a bad trip and conjure his own response to a place filled with phoney humans. But Jus saw something appealing in the Hells Angel philosophy: that they stood against the time they lived in, in the same way that The Living Dead committed themselves to immortality or death. What was there left to love in a doomed world?

Around the corner from Jus's childhood home is Avenue Road, where the writer Thomas Hardy once lived. Hardy moved to Wimborne in 1881. He wasn't the only person of renown on the street. Nine years earlier, in 1872, a local businessman called John Low moved to Avenue Road after permanently shutting the stationer's shop he ran on the high street. He was known for closing the shop whenever he was offended by a customer, only reopening when he had recovered from the insult. When he moved to Avenue Road, he ordered that it not reopen for the rest of his life. It is now part of the Museum of East Dorset.

Hardy wrote the novel *Two on a Tower* while he lived in Wimborne. He fictionalised the town as 'Warborne'. The book is not considered one of his best, but it is full of his customary acuity about the doomed spheres that human beings occupy. It tells the story of a young aspiring astronomer called Swithin St Cleeve and his affair with Lady Constantine, ten years his senior. A lot of the action takes place on a tower on Constantine's land, where Swithin has improvised the construction of an astronomical observatory. Hardy said his intention was to 'set the emotional history of two infinitesimal lives against the stupendous background of the stellar universe'.[13] The fictional tower was based on similar structures near Wimborne – Horton Tower and Charborough Tower.

Hardy had observed Tebbutt's comet the year he moved to Wimborne on 25 June 1881. He incorporated the upcoming Transit of Venus in December 1882 into his story, with Swithin determined to journey to the Pacific region to get a good observation point. Not long after he moved to Wimborne, Hardy and his wife Emma were given a coach tour of the surrounding countryside. On passing Charborough Park to the north, their driver, William Young, told them the tale of the spinster lady of the house and how her mother had been courted by a man twelve years her junior. This fed into the premise of the relationship in *Two on a Tower*.[14]

The study of astronomy is a double bind. The magnitude of the universe reduces the troubles of the mind, but it also reduces *everything* to insignificance. Through Swithin, Hardy makes it clear that there is an innate horror in the observation of the void of space and its '[i]mpersonal monsters, namely, Immensities.'[15] In an early scene, Swithin explains why this is so to Lady Constantine: '"There is a size at which dignity begins," he exclaimed; "further on there is a size at which grandeur begins; further on there is a size at which solemnity begins; further on, a size at which awfulness begins; further on, a size at which ghastliness begins. That size faintly approaches the size of the stellar universe. So am I not right in saying that those minds who exert their imaginative powers to bury themselves in the depths of that universe merely strain their faculties to gain a new horror?"'[16]

Whether Freewheelin Frank or Swithin, who is prepared to evaporate into the cosmic consciousness? It's hard to feel ready for that. But Jus embraced this possibility. His experiments with acid were a way of opening an empty space within himself that was commensurate with the immensity of space. Once that emptiness was internalised, the creative possibilities were endless. Even before he was a teenager, Jus was already obsessed with the vastness of the universe, witchcraft and the occult. Black magic offered him both liberation and dissimulation. At primary school he was nicknamed 'The Omen' for his habit of fixing other pupils in his stare for uncomfortably long periods of time. It didn't make him popular.

Jus was an anxious child. It created an emotional separateness from his environment. 'I think the fears and the anxieties make me an outsider. And then being an outsider creates the situation where you can't integrate with society,' he said in an unusually open interview with *Psychology Today* in 2018.[17]

He first got into heavy metal because he was attracted to the imagery. Jus's mum, Rosemary, listened to AC/DC, Thin Lizzy, Free and Led Zeppelin. She had been a sixties' flower child in her youth, with a Mary Quant haircut, and had attended the Rolling Stones concert in Hyde Park in 1969 – supported by Robert Fripp in King Crimson with security provided by the Hells Angels. She listened to Pink Floyd's *Ummagumma* constantly while she was pregnant with Jus. He was quite literally 'Rosemary's Baby'.

Mike Oborn made the young family listen to *The Dark Side of The Moon* and *Tubular Bells* in the dark, from start to finish. The first time Jus smoked weed himself, someone suggested they put on Pink Floyd's *Live at Pompeii* concert film. Pink Floyd has been lurking in the sound of his music ever since – sometimes deep underneath and other times nearer the surface.

On Jus's first day of secondary school, at Corfe Hills school (in Broadstone, between Poole and Wimborne), he sat next to a boy who told him he could play the Hammond organ. This was the conversation that steered Jus away from a life of delinquency to one of music and delinquency. After chatting for a bit, the boy told Jus that there was a Pink Floyd concert on the radio that night. Jus missed it, but tuned into Tommy Vance's *Friday Rock Show* on BBC Radio 1 instead and a load of music he'd never heard before: Iron Maiden, Saxon, Metallica and Slayer. Later on, he bought the latter's 1986 *Reign in Blood* album in Italy when it was banned in the UK, popping over the border when the family was on holiday in Austria. Square Records didn't stock heavy metal (the in-joke being that the record shop stocked 'square' music) but Woody's records in nearby Ferndown did. Jus became a regular visitor.

There was no moving on from metal music. It became a lifelong obsession. There was community and consolation in it. Jus was also turned on to Hawkwind, when he was told by the coolest goth kid in town to stop listening to Morbid Angel and try Hawkwind's 'Angels of Death' (from 1981's *Sonic Attack*) instead. The goth also played The Stooges to Jus for the first time. The range of sounds Jus ingested increased in diversity like the drugs – everything was being absorbed at once.

Turning left on Leigh Road back into the centre of town, we came to St John's Church. Here, Electric Wizard bassist Tim fell from the front of the church when he tried to steal its cross. He smashed through a skylight window and had to repaint it for community service. The church is within spitting distance of the fish-and-chips shop where drummer Mark worked. The band blagged food here after rehearsals. They also tried to steal the cross from the Pentecostal church just up the road. Such was the desire for stage decoration, Jus's earlier band Lord of Putrefaction even tried to lift some gravestones at one point. The police arrived at his house the next day.

'You know what we're here about.'

'It's there,' they said sullenly, pointing at the gravestone leaning against the wall.

As we stopped for Jus to buy rolling papers from the
WHSmith opposite the *Psychomania* supermarket, Liz Buckingham spoke about her time in Long Island and Connecticut.
Her father, Raymond Buckingham, was an English opera singer
who did turns on *The Morecambe & Wise Show* and became a
minor celebrity in the UK, and she lived in New York after her
parents divorced. She has dual citizenship and moved to the UK
after she joined Electric Wizard. Jus and Liz tried living in Los
Angeles while they waited for Liz's passport to be sorted out.
She thought he wasn't suited to life in Los Angeles. He thought
that if it had worked for Lemmy it might work for him but soon
he agreed it felt wrong. In the clear light of a summer's day, he
doesn't look like he belongs in Wimborne either.

We made our way back around the Minster green in the
early evening. It felt more like a communal spot in the softer
light and long shadows. As we walked back past the Minster
to the car park the Quarter Jack rang out for 5.45 p.m. Over
the road on the other side is Wimborne's model town, where
its structures are replicated at one-tenth scale – the perfect
surrounding to pretend to be Godzilla once the acid had
kicked in and the mental anchor of the church had been
abandoned.

We drove past the police station, opposite the place where Jus
set fire to a three-wheeler Robin Reliant in 1998. He was trying
to start a revolution. It resulted in a cycle of court cases. He got
busted for weed while on probation. It set his parents against
him. Since then, he has played the quasi-prodigal son – but
instead of frittering his life away, he has returned with evidence
of Electric Wizard's success. Yes, he did a lot of drugs, but look
how successful he's been on them!

Heading east out of the town is the Leigh (pronounced 'lie') Park estate. No. 13, Day's Court, was Jus's home during his early twenties. 'Thirteen', as it became known, was a council house and the Wizard's headquarters – a den of iniquity, LSD, jamming and twenty-four-hour parties. A few of the attendees who spent too much time in Thirteen's vortex ended up at St Ann's, the psychiatric hospital near Poole. They returned to Wimborne as ghostlike versions of themselves. Thirteen was a staging post for drugs coming into town. Once, the occupants took a delivery of a huge number of shrink-wrapped bars of weed. They arranged it into a chair-like arrangement to sit on. It was called the 'dopethrone'.

In 1994, after multiple busts by the police, the punk-rock mayor rang Jus to warn him the law was about to come down hard on him and it was best that he left town. A friend's dad had a house in Bournemouth he could move to, so he made an initial escape from Wimborne, aged twenty-three. Jus had got to know some of the local policemen during his time in Wimborne – well enough for them once to call him after he'd moved to Bournemouth to say his gran had left her front door open. Jus regularly returned to Wimborne after moving, mainly to rehearse and party.

The police had been strangely pliable at times. Early on, they arrived to shut down an Electric Wizard rehearsal in the front room of Thirteen. The band was able to reason with them that they were just doing their job. A job where friends and hangers-on partied into the night, screaming and going ape. The police looked at each other and shrugged, then repeated back to them as if in a trance, 'Yes, you're just doing your job,' and left. They eventually came to an understanding that the band could rehearse between midday and four o'clock – before the estate's kids got home from school. The locals still complained about them playing.

Their neighbour was a weird older man who was one of several residents sent down from sink estates in bigger cities like Manchester and Glasgow to cool off in Dorset. I tried to imagine what it would feel like to escape an inner-city hell and end up living next door to Electric Wizard.

In any case, the neighbourhood was far from salubrious – plenty of junkies occupied the other houses in the close. In the 1960s, moped-owning mods had populated the estate, whereas the bikers lived in the surrounding countryside. This consolidated the image of bikers as rural outlaws. The estate backed onto Wimborne market, which had been established in 1855 on land bordering the railway line. The market originally traded livestock, with the smell of animals wafting over the estate. By the early seventies, the livestock business had ceased, and it transitioned to become one of the largest open and covered stall markets in the south of England.

We drove out of Leigh Park and continued east. We passed the turning for the aviation company where Mark, the Wizard's first drummer, worked as a cleaner. Mark now lives in Bournemouth.

When he rejoined Electric Wizard in 2014 Jus asked where he was working: 'You're not still working there as a cleaner, are you?'

'No, I'm head cleaner now,' Mark replied. He also boasted he had his own office.

We passed Mark's mother's house. Jus and Mark's families have a relationship stretching right back to the very beginning. Their mothers were in beds next to each other in the maternity unit when Jus and Mark's older sisters were born. Mark's mum used to babysit Jus.

We entered Colehill, the more upmarket part of town, with its big, detached houses. Jus pointed out Canford Bottom, where Adam Richardson used to live. Adam played guitar in one of the bands formed by Jus preceding Electric Wizard in the early nineties: Lord of Putrefaction. If Wimborne was the setting for *The Outsiders* (S. E. Hinton's novel or Francis Ford Coppola's film of the book), you could say that the 'socs' (the socials) – the wealthier kids – lived in Colehill. But Adam was also a 'greaser', a punk and metal kid. He moved freely between the two worlds.

Lord of Putrefaction was influenced by Paradise Lost from Halifax, and the death-doom sound they invented – gothic lyrics roared over slow guitars that exuded the cold misery of Saddleworth Moor and spiritual destitution of Brontë country. Lord of Putrefaction imported this sound to Dorset before Jus evolved it in subsequent bands into the fully-fledged cosmic abomination of Electric Wizard.

We arrived at Colehill Memorial Hall on Cannon Hill Road. There was a youth club here in the late eighties. A few years before Electric Wizard got banned from rehearsing in every village hall in the area, Jus played his first gig here aged sixteen with first band Putrefaction. Putrefaction was the prototype of Lord of Putrefaction, more of a death metal and grindcore band, influenced by Autopsy, Repulsion and Azagthoth amongst others. We're not counting his true first band, Dead Meat, who played some horrible gigs at school, torturing the blues. Their first performance featured both Black Sabbath's 'War Pigs' – the first song Jus attempted on guitar, even if it was only the 'duh-dun!' two-chord opening – and 'Benny the Bouncer' by Emerson, Lake & Palmer. Greg Lake is another of the musical forefathers from the region: he was born in Poole. In fact, the father of Putrefaction drummer Steve Mills had been in a local band with Robert Fripp and Pete Giles before they formed King Crimson.

Putrefaction practised on Saturday mornings and spent Saturday afternoons taking LSD. Their demo was delayed after being threatened with legal action due to the excessive volume of rehearsals. They patiently waited for the rehearsal space

to be soundproofed before they recommenced. When it came
to playing that first gig, Putrefaction's aim was to punish the
village and raze it to the ground. It didn't start well. Jus had
managed to forget his guitar. His dad had to go home to get
it. He vowed never again – telling Jus to get a proper job, etc.
Putrefaction didn't shock and awe quite as they intended. But a
group of punk kids from the nearby village of West Moors got a
mosh pit going and knocked over the vicar. It was the first and
last time Jus's parents saw him perform live.

The band was supporting local goths Ryders of the Storm, featuring a guitarist called Gavin Gillingham, who later joined Jus
in Thy Grief Eternal, a band that started to get noticed beyond
Wimborne's boundaries. Gav liked to wear a wide-brimmed
hat, so he looked like Carl McCoy from goth legends Fields of
the Nephilim. Thy Grief Eternal later evolved into Eternal,
influenced by the 1990 self-titled release on Rick Rubin's Def
American label by the Illinois band Trouble. Trouble's overt
Sabbath style, and vocalist Eric Wagner's semi-screeched, clean
singing, were enough to convince Jus to turn his back on the
growling primitivism of the death-doom genre for good.

Jus was later kicked out of sixth form at Corfe Hills for
smoking and blasphemy. When asked to cover a textbook with
sticky-back plastic, Jus got creative. He cut out autopsy photos,
made collages of Page 3 models with skulls for heads, then
added newspaper reports about black magic, rape and murder.
He had not been a great student. The textbook was the final
straw.

It was not his first brush with blasphemy. When he was
fifteen, Jus was an active member of the international metal
tape-trading scene. A package meant for him arrived at a
woman's house with a similar name. She opened it and found
a death-metal cassette full of outrageous songs involving
Jesus Christ depicted in various compromising positions which

resulted in the police paying Jus a visit. It didn't help that the letters sent with these tapes were juvenile to the extreme, beginning with exhortations as to how many nuns the recipient had raped recently, and so on.

We drove north out of Colehill towards Horton, past God's Blessing Lane, where the final case of Black Death was recorded after it landed in Melcombe Regis, now part of Weymouth, in 1348. The Black Death routed Wimborne as it did most of the country, killing up to half of the nation's population. As the landing point for the plague, Dorset has been long hardened against epidemics. We drove past a hand-painted sign for Gaunts House, in a curly retro-seventies font adorned with pictures of leaves. I thought the name sounded familiar and later remembered that Merope Gaunt is the mother of Tom Riddle, aka Voldemort, from the Harry Potter books. 'Recently wizards got a bad name due to fucking Harry Potter and *The Lord of the Rings*, and they're not as cool as they used to be,' Jus complained to *Kerrang!* magazine in 2017.[18]

Gaunts House is Sir Richard Glyn's ancestral home. Sir Richard is a descendent of one of the society families that moved into Wimborne and the surrounding area during the Georgian period. Glyn runs new age workshops and events from Gaunts House. It was built by a former Mayor of London and the estate was connected to John of Gaunt, the third son of Edward III (and father of Henry IV), who is thought to have had a hunting lodge in the area in the fourteenth century. The mansion is home to a charitable foundation that, according to its website, seeks 'Realisations of life through wisdom, teachings, mindfulness, conscious awareness and pure intent in thought, expression, and action.'[19] Glyn is reported to be preparing his disciples for an apocalypse event in 2050.[20]

Glyn allegedly rented his many properties in the area based on the vibration of the prospective tenants – many of whom were the fading lights of seventies entertainment. When he encountered Electric Wizard wandering around town wearing dark colours, he admonished them that turquoise was better at getting them on the right kind of wavelength. He was known to help local bands but declined to help the Wizard for the simple reason they wore black.

On our drive, Horton Tower suddenly appeared out of nowhere. On top of a small hill, it is strange and arresting – akin to Glastonbury Tor, or the effigy of the Wicker Man. It rises out of the landscape like the giant, multi-limbed dominatrix on Electric Wizard's 1998 EP, *Supercoven*.

At the beginning of the Robert Fripp documentary he walks into the derelict tower on a winter's day. The six-storey brick tower is forty-three metres high and was commissioned in the mid-1700s by Sir Humphrey Sturt, another local landowner and Dorset MP. It was possibly built as an observatory for stargazing or so Sturt could watch the hunt. Now, the entrance is bricked up and the edifice has hosted mobile phone masts since 1994.

We walked up the chalk path to the tower. A monument to decayed splendour, there are clusters of fir trees nearby, suggesting it also inspired Hardy in creating Swithin's observatory in *Two on a Tower*, set atop 'a circular isolated hill, of no great elevation, which placed itself in strong chromatic contrast with a wide acreage of surrounding arable land by being covered in fir-trees.'[21] Another Hardy connection is that they filmed the cock-fighting scenes in the 1967 movie version of *Far From the Madding Crowd* here. These were later cut from the finished film.

A tractor hummed as it wrapped up bales of grass in the field we stood in. Still, it was unusually quiet up there. Jus described how you used to be able to see Charborough Tower, aka Drax

Tower, on its estate not far from here, but now the view was obscured by trees. He told me that King Alfred's Tower on the Stourhead estate in Wiltshire, just over the Somerset border, also has a similar architecture to Horton, with its three turrets.

When Jus and his friends came to party up here back in the day, the inside of the tower had an uncanny and unsettling vibe. It smelt damp and rotten. Stalactites of accumulated bird droppings hung from its interior ledges. The walls were green with algae. There was human shit at the bottom. It was slimy and unholy.

A tower such as this provides protection and an advantageous position to gaze both outwards and inwards. In 1969, acid guru Timothy Leary set up a lifeguard tower on the beach at Zihuatanejo, Mexico, for his esoteric community, the International Federation of Internal Freedom. Like ancient shamans, people would climb the platform alone on massive doses of acid and confront the void.[22]

At the base of Horton Tower, there is a panoramic view of the landscape with Poole harbour visible to the south. The smuggling route to Wimborne is practically a straight line. This part of Dorset is not hilly – it undulates.

'If I had to explain why Electric Wizard is slow,' said Jus, looking across the fields to the north, 'I think of this landscape. This is the epicness. The slow, epic feel would always come from this. This tower, this landscape. It's not chocolate-box England, all little valleys. It's open. There's a big horizon. Everything's a long way away.' In a place like this, with people removed from each other, Electric Wizard played louder, harder, slower and deeper because they wanted to be heard.

As we drove back, we passed the secluded barn and farmyard that used to be occupied by some hippy girls. Electric Wizard sometimes rehearsed and played squat parties there. Sir Richard Glyn interrupted one session when he appeared in a full suit of armour, brandishing a sword – he demanded they cease the booming racket. Presumably the soundwaves unleashed by the Wizard had travelled over the field, across the boundary into the grounds of Gaunts house, and interfered with whatever cosmic wavelength Glyn was tuned into at the time.

Returning to the outskirts of Wimborne, Jus pointed in the direction of a weir and old mill house where Electric Wizard often smoked bongs, filled with whatever they could get their hands on. When they first got proper skunk weed in the town, what they called 'flowering heads', it was a big deal. Usually, they had to make do with a black substance that tasted like rubber or petrol with a tiny amount of hash mixed in.[23]

There used to be some graffiti on the wall of the mill house. When Jus lived in the town it simply read, 'We kane. We kill.' But after he came back to the spot on a night out after moving to Bournemouth, the graffiti had been overwritten with another declaration: 'We kane harder.'

Badbury Rings is magical on a summer's evening. Located a few miles north-east of Wimborne, it is an iron age hill fort surrounded by three concentric earthwork circles. It was a Roman settlement near a junction of major Roman roads, one of which is connected to Old Sarum near Salisbury, the others to Hamworthy, Dorchester and Bath. This is also one of the supposed sites of the mythical Battle of Mount Badon, which King Arthur fought around 500 AD, as the Britons beat back the Anglo-Saxons. The Welsh chronicler Nennius (writing several centuries later) wrote that over nine hundred men died at Arthur's own hand.

From Wimborne, I drove up the Blandford Road to rendezvous with Jus and Liz. Thomas Hardy had taken this road with his wife and sister to visit Badbury Rings in the hired wagonette when he spotted Charborough aka Drax Tower, over the wall of the estate.

Private now as it was then, the estate is still home to the Drax family. Richard Drax, the Conservative MP for South Dorset, currently lives there. It is surrounded by a wall known as the 'great wall of Dorset', which is three miles long and comprises three million bricks. Drax is the biggest landowner in the county. His family built its fortune from seventeenth-century ancestor James Drax and his sugar plantations in Barbados on which tens of thousands of slaves are thought to have died. The Drax Hall sugar plantation dominated the physical and mental terrain of Barbados. The plantation is still owned and run by the family.

When Robert Fripp showed the cameras around in 1985, it was winter as they zoomed through the leafless, claw-like trees lining the road. As a child, Fripp played on the slopes of the rings with his sister. When they were young, Jus and his friends could just about make the four-mile journey to the rings on their bikes.

As we walked up the avenue through the rings, Jus pointed out a small area of woodland nearby, known as Satyr Wood. The satyr used to pop his head out to spy on young lovers, but he's not been seen since the seventies. We got a clear view of Drax Tower as we walked up into the wooded clearing at the centre of the rings.

After the pubs closed on weekends, there were parties here – the site is managed by the National Trust but is accessible all hours, though the authorities have tightened up the security over time. One evening, once again on acid, Jus was moved along from the site and his group relocated to the New Forest, only to stumble across a ritual magic ceremony in the dead of night. They were chased by naked people on horseback. There was a huge fire, and the gathered mass was worshipping what appeared to be a giant chicken. Jus dismissed this as an acid-induced hallucination until years later he came across a photo of the occultist and high priest of Wicca, Alex Sanders, in a ceremonial outfit resembling a chicken.

Sanders was the self-styled King of the Witches in Britain, supposedly introduced to witchcraft in his teens when his seventy-four-year-old grandmother took his virginity and pierced his scrotum with a pen knife. Sanders went on to write lyrics for Black Widow, a seventies occult rock group. His wife, Maxine, once simulated a naked Wiccan sacrifice during one of their concerts. Sanders even introduced the actor Sharon Tate to witchcraft during the filming of *13*, aka *Eye of the Devil*, in 1966.[24]

For Sanders – and many who followed Alexandrian witchcraft – Diana, goddess of the moon, was their mother and Lucifer their father. The ley lines which criss-crossed England, including near the site of Badbury Rings, mirrored their parental gods' pathways across the sky. Groups of standing stones were observatories to observe these wanderings. The gods were controlled by priestess witches, and their drawing down of the moon.

A master of getting himself publicity via chat shows and print interviews, in a 1970 documentary called *Legend of the Witches* Sanders performed a black mass in full priest's garb. Freewheelin Frank also describes attending a memorable black mass at the Wax Museum, San Francisco, one Halloween:

'In the darkness of flaming scarlet a magician performed a hellish ritual that dates back through thousands of years of devil-like ceremonies sacrificing a beautiful maiden. The people that witnessed this black mass were all of a high social standing. It was no joke. One Greek lady I can still remember with her long reddish-like hair and her fiery eyes. I wished I could remember every word, word for word, of the ancient old tongues that were spoken and quoted and read from a paper by the magician who performed the ceremonial black mass.'[25]

The maiden's sacrifice is performed on a waxwork – 'there was no blood except in the imagination'. Frank is surrounded by effigies of grave robbers and even Frankenstein in his lab. Frank is impressed, entranced with the ceremony and its attendees: 'In darkness I roared into the night. Unfollowed. But yet were all unseen.'[26]

Badbury Rings was frequented by Gandalf-like hippies and cult acolytes, drawn to this ancient meeting point. Jus saw a centaur here once. He had run out of the back of a tent to escape a rave when he came across it. The centaur had two smaller, female centaurs with him. They locked eyes with Jus, turned, and disappeared into the trees.

Lying on one of the rings and tripping, with the distant town of Blandford Forum bathed in the light of the setting sun, Jus felt like he could see the whole world. In the right weather conditions, hundreds of cumulus clouds made their way overhead like a battalion of blissful UFOs. Here, Electric Wizard imagined the wizard from the song 'Electric Wizard' on the band's 1994 debut album, who arrives on the back of a dragon and takes the band on a journey into space 'where on the edge of time there stood two towers black'.

The growth of rave culture shifted the attention of Wimborne's youth from squat gigs and outdoor gatherings where the audience predominantly took acid, to techno parties in warehouses where everyone was on ecstasy. There were early signs of this sea change while Jus lived at Thirteen as the nineties dawned, and then it surged with unstoppable momentum – from the Spiral Tribe sound system at the headline-grabbing Castlemorton Common Festival rave in May 1992 onwards. As rave culture got watered down for wider public consumption, Jus and his friends referred to it as 'Southampton music'. At first, he tried to escape it, but trance, techno and the repetitive loops of dance music made an indelible mark on Electric Wizard, which in the realm of heavy rock was also a small revolution.

The sun was setting when I left Wimborne. I had seen the town in the warm light of a summer's day. It did not strike me as a sinister place. It is perceived as a bastion of English values and stability. It was even credited as the place where most people were married in all of the country – with two-thirds of all adults hitched.[27] A picture postcard of conservative respectability. But thirty years ago, according to Jus, it was hard not to feel Dorset was 'the most backward part of the country'.[28]

And where the sunlight reaches, shadows are created. There was a web of half-spoken truths and half-glimpsed revelations about the town. I was only getting a sliver of it. Wimborne might not be the centre of the universe, but it was a key part of the mental and physical topography of Electric Wizard's life. The town was the miasma out of which the band grew: it contained the experiences that remained encoded within Electric Wizard, and the echoes of what was to come.

Wimborne is the gate.

Chapter Two
The wizard in black reveals the sign

Come My Fanatics . . ., Electric Wizard's second album, released in 1997, is the sound of dying amps roaring out across a dead planet. It begins with the destruction of a person and ends in the desolation of space. Throughout the album, the band is grasping at something otherworldly – a new form of heaviness.

Come My Fanatics . . . is where the band truly begins. It was designed to be all-encompassing, misanthropic and millenarian. It defined Electric Wizard.

'Engulfing heaviness. Escapism. Total oblivion,' Jus said of the sound. 'The music that I like is music that takes me away from my body, almost. I'm transported into something else. That's what our music is about. It's not heaviness for effect, but as a drug, as a numbing force.'[29]

In 1997 there was nothing like it. The layers of distortion, phased guitars and buried drums came close to total meltdown – 'never was an organic brain nearer to utter annihilation in the chaos that transcends form and force and symmetry'.[30]

Come My Fanatics . . . conjures a super-harsh psychedelia. Spiritually, it aligns with the nightmarish images of vampirism and violence imagined by the droog Alex in the film of *A Clockwork Orange* as he trips out to Beethoven's *Symphony No. 9*. Alex says the music is like 'silvery wine flowing in a spaceship'.

Like the imagery and Nadsat droog-speak of *A Clockwork Orange*, the album devised a new language to express alienation – a musical expression which had touchpoints elsewhere but as a whole was hitherto unknown and remarkable.

Electric Wizard found the album's producer, Rolf Startin, advertising his services in the *Yellow Pages* telephone directory. He had worked at The Manor studio, originally used by Richard Branson for his Virgin label. He supposedly programmed the keyboards on Neneh Cherry's hit single, 'Manchild' (though this is difficult to verify), and he worked on Alexei Sayle's studio recordings.

After the mayor had warned him about staying any longer in Wimborne, Jus had moved to Bournemouth, known as the 'Costa del Dole' due to its high unemployment rate.[31] Tim followed, but Mark remained in Wimborne at his mum's house, sometimes disrupting recording – especially when Mark dropped acid and got lost in a field on his way to the studio the day he was meant to lay down his drum tracks.

No more games, Jus resolved. Music could, and should, overwhelm the senses. It must perturb, disorientate, saturate and overcome its human conduits. The Wizard needed to succumb to its powers to succeed. They had to let heaviness win. *Come My Fanatics . . .* tore a huge hole in the fabric of reality and let heaviness pour in.

The opening of *Come My Fanatics . . .* is like a roar of a motorbike – feedback billows out of juddering speaker cones. 'Return Trip' is the heaviest album-opener of all time. It was one of three songs that Jus had written before going into the studio, alongside 'Wizard In Black' and 'Son Of Nothing'. The band were keen to jam out the other three and make the most of their recording space, Red Dog studios (which they had helped to build in an old bank vault), and Rolf's engineering expertise. They were excited by the studio and wanted to get hands on.

This was before digital recording was the norm. They intended to do what the fuck they wanted to fulfil their vision.

There is something shocking, almost hateful, about the sound of 'Return Trip'. Out of the murk of the cacophony, Tim's two-note bass riff sways side to side with the unbidden malevolence of the walking dead. Mark's drum patterns are barely discernible as they rifle and pitter-patter about the motif. Jus joins the fray with a blues descent that sounds like an avalanche. There is a ridiculous amount of fuzz, but it lacks warmth. It has the cold intensity of a black hole sucking the listener into unbeing. After a loping second riff sequence, the song sounds on the verge of collapse as the valves of the amps hum and crackle. You only know it when the band piles in, but underneath that noise Jus is resuscitating the song with its slow, heaving, *grooving* main riff – heralded by a sample from Umberto Lenzi's 1981 film *Cannibal Ferox* (*Make Them Die Slowly* in the US): 'Get off my case, motherfucker!'

When he was fifteen years old, Jus compiled a VHS edit of his favourite horror film dialogue snippets and musical themes. He used it a few times for the demos of his previous bands. On another cassette he recorded the audio of an American documentary special from the ABC news strand *20/20*, called *The Devil Worshippers*. That was made during the height of the eighties 'satanic panic'. The events of this period are well known: Judas Priest and Ozzy Osbourne had to defend themselves in court that their music didn't lead to suicide. Tipper Gore founded the Parents Music Resource Center which slapped 'Parental Guidance: Explicit Lyrics' stickers across albums that were deemed profane. Heavy music was branded as inherently dangerous, to the delight of artists, record labels and its audience.

Jus recorded the audio of full-length Hammer horror films so he could rewatch them in his imagination while listening to the cassettes during school lessons. This was more than enjoying the soundtrack – it was total immersion in a discomfiting audio-visual world. Jus used the recordings to trigger his imagination, in the same way he used LSD – to open up a void for his creativity to fill. Conjuring cinematic visions with music (both pre-existing or Electric Wizard's own) was integral to the making of *Come My Fanatics . . .* , and became the band's modus operandi.

'Return Trip' is in three movements. The opening riff was lifted from the New York band 13, and their song 'Whore', released on a split with Eyehategod in 1994. Jus had a photo of their guitarist, Liz Buckingham, on his wall. The main riff itself was an amended version of a riff Electric Wizard used on their song 'Stone Magnet' from their first, self-titled album and, before that, on a demo – with a tweak to the tail.

Jus made the demo for 'Return Trip' on a four-track recorder with a drum machine. It was only really for his reference. He had seen a Pink Floyd documentary in which they wrote their arrangements on a blackboard to brief the members. This approach worked for Mark and Tim. Jus showed the band the different parts and they jammed it out. 'We'll work out a song maybe half an hour before we record,' Jus told *Bad Acid* in the first issue of its fanzine in 1998. 'I think it sounds fresher, more dangerous and aggressive 'cos the song is so new.'[32]

The opening couplet of the song is zoomed-in cinema of the mind: 'The sun burns in the stranger's eyes/Just one tear before he dies'.[33] It feels like the song is hurtling towards its own destruction along with its protagonist. Tim encouraged Jus to swear on the song. He was impressed with the gang-chant vocal refrain in the Machine Head song, 'Davidian': 'Let freedom ring with the shotgun blast!'

Machine Head's debut album, *Burn My Eyes*, was released in 1994. It was a brutal reimagining of thrash metal that distilled the technicality and speed of the genre to favour heft and groove.

It also dealt with realism and social issues: '1994 – corruption, racism, hate' singer Robb Flynn growls at the beginning of its single, 'Old'. It's an interesting point of reference for Electric Wizard because they instinctively rejected material reality whilst being obsessed with the world around them. *Come My Fanatics . . .* works as escapist allegory *and* social commentary.

When Jus came up with the lines 'I hope this fuckin' world fuckin' burns away/And I'd kill you all if I had my way', Tim was satisfied. It gave the song a nihilism which was direct, cataclysmic and fuck-you.

After free-rein guitar solos, panning in and out of the song like spacecraft strafing the skies, the Wizard saved the heaviest part for last. Again, the song comes to a virtual stop. Then the last movement is the sound of guitars wrenching the planets from their interstellar pathways by exerting an enormous magnetic force on them. Jus improvised some repentant screams amongst it all, like the sound of a man breaking up on re-entry, with the hollow conviction of someone trying their luck with a God they know doesn't exist: 'Lord forgive me, for I have sinned. But I'll never sin again. No, no, no, I'll never sin again!'

In another *Bad Acid* interview, from September 1998, the band spoke about how they 'geller' riffs. Tim explained it was a tribute to Uri Geller, infamous psychic, friend of Michael Jackson and spoon-bender. 'Yeah, when we do our riffs the necks bend on our guitars!' exclaimed Jus.[34]

Electric Wizard wanted a regime change in heavy music. They had grown up during the eighties' arms race for heaviness. As the decade progressed, there was constant one-upmanship between bands. In terms of speed, this culminated with grindcore and its incomprehensible blasts, typified by Napalm Death in the UK and Anal Cunt in the US. At the other end, the bands Thergothon, Winter and Disembowelment were making the slowest forms of doom metal imagined.

Studying music at school, Jus had been repelled by modern production techniques: recording musicians separately and playing to a click track was sanitised and safe. In his mind it suited the Stock Aitken Waterman pop of Rick Astley and his ilk, but had no place in heavy music. Nonetheless, it was creeping into the production of death metal: what should be abysmal and raw was becoming sterile and quickly dated. Jus felt great heavy music must reject trends – it should sit outside of time and space itself.

Electric Wizard also wanted to express something about where they were from. American sludge bands like Eyehategod reeked of the bayou of New Orleans. Black metal, when its second wave broke in Norway in the early nineties, was redolent of ice fields and pine forests. 'We were from a small town, unemployed, smoking a lot of drugs,' Jus told *Kerrang!* in June 2009 about the emotion expressed on *Come My Fanatics . . .* 'There was a lot of paranoia thinking people hated us, and we had a lot of trouble with the police as well, getting arrested and stuff. It was youthful arrogance: "Fuck you, fuck everyone!"'[35]

The Wizard learned the hard way in Wimborne that people ostracised you for having long hair, tattoos and liking heavy metal and acted up to the image, as was expected of them. Their run-ins with the police sometimes verged on the staged – rehearsing on a council estate in the middle of the day and setting fire to cars was going to attract the law's attention.

The beginning of the second track of *Come My Fanatics . . .* , 'Wizard in Black', uses a telling sample from the 1974 film *The Living Dead at the Manchester Morgue* (directed by Jorge Grau, the movie is also known as *Let Sleeping Corpses Lie* and *Don't Open the Window*) where a cop berates a youth: 'You're all the same the lot of ya, with your long hair and faggot clothes. And you hate the police, don't ya?' 'You make it easy' is the response.

Jus was fascinated by the second wave of black metal that gripped Norway, especially the associated church burnings that began in 1992. It was the satanic panic of the USA revived – and with real teeth. Jus corresponded with Jon 'Metalion' Kristiansen (founder of Norwegian fanzine *Slayer*) and Euronymous, guitarist of black metal band Mayhem, who was later murdered by his bandmate, Varg Vikernes (both implicated in the arson attacks).

In their letters they discussed the power of magic mushrooms. In Norway, it was not easy for the young black metallers to access drugs, and they relied on nature's bounty. The psychedelic origins of black metal have since been usurped by the church burnings and killings that followed. The mushroom-inspired artwork in Kristiansen's *Slayer* magazine was strangely expunged from its recent compilation edition. To what extent magic mushrooms might have prompted Berzerker-like outbreaks of crazed violence in Norway's black metal scene remains a mystery. (Berzerkers were the frontline warriors in Viking invasions, whose raping and pillaging have been partly accounted for by them being massively intoxicated at the time.) Growing up, Electric Wizard sourced their mushrooms at Horton Tower and Gaunts Common outside Wimborne. But they were only seasonal, and acid was more reliable for year-round tripping.

On 'Wizard in Black' Jus sings, 'A tower stands on the edge of time', behind which the 'chaosphere seethes'. Here a wizard reveals a sign to those gathered in 'Eye of ultra soul': 'I am a god, I am the one/Into the chaos see my time has begun'. This is the recourse left to those threatened to be swallowed up by the vastness of the universe – to stand against it with godlike demeanour. Otherwise, like Hardy's aspiring astronomical lovers in *Two on a Tower*, they would be 'oppressed with the presence of a vastness they could not cope with even as an idea, and which hung about them like a nightmare.'[36] The song elevates the

49

juvenile mushroom-picking at Horton Tower to the astral plane. There's a pacier tempo, with near-jazzy, diminished chords. The establishment and its power melts into sonic oblivion.

Jus found in black metal the foul, fucked-up sound he wanted Electric Wizard to espouse. But the band's attitude to black and death metal at the time was confusing. In their first *Bad Acid* interview, Jus sought to distance himself from black and death metal, in favour of the doom genre as an expression of his background.

'Well, the way that I see it is that death metal and black metal and indie and dance is fuckin' rich kids wanking about, especially death and black which is blatant "Look, Mummy and Daddy, I'm really naughty." Doom and downer stoner is fuckin' soul, but it's like urban nineties' soul, y'know? Working in factories and the dole and shit, just makes you wanna lose your head on dope and numb out to heavy shit.'

In their second *Bad Acid* interview, asked whether they are 'stoner rock', Jus baulked that they were a 'fucking heavy stoned band'. Tim responded by calling themselves a 'black death' band.

At the time, 'stoner rock' was an easygoing, fuzzed-out type of music which was associated with surfing, skating, muscle cars and the desert landscape – it was Californian music. Fu Manchu were the prime example. From southern California and part of the Palm Desert scene, Fu Manchu's 1996 album *In Search Of . . .* had a cover featuring an illustration of Mustang and Chevelle muscle cars poised to drag race in the desert and a hippy chick about to drop the bandana to get the race started. But Jus admits today that the album's gnarly guitar tone, generated in large part by a Crown model fuzzbox, blew him away and partially influenced what he wanted to achieve on *Come My Fanatics . . .*

'I fucking hate that term, I hate that label,' Jus said of 'stoner rock' to the *Midwest Metal* fanzine in 2001. 'I hate when we'll go play a gig man, right? So we go to Holland and they have posters up and it says Electric Wizard, ya know? Stoner rock from wherever! I mean stoner rock means you play like Kyuss or Fu Manchu or something like that. So at our gigs people of all kinds would turn up with their Fu Manchu shirts and shit and they'll usually end up walking out!'[37]

Electric Wizard's main problem with stoner rock bands was that they couldn't handle their weed. The Wizard told *Midwest Metal* they got the band Orange Goblin so high with a homemade 'hash lung' smoking device that they vomited. 'But they're from the city, small town smokers are the hardest,' reasoned Jus.

When asked by *Bad Acid* whether Electric Wizard was a 'space doom' band, Jus cut to the chase: 'I don't know what our music is called, it's just some serious, drug-inspired noise. I wanna appeal to other drug fiends, not just a particular music scene. I hope anyone into dope will dig and understand our message whether they're into metal, hip hop or jungle. We wanna fuck you up.'[38]

The studio sessions of *Come My Fanatics . . .* began with Jus's amp catching fire while recording the song 'Doom-Mantia'. When a valve amp starts to short, the electricity begins to arc under and between the valves and not up into them. It produces a weird echoing effect. This cosmic atmosphere was captured on the final version of the expansive jam invoking a black-mass ritual where 'Thirteen gather on a moonless night/The morning star is burning bright'.

Jus went to the music shop Langdons in Boscombe, part of Bournemouth, to replace the Fender amp that had gone up in flames. He had seen enough episodes of shows like *Beat Club* repeated on satellite television to know he wanted a serious and powerful amp, made by Orange or Hiwatt.

Electric Wizard's instruments and equipment were their chopper motorbike equivalents: stripped-back, powerful and frightening. But he couldn't afford one of those big-brand amps. Instead, he was taken out back and shown a Sound City amp and cabinet, made by a London-based manufacturer. The Sound City amp and cab cost £150 but more than did the job and has been used on every Electric Wizard recording since. Put through the Boss FZ-2 Hyper Fuzz pedal Jus preferred to use at the time, the amp roared like a Harley.

Electric Wizard tuned as low as they could go before the strings fell off. Downtuning became the norm with the growth of nu metal over the next couple of years, but it was still hard to get higher-gauge strings which made lower tunings easier. The band couldn't afford digital tuners either and the analogue tuners struggled with the abnormal low sounds. Staying in tune during the recording of *Come My Fanatics . . .* was a challenge.

'Doom-Mantia' exudes the total mental disruption the Wizard wanted to achieve on the album. The rhythm tracks are piled on top of each other, many processed through a phaser, giving the panning effect of afterburners powering into the night sky. Jus's vocals sound like they are being spliced apart by some sort of alien interference. His guitar soloing unravels across the vast, eight-minute-plus expanse of the song, as if to infinity. It is the drug-propelled jamming of krautrock and Hawkwind multiplied a thousand-fold.

There is a Janus-face quality to Electric Wizard's use of amplifier damage. They were out to challenge power structures and change the world with heavy riffs, but in two different ways at once. Their first instinct was to crush everything, let the world crack and burn, and enjoy the spectacle. But 'Doom-Mantia' shows the other approach – to draw people into their tractor beam with freeform, occult improv. Tim told *Terrorizer* magazine in 2000 that this was a form of 'hypnotherapy'.[39]

If Electric Wizard's music is used for meditative practice of any kind, it should be treated with caution. The 'dark night of

the soul' has been known in mindfulness practices that get out
of hand. Turning inward during an intense, contemplative act
can trigger the unearthing of pornographic and violent images,
like those in *A Clockwork Orange*. Or a profound emptiness
fills the subject as their world turns to grey. During meditation,
practitioners often pass through a period of emotional uncertainty, negativity or confusion. But sometimes they get stuck
there, in what the Buddhist tradition has called 'falling into the
Pit of the Void'. Listening to this period of Electric Wizard can
feel like being hypnotised by one of Uri Geller's bent spoons, but
you need to want to let in the void – just as the band dropped
acid to feel the spiritual emptiness that terrifies people when
meditation 'goes wrong'.[40]

'I got a fucking library of the occult and supernatural, I'm
almost obsessed by it,' Jus said in the 2000 *Terrorizer* interview.
'I was into a lot more when I was a satanist when I was
younger. That just starts you on the course of learning about
shit. It's always been part of the band, it's the idea that music is
a spiritual thing, we're on a spiritual level when we're jamming.
I just think you can have this great power and magic with
music, and through feedback. Electric Wizard, that's the idea,
we're using the electric to make wizardry.'

Rather than reaching a communal state of mind in which
Electric Wizard drew their listeners under their spell, the second
half of *Come My Fanatics . . .* was conceived as a single story
about the disastrous results of attempting to escape the planet.

The first song in the sequence, 'Ivixor B/Phase Inducer', is the
album's most experimental. It opens with a reverberant drum
and bass jam, overlaid with a neo-eastern wailing vocal which
the band sourced from a sampler CD from the cover of a dance
magazine left in the studio. The Wizard were already drawn to
the darkness and intensity of drum 'n' bass and its heavy use of
samples, such as on the tracks '6 Million Ways To Die' and 'Dark

Stranger'. The latter was released in 1993 by Boogie Times
Tribe and has ascending keyboard motifs which sound like alien
communication, as well as samples of Gary Oldman saying 'dark
stranger' and Anthony Hopkins saying 'dark side', from a documentary made about 1992's *Bram Stoker's Dracula*, directed by
Francis Ford Coppola. This was the drum 'n' bass that appealed
to metallers: portentous and menacing. They could deceive themselves that they were leaving their juvenile interests behind
when they started listening to drum 'n' bass and jungle, but they
were always on the same heavy-music continuum.

When Electric Wizard came across this particular vocal
refrain on the sampler CD, Jus thought it might work with the
key of the jam they were working on. It also fitted with the
concept of an alien siren luring a spacecraft to its doom. He
had come across the planet Ivixor B as a child in *The Alien
World: The Complete Illustrated Guide* by Steven Eisler, published in 1980. The book is from the era when publishers treated
children as deserving of mind-bending and often frightening
near-truthful concepts of the alien and the afterlife (see also
Usborne's *The World of the Unknown: Ghosts*, published in
1977). The copy on its flap described it as 'the first sensible
treatise on the fictitious world of expanding and contracting
galaxies and their alien life.'[41]

Written around some jaw-dropping, full-colour visions of alien
life, the book is organised into different fictional sectors. Ivixor B
is in the Oisir-Raxxla sector. This race of aliens are classified as
'gigantiform, exoskeletal reptiloid analogues'[42], or in other words:
giant lizards. These creatures are depicted by science-fiction
artist Tony Roberts, who illustrated books for Isaac Asimov,
Ursula Le Guin, Frank Herbert and Robert Heinlein.

Ivixor B is a giant red sun supporting over forty planetary
bodies. In the atmosphere of seven of these planets drift the
sirens of Ivixor B, the Kiiry – 'gigantic, medusoid creatures,

54

which float through the hydrogen seas of the worlds on gas-filled bells, trailing limbs down into the denser atmosphere.' They are capable of swimming in the void of space between worlds, but colonised these planets, Eisler explains, 'in the same way that a herd of beasts might spread out to occupy the whole of a river valley.'[43]

Detecting subspace emissions from ships and repeating them as 'tunes', the Kiiry 'sing' on subspace frequencies to seduce spacecraft into their field of influence. In the book, these enormous alien creatures are illustrated by Roy Virgo. Jus imagined their energy tendrils, up to two thousand kilometres long, having actual female human faces, singing out like the sirens to Odysseus and his shipmates in *The Odyssey*. The bass riff of the song stretches, contorts and twists back on itself like these appendages.

'Ships are attracted into the solar influence zone of Ivixor B,' writes Eisler. 'Once there, the life spirit of the occupants is drained by the drifting sirens; ships orbit endlessly, their desiccated crews never having known the final moment of death, so entranced were they by the songs of the Kiiry being transmitted through the subspace crystals of their communication controls. The space around Ivixor B, thus, has become a Sargasso Sea of wrecks, through which the Kiiry swim in lazy, almost innocent abandon. Why they are destructive is not known; and what they achieve by the indolent killing of other races has never been divined.'[44]

The 'Ivixor B' section of the song fades into lifelessness, drained by the Kiiry. When it came to the 'Phase Inducer' section, simulating the atmosphere of the dead spaceship drifting in space, the three members of the band jumped on a Korg synthesiser lent to them by someone who lived upstairs from Tim. They pressed buttons and turned dials, making a whole host of glitchy noises. The band were mainly just fucking around

and elbowing each other out of the way, but Rolf told them he
had recorded it and it sounded great.

They also wanted a lost-in-space transmission to be read out
during this section of the song. They had in mind Hawkwind's
'Black Corridor' from 1972's *Space Ritual* – a spoken-word piece
by Michael Moorcock which describes space as 'remorseless,
senseless, impersonal'. Jus tried to improvise something, but
they fell about in hysterics. Mike Hurst, who was engineering
the album, said he did some amateur drama on the side and
would have a go. He sounded much better but making it up on
the spot wasn't working. So Jus went back to *The Alien World*
and gave Mike the fragment of a fictional transmission from one
of the doomed spacecraft of Ivixor B.

'. . . a sun not dissimilar to Algol, but with the fire of hell
burning from its surface . . . forty-three worlds, clustered
in a narrow plane, and most of them giants, their gaseous
atmospheres curling wraith-like into the void . . . colours, so
beautiful, the richness of reds and purples, and the scores of
rocky moons . . . ruins, I think . . . yes, ruins, the hulls of ships
and stations, the closer I go the more I see, thousands, millions
of wrecks . . . the singing is louder now, a strangely haunting
whistling through the transceiver sets; the rubidax crystals have
changed colour and when I cool them they emit this strange
song, all scales and strange combinations of notes . . . I feel
oddly drawn towards the world, an image in my mind tells me
my great-grandfather is here . . . I can sense his ship, lying in
the void, and his voice seems to be calling to me through the
song voices of the worlds . . . I must go closer and seek him,
but the wrecked ships are clustered so closely about each world
that I am in danger of collision. End report.'[45] Hurst's voice is
just about discernible in the mix. Without the script, it is like
tuning into one side of an extremely faint interdimensional
conversation. Hurst is trapped in the sub frequencies of the song

56

itself. There are shades of Stanislav Lem's novel *Solaris* here in the notion of astronauts hallucinating dead relatives in thrall to a distant sun.

The book that influenced the following song, 'Son of Nothing', was *Childhood's End* by Arthur C. Clarke. This track serves as a flashback to tell the story of man's escape from a dying sun and impending environmental disaster. Destination? 'The sun of nothingness'. The demo of the song was called 'Return to the Sun of Nothingness', a tribute to the working titles of Pink Floyd's 'Echoes' (from 1971 album *Meddle*) where 'No one flies around the sun'. The song is slovenly, with a main riff that chugs out to eternity. 'Will we ever reach our journey's end', to start life again on a planet away from the 'war pigs' of Earth? Jus sings. The demo contained a final glimmer of hope which was cut from the final version: 'Oh baby, just maybe, we'll return'.

Childhood's End, written in 1953, had made a strong impression on Jus. In the novel, a race of aliens known as the 'Overlords' suddenly arrive and station their ships above the key cities on Earth. One of the Overlords, known as Karellen, Supervisor for Earth, is the principal communicator with the Finnish UN Secretary-General, Rikki Stormgren. The Overlords resolve the conflicts of our planet and insist on the end of certain practices such as cruelty towards animals. They achieve this through terrifying displays of supernatural power, such as making all the attendees of a bull fight feel the searing pain of the wounded animal as it is lanced. One character, Jan, makes himself a stowaway and gets transported to the Overlords' home planet. He returns to a human race changed beyond recognition: 'Jan had glimpsed the universe in all its awful immensity, and knew now that it was no place for man.'[46]

Clarke acknowledges the oppression of the aliens' 'benevolent' colonial power, drawing comparisons with the British Raj in India. In opposition to the Overlords from the outset is the

Freedom League. Members of this resistance kidnap Stormgren
and transport him to an underground location where they think
they are beyond Karellen's powers of oversight. They see the
willing multitude above ground as an enslaved people – enlightenment is below ground. Later in the novel, an island colony is
established, Athens, which models itself as an enclave of social
engineering, drawing together the cream of society to advance
the arts and sciences. One of its citizens bemoans the world
which is now 'placid, featureless and culturally dead'.[47]

On this part of *Come My Fanatics . . .* , Electric Wizard
wanted to convey an insular and in-the-know feeling that there
was an intra-planetary Overlords-style master race calling the
shots. Or at the least, make a target out of the blank masses
sleepwalking through their days, making shit music. Liberation
and like-minded rebels dwelled underground. Wimborne was a
microcosm of a larger truth in society: there are secrets which a
few have access to and that are hidden from the broader popu-
lace. If these horrible things bubbled up and surfaced in society,
the wheels of bureaucracy and power would soon squash them
and obliterate all traces.

Today, these notions of planetary control, raging epidemics,
environmental catastrophe and warfare are overground and
for all to see. *Childhood's End* sees these conclude and with it
an awakening of humanity to a wider consciousness beyond its
control. As its children begin to develop extrasensory powers,
the Overmind develops like a multi-nodal network. If Electric
Wizard's music destroyed, it also soothed and laid the pathways
for this connectivity for those willing to understand them: the
union of a cohort, or a coven, of the chosen few.

In the late nineties, this felt like a subversive point of view:
'Back then you were considered quite a paranoid, underground
freak if you thought the world was controlled by the powers that
be and no one really cared about us,' Jus told me in an interview

for *The Quietus* for the album's twentieth anniversary, conducted
on the day when Donald Trump was inaugurated president of
the United States on 20 January 2017.[48]

The idea of underground culture here is of a bunker mentality
also found in the subterranean world of 1970's *Beneath the
Planet of the Apes*, inhabited by what its poster described as
'radiation-crazed super humans' – telepathic descendants of survivors of nuclear holocaust. They have mutated over centuries
and worship an ancient nuclear bomb. The planet is destroyed at
the end of the film by the doomsday bomb. The closing narration
of the film is sampled at the end of 'Son of Nothing' as the song
picks up tempo and rages out of control: 'In one of the countless
billions of galaxies in the universe, lies a medium-sized star,
and one of its satellites, a green and insignificant planet, is now
dead.'

The nuclear threat is also at the heart of Leigh Brackett's
1955 novel, *The Long Tomorrow*. Brackett went on to be the
screenwriter for *The Empire Strikes Back*, the most brooding
of the *Star Wars* franchise. In the novel, a catastrophic event
referred to as the 'Destruction' has wiped out the city centres
of the United States. The exact nature of the conflict that led
up to it, and the cataclysm itself, gives the novel its strange
vision of a society that has regressed back in time and added an
amendment to its constitution: 'No city, no town, no community
of more than one thousand people or two hundred buildings to
the square mile shall be built or permitted to exist anywhere in
the United States of America.'[49]

In one of the country's sparse, technologically backward
and religiously minded communities, two young men dream of
escape. There have been rumours of a city called Bartorstown,
a pre-war, top-secret military installation named for Waltham
Bartor, the Secretary of Defense who built it. Eventually, not
without trials, they are taken to Bartorstown. It is hidden

within the bowels of a mountain. Within it is a nuclear reactor – the object of fear and fascination. The same energy that was unleashed to bomb humanity back to the pre-industrial era is being harnessed again to rebuild it. The book is a cautionary tale of the perils of progress and striving too hard to uncover what should remain hidden, lest it destroy your relationship with reality. The canyon walls protecting supernatural power can begin to feel like a tomb. As Joan, one of the women of Bartorstown bitterly comments: 'You have to be a fanatic to feel that it's all worth while [sic].'[50]

Come My Fanatics . . . was an atomic explosion in metal's landscape. Electric Wizard were emissaries from a paranoid future. For a band who were proselytising the ways of the underground, the record heaved them overground – into a near-blinding sunlight of wider consciousness.

Lee Dorrian, the Napalm Death and Cathedral singer who ran the label Rise Above Records, which released the album, told me that *Come My Fanatics* . . . was the 'turning point of everything': '*Come My Fanatics* . . . blew everything apart and sent everything off the scale because it was a completely fuck-off sounding record. No frills but done with such fucking venom but also otherworldliness. When I first listened to it, I was like, "Fucking hell, I can't hear the drums", but realised that it was a good thing that they were completely buried. I just got completely stoned and listened to it on my bed and thought it was the most amazing thing I'd ever heard.'[51]

When it sent the album to the media, Rise Above's press release didn't hold back: '*Come My Fanatics* . . . is a flash-back-inducing trip of sub-sonic-shit-yer-pants, low-end vibrations blended with wild unkempt drums and full-on feedbacking amps overdriven by cheap electronic mood modulators.'

'It's a very technically inept album,' Jus told me in the interview for its anniversary in 2017. 'It's very difficult to deliberately do things badly. It just happened. It was exactly the sound we were trying to create.'[52]

The first pressings of the album featured artwork by Jus of the band's name across the front of the cover, with black flames licking the base of the letters. A horned, bearded, red-eyed devil man with a cross hanging off his neck was positioned in the centre. Later versions depict Anton LaVey and his disciples in a still from a 1971 documentary called *The Power of the Witch*. At the time, Jus had to pause his taped copy and trace the image of this crew from his television screen. He later provided the incandescent universe as background, to pull the coven out into space. The band's name and logo are placed in a discreet, sans-serif font in the bottom left corner. The album's title had four points in the ellipsis: *Come My Fanatics* . . . . One more than the convention. One louder.

On the cover of the issue of *Kerrang!* published on 11 January 1997, the bands Korn and 3 Colours Red were being touted as the 'future sound of music'. Korn had released their second album in October and, with it, nu metal was consolidated as the explosive trend of that period. 3 Colours Red were the Creation label's alternative rock hopes at the time and received a huge amount of support in *Kerrang!* and elsewhere – though who speaks of them now? There was a photo of Lars Ulrich from Metallica's recent UK tour with his controversially short hair-style. Keith Flint from The Prodigy poked his head out of the bottom of the cover. There were images of members of Deftones, No Doubt, Terrorvision and Feeder. Metal was changing in front of our eyes.

In the review section, the editor Phil Alexander gave *Come My Fanatics* . . . a full score 5K review. He described it as 'one of the most punishingly heavy albums in recent memory' with nods to 'Sabbath at their trippiest', singling out the 'barking space doom' of 'Ivixor B/Phase Inducer'. 'Classic is the only word for it,' he concluded. He also gave some sonic reference points: Eyehat-egod, Kyuss (which didn't help the stoner rock tag that bothered the band) and the early material of New Jersey's lysergic space freaks Monster Magnet. The review was accompanied by a black-and-white photo of the band standing at a gate. Mark has his arms crossed and is looking upwards, as if suspiciously. Tim is holding the gate open and gazing at nothing in the middle distance. A leather-jacketed Jus is eyeballing the camera in the background.

The review was unexpected and its praise unprecedented, although Jus had noticed Alexander sometimes wore T-shirts of doom acts like Penance and Saint Vitus when he presented his *Raw Power* TV show. *Kerrang!* was the biggest metal magazine in the world. Electric Wizard were very happy with the reaction – they couldn't deny it. But there was a potential problem. Could they begin to adjust to a new reality of success when they had been comfortable in the Dorset underground?

The *Terrorizer* review of *Come My Fanatics . . .* took a swipe at the band for being unreliable: 'The Wiz have made a great stoner doom record . . . Now if they can work out details for actually showing up for gigs when they are booked to do so, they'll be able to swab this madness around a bit further.'[53]

The truth is, the Wizard wanted success. Unlike the space-craft of 'Solarian 13', which closes *Come My Fanatics . . .* , they didn't want to drift forever. That song contained the promise of something different in their sound. Its pentatonic groove moved in a different way. It burned slowly, even sexily. It began a tradition of the final tracks on their albums pointing the way forward to the next record. The EP that followed would express something that built itself up like a smouldering ball of energy before unleashing something overwhelming – annihilating, even.

Come My Fanatics . . . was the true birth of Electric Wizard. In its blown-out vision of a world riven with conspiracy and

environmental disaster it seemed to spawn the twenty-first
century itself. What was absurd and freakish about it when
it was released seems prophetic now. It also set up a conflict
between a world that the band struggled hard to create and
express, against the effort and mundanity of the day-to-day lives
they inhabited. It was the start of a war with reality; a war it
was unlikely the Wizard could win.

Chapter Three
Mindless slaves to the black god

'We're just three depressed fucks from a small town. It's got to be good to turn all that negative energy into good music, but the whole idea that people getting stoned are a bunch of happy, flower-giving, hippy fucks is what Electric Wizard is against in the most extreme way.' – Jus in *Kerrang!* magazine, October 2000.[54]

Electric Wizard asked themselves a question: are we three reprobates from Wimborne, or is there something deeper, darker and more intricate behind it? Was theirs a higher purpose – to be a violent revolutionary force and to rise up and liberate the exploited substratum of society from the Duke of Normandy? Or were *they* the hidden power themselves, waiting for that moment to seize control and establish a new world order?

Electric Wizard had formed when Jus left his band Eternal to join Tim and Mark, who were jamming Black Sabbath covers. 'My older brother went to school with Jus,' remembered Tim in 2006. 'I was looking for a guitarist and I'd been best mates with Mark since I was thirteen. Through my brother, I phoned up Justin and, you know, "D'you fancy having a jam?" and immediately it clicked.'[55]

In the early-to-mid-nineties, Black Sabbath's stature was reduced to that of a cult band. Adrift, and with only guitarist

64

Tony Iommi involved throughout as a founding member, Sabbath
had struggled to navigate the fallout from the eighties' hair
metal explosion with its epicentre in Los Angeles. Jus, Tim
and Mark kept faith with Sabbath's earlier material from the
seventies, as did bands in Seattle – Tad, The Melvins and
Soundgarden, amongst others – who captured some of Sabbath's
unorthodox and titanic songwriting in the form of grunge. When
grunge's popularity suppressed the excesses of the eighties
(along with a lot of previously popular heavy metal) for a time,
the iron men of Sabbath had their revenge by proxy.

'A lot of people I knew were like, "Oh, you have to listen to
Hawkwind when you're on acid,"' Jus remembered in 2006. 'And
I was like, "Nah, I wanna listen to death metal." But it sounded
harsh, so then we listened to Sabbath on mushrooms, and went,
"What the fuck are we doing? This is the greatest band that's
ever fuckin' existed."'[56]

Black Sabbath's 'War Pigs' was the first song that Jus
learned to play on guitar. 'A lot of English people really relate
to Sabbath because of their background,' Jus told an American
journalist in 2001. 'Led Zeppelin were rich boys – well, a couple
of 'em were rich boys – I don't relate to them so much. Sabbath
was a big inspiration – you could play the heaviest music you
could play, come from a fuck-all background with no money and
still be a superstar and fucking destroy the world.'[57]

Electric Wizard originally called themselves Doom Chapter.
They wanted to establish their own biker chapter equivalent
within doom metal itself. But when they started working with
Rise Above, the label insisted they couldn't be a doom band
with the word 'Doom' in their name. They were told they had
to find another name. In his previous band Eternal, Jus had
recorded a cover of Sabbath's 'Electric Funeral' (from the 1970
Paranoid album). 'Electric Funeral', with the semi-tonal crush
of its main riff, turns the 'obscene fire' of nuclear holocaust into

a supernatural entity overlooking mankind: 'And so in the sky/ Shines the electric eye/Supernatural king/Takes Earth under his wing'. When it came to finding a new name for the band, Jus chose the title of one of Doom Chapter's new songs, 'Electric Wizard' – its title a composite of 'Electric Funeral' and, from Sabbath's first album, 'The Wizard', a jaunty track about how a trickster figure can enter and upend your life at any moment.

It took four years for Electric Wizard to evolve in Wimborne, if Putrefaction is considered the band's primitive beginnings. Putrefaction released their *Necromantic* demo in 1989. It saw Jus play guitar alongside Adam Richardson with Dave Gedge on bass, not long before Gedge founded the Bad Acid record label and fanzine. Harry Armstrong, another principal musician in the late nineties/early twenty-first-century English stoner and doom rock scene, in the bands Hangnail and End Of Level Boss, had also played bass in the band.

Putrefaction, and then Lord of Putrefaction, were heavily indebted to the sound of the English death metal and grindcore bands on the Nottingham-based Earache label: Bolt Thrower, Carcass and Napalm Death. Lord of Putrefaction recorded a split with a band called Mortal Remains in 1991 and another demo titled *Wings Over a Black Funeral*.

From that demo, the song 'Wings Over a Black Funeral' is a lacerating blast of death metal. 'At The Cemetary [sic] Gates' gamely rips off the breakdown from Slayer's 'War Ensemble' (on the 1990 album *Seasons in the Abyss*), whereas 'Dark Prayers' has the funereal pace of the emergent death-doom scene centred on the city of Bradford and its surrounding towns in Yorkshire. In that region, Paradise Lost and My Dying Bride were transmuting goth into pitch-black evocations of the tomb.

Jus's next band, Thy Grief Eternal, continued with the morose sound and gruff vocals. Adam had left but Gavin Gillingham of Ryders of the Storm joined on guitar. They recorded a demo

called . . . *on Blackened Wings*. As well as torturous guitar bends
and Thor's Hammer drumming, the song 'Swathed in Black'
exhibits some new melodic ideas – including more graceful
accents to the riffs. In a similar way, the title track has the
same chilling harmonies that gave Cathedral's early music its
beauty. The song even features a competent guitar solo over a
stirring, uptempo chug.

Cathedral's Lee Dorrian liked what he heard of the Lord of
Putrefaction demos and when they changed their name and
slowed down, his favour grew. He invited Thy Grief Eternal to
support Cathedral at the Marquee Club in London and paid for
the sessions that became the . . . *on Blackened Wings* demo. The
'ceremony' (as the liner notes described it) took place on 26 and
27 October 1991 at Rhythm Studios near Bidford-on-Avon, not
far from Stratford-Upon-Avon. The producer/'funeral director'
was Paul Johnson, who had produced Cathedral's debut album
that year, *Forest of Equilibrium*. Dorrian hoped to include one
or more Thy Grief Eternal tracks on an instalment of his Rise
Above compilation, *Dark Passages*. This never happened, and
other plans for an album, and then an EP, fizzled out.

The band morphed again. James Evans, who had played
drums in Lord of Putrefaction and Thy Grief Eternal, was
replaced with Gareth Brunsdon. Eternal was born. Rise Above
weren't the only ones interested in the band. Earache Records
fronted the cash for Eternal's *Lucifer's Children* demo in 1993.

Proper recognition of the impact of Earache and Rise Above
on British musical culture has long been neglected. Their bands
played Peel sessions, inspired legions of imitators worldwide,
and founded their own subgenres in the process. They were com-
mercially successful too, to the point that Columbia Records (a
division of Sony) licensed Earache's roster in the early nineties
for distribution in America. Both labels also benefited from the
UK Conservative government's Enterprise Allowance Scheme to

get started, with the ironic result that Thatcherism invested the creative capital for a host of abrasive, anti-capitalist bands.

The DNA of Electric Wizard is clearest in Eternal. 'Magickal Childe' begins with the 'long hair and faggot clothes' sample from *The Living Dead at the Manchester Morgue* later recycled for 'Wizard in Black' from *Come My Fanatics* . . . Likewise, the thirteen who are gathered on a moonless night on the slow-motion 'Lucifer's Children' found themselves reconvened on 'Doom-Mantia'. The lyric was stripped back on 'Doom-Mantia', just as the music was queasily overloaded with drugged-out formlessness.

The influence of Jus discovering doom legends Trouble (more of whom later) came first in his cleanly sung vocals in Eternal, then in his more supple guitar playing, and the inclusion of choruses and bridges in the songs. The music lopes and gambles because it is instilled with more life – it still trudges when it wants (as on the momentous first half and tortured ending of 'Lucifer's Children' – 'This planet's fucking dead,' Jus screams). The second riff sequence on 'Magickal Childe' was massaged into the main riff to 'Mourning Prayer' on Electric Wizard's debut album. The excellent cover of Black Sabbath's 'Electric Funeral' is another signpost to the band that followed.

The main connecting thread between Eternal and Electric Wizard is the fourth song on the Eternal demo: 'Chrono-naut (Phase I–IV)'. The song is an epic in four 'phases' about interplanetary and intertemporal travel because, frankly, 'Reality's too slow,' as Jus sings. 'Chrono-naut' is a fifteen-minute-plus, cosmic stoner-rock masterpiece. It's not a surprise that Electric Wizard later re-recorded it for a split EP with Orange Goblin in 1997, though Jus never really owned it as an Electric Wizard song.

The Eternal version is nimbler than the later version, which Rolf Startin roughed up into a gnarlier, growlier mindfuck. Mark also played a blinder on Electric Wizard's version. Eternal's rendition is more wide-eyed and less LSD-fried. It is overtly catchy in a way Electric Wizard shied away from being. Its massive second-phase hook is testament to that, but nothing like the prolonged, blissed-out mid-section with a slather of guitar solos and Kyuss-like trippy vibes.

It's an optimistic, mind-blown track which delighted the locals in Wimborne when Eternal played it, pledging to stand on the shores of the chaos seas 'where dreams become reality' to 'witness a billion suns'. At this point in the lives of Wimborne's children, the spaceship is not lost but just keeps going, and the last chapter of mankind is not obliteration but a union with the stars where 'peace and love will at last be ours'.

It is a power bestowed upon them by the Electric Wizard himself, before the band that formed under his name burned up on re-entry and emerged with a far bleaker perspective on humanity.

> The wizard gave us the key – yeah
> Placed it in our veins
> A spaceship powered by sorcery
> We'll never be the same
> Jetting through the multiverse to find a new sun
> Chrononaut through time and space
> Our minds will be as one
> Yeah

Jus doesn't like Electric Wizard's first, self-titled album.

He sees it as a misstep for two reasons. One was Paul Johnson's production – again at Rhythm Studios – which was too dry and too staid for the sound they wanted to get. My personal

feeling is not to downplay its thick, powerful tones – it has a
solid classic doom sound with some great songwriting. But one
listen to the tracks from the 1993 Doom Chapter demo included
on the 2006 reissue of *Electric Wizard* – 'Illimitable Nebulie' and
'Mourning Prayer, Part 1' – attests to the sprawling, seething,
jammed-to-fuck low-fidelity potency of the band this early on.

A sample of Sardu, master of the Theatre of the Macabre
from 1976 film *Bloodsucking Freaks*, introduces an even earlier,
rougher demo of the song 'Wizards of Gore' which bound
together the savage filmic horror show of much later Electric
Wizard to the gargantuan striking doom chords of Thy Grief
Eternal. This demo's main riff presented itself again in one form
on 'Stone Magnet' from *Electric Wizard* and later in another on
'Return Trip' from *Come My Fanatics* . . .

The difference between these early Electric Wizard demos and
a song like 'Chrono-Naut' is how the hidden world sounds like it
is encroaching on the band unbidden, versus the band gleefully
traversing the unknown with a polished sound. Jus's vocals
sound like an alien entity trapped underneath the rehearsal
space in the demos – sanding down the rough edges of their
sound on their first album did them no favours.

The second misstep on the debut album was Dave Patchett's
cover artwork, which Jus still detests to this day. It depicts a
dragon-like seahorse riding the cosmic seas with a priestess on its
back – strange planets, Buddha-like stone figures and even flying
dolphins provide the background. The band's logo mimics the font
of Black Sabbath's first album. As a piece of art, it wouldn't look
out of place in one of Glastonbury or Tintagel's tourist trinket
shops, but for Electric Wizard it was way off the mark.

Johnson and Patchett both worked on Cathedral's albums.
That's why Rise Above believed they would be a good fit to
tackle the recording and artwork of Electric Wizard's debut.
It sealed the fate of the album as a solid but not groundbreaking

doom metal release. It remains a stepping stone towards the extraordinary breakthrough of *Come My Fanatics* . . .

'I've pondered the fact that our first album was shit,' Jus told *Decibel* magazine in 2011. 'A lot of bands start off with a really good album and then they just go downhill. Luckily, we started with a shit album so we could only get better, really. Bands should consider doing their first albums quite badly. It could help their careers.'[58]

Electric Wizard is not shit. The riff of 'Behemoth' is enormous, encompassing the 'blackened wings', inherited from the imagery of Thy Grief Eternal, that 'shadow the earth'. But the song does not do anything to innovate on the deathly slow doom template laid down by band favourites Dream Death and other more established doom acts like Solitude Aeturnus, who recorded 1994's *Through the Darkest Hour* with Paul Johnson at the same studio.

The instrumental 'Mountains of Mars' presaged the psychedelic excursion of 'Ivixor B/Phase Inducer' from *Come My Fanatics* . . . This bass-led somnolent drift over an alien landscape was a spiritual successor to Black Sabbath's hushed and trippy 'Planet Caravan'. Both the Wizard's and Sabbath's songs stop me dead in my tracks when I hear them, giving any moment or situation a lysergic sheen. The album's opening track, 'Stone Magnet', also looked ahead – the verse Jus sang over it set the tone for the pessimism that fuelled the band thereafter: 'But look around you, what you got/No hope, no future, no fuckin' job'.

The relentless, chugging intensity of 'Devil's Bride' depicts a satanic wedding – *The Devil's Bride* was the US title for Hammer film *The Devil Rides Out*, which came to symbolise more in the band's later incarnation. The song itself is an out-rider for the occult obsessions of later Wizard albums *Witchcult Today* and *Black Masses*, but in its latter part also shows how

71

the band could let a song run out of steam, ending as it does in a furious barrage.

Cosmic horror and druidic invocation of the 'ancient ones' are centre stage for 'Black Butterfly', which shows how Jus reintroduced the distended, slow-motion riffing of Thy Grief Eternal as a way of setting Electric Wizard apart from the more exuberant Eternal. Thirteen is the magic number again on this song – the number of 'maidens' to be sacrificed, as the song spirals out. This section delineates the 'Open caverns of eternal midnight' of its best and final line. But at this point the Wizard were lacking that confidence to simulate complete existential collapse, and they rein it all back in for a steady gallop to the song's conclusion.

Tripping out at Badbury Rings, the band envisaged a wizard descending to earth on the back of a dragon, then whisking them off for a journey through the astral gates. The album's final and title track, 'Electric Wizard', documents this extraordinary voyage through the 'virgin universe' where the band play on the dragon's back, coming upon the two towers on the edge of time and space, 'Creating and destroying with the music we made'. The song is the band's own creation myth – an expanding universe with this line-up's implosion seeded within it.

In the most audacious part of 'Electric Wizard', and perhaps the most memorable piece of music on the album, they take it all down to a whisper in anticipation of the wizard addressing them: 'The wizard turned and spoke to us and this is what he said'. Instead of expressing himself in words, Jus channels the wizard by playing an exquisite, light-touch blues-infused guitar solo. They are so enthused with what they're doing by this point of the song that the whole band surges back in and Tim even takes a bass solo.

The album ends with a song called 'Wooden Pipe', a sample from the 1968 BBC dramatisation of *The Hobbit*, as narrator

Anthony Jackson describes Bilbo Baggins standing in front of his home: '. . . smoking an enormous long wooden pipe'. Tolkien's heavy hints that the hobbits were stoners pleased Electric Wizard. They used the Tolkien sample before the band disowned Gandalf as a shit wizard just as peremptorily as they disowned their debut album.

A better model for a wizard is Simon Sinestrari, played by Andrew Prine, from 1971's *Simon, King of the Witches*, a film directed by Bruce Kessler (also a racing driver). Simon is a magician who lives in a storm drain in Los Angeles but that doesn't stymie his insouciant charm. He is a leonine medallion man in his mid-thirties, who dresses in a purple neckerchief. He is morally ambivalent, in the mould of Charles Manson. Ambitious, nonchalant and inscrutable, Gandalf he is not. In his words, Simon makes money through 'spells, incantations, charms, curses'. For him, psychics are too passive, and he prefers to divine the future: 'I see what I will to see'. Simon sides with the weed smokers and denizens of underground society against law enforcement. He manipulates energy to create strange electromagnetic charges in objects and people – 'he's pretty much an Electric Wizard,' Jus once said approvingly.[59]

Electric Wizard is a marker in time. Weirdly, it received a short review in *Front* magazine in its July 1999 issue (five years after its original release), with Jordan, aka Katie Price, dressed in a stringy Union Jack bikini on its cover. Alongside a glowing feature review of Pavement's *Terror Twilight*, the magazine describes Electric Wizard's debut as 'chock full of doom and gloom' – 'Motörhead on barbiturates, with Lemmy's bass turned up to 11 . . . Mind- and speaker-blowing.' Electric Wizard were rarely compared to Motörhead. They have always preferred the association with Hawkwind, Lemmy's previous band. But like Motörhead, Electric Wizard have staked a claim to be regarded as one of England's most influential and important bands – a symbol of the heaviest forces awaiting wider recognition.

In the mid-to-late nineties, Electric Wizard recorded their jam sessions and frequently distributed them as demo tapes. They had one instrumental jam titled 'Witchcoven (Live California Jam '74)'. They prefaced the music with crowd noise sampled from the California Jam gig played by Black Sabbath at the Ontario Motor Speedway, California, on 6 April 1974, subsequently broadcast on ABC. The demo is a nasty, tar-thick, proto-song, but at the three-minute mark there's a major-key sequence with an unusual, ecstatic quality that lifts it to a different zone. It was too good not to be reused in 1998, in a song which came to define the band.

When Jus was in the two gruff, Wimborne-based death metal bands that preceded Eternal – Thy Grief Eternal and before that Lord of Putrefaction – he noticed a problem with death metal: there were no women in the audience. For straight male musicians, a lack of women meant a dearth of sexual energy at gigs. Death metal was sexless and that was no fun. Electric Wizard were fascinated by the Austrian psychoanalyst and contemporary of Freud, Wilhelm Reich, and his concept of 'orgastic potency'. This was manifested in what Reich called 'orgone energy', a kind of cosmic lifeforce. The Wizard started working on a song that built, arrested and then exploded in an orgasmic climax.

At first, the resulting song, 'Supercoven', sounds like another lost transmission intercepted from the depths of space, presaging the song's first movement. There's the barely audible, ghostly exchange between Martin Landau as The Colonel and Robert Shaw as The Priest sampled from a 1971 occult-inflected spaghetti western called *A Town Called Bastard* (aka *A Town Called Hell*): 'So you're trying to crawl back to God, uh?' asks Landau; 'I would if I knew where to find him,' responds Shaw. Set in Mexico, the film also features a pallid Dudley Sutton (most famous as Tinker in *Lovejoy*) as Spectre, styled exactly like WWF's The Undertaker. 'Supercoven' as a song crawls back to a god, but certainly no Christian deity.

Electric Wizard had been playing around with a bolero-type construction in 3/4 time that emerged from nothing and then enveloped the listener in a blanket of harsh riffing. This played to Mark's strength as a drummer. He liked to take it easy on the snare and roll around the beat of a song, in the style of Cream's Ginger Baker, The Who's Keith Moon and Slade's Don Powell. As they developed the opening section of this new song in the studio, Mark was wrenching the song onwards, like Sisyphus barely able to push his monstrous boulder to the top of the mountain.

Mark played on a tatty drum kit – he hadn't changed his skins since the band recorded their first album four years earlier. Jus rarely changed his strings: 'The poorer you are, the heavier you are!' he boasted. Asked how he developed his drumming style, Mark replied: 'Some black men taught me! I'd go down on the back streets and beat on the bins. And from that day I've never forgotten how to drum in that style, from beating those bins.'[60] He played the drums like they deserved to suffer: 'You can't really go out and slaughter someone in public, so I play the drums like I'm killing someone!'[61]

If Mark played like a murderer, then 'Supercoven' was the sound of him erratically digging a shallow grave. Electric Wizard recorded again with Rolf Startin at Knighton Heath College in Bournemouth (now the Bournemouth Academy of Modern Music) over three days in February 1998. In each session they spent a few hours doing nothing, got loaded up on vodka and

weed and began piecing the song together. The jamming took
up to forty-five minutes. 'Most of our songs are ended by the
tape running out (ha, ha)!' Jus told the *Serpent Eve* fanzine. 'We
usually see Rolf, our producer, waving his arms about in the
mixing room pointing at the tape machine 'cos it's about to
run out.'[62]

If the planet was destroyed, 'Supercoven' is the incantation
the survivors would sing to their apocalypse-god: 'Black sun
master/Under starless sky/Black stone altar/They pray to the
sign,' Jus sings, a high priest wailing above the maelstrom. The
song is both a paean and a condemnation of the 'black god', for
whom human suffering is merely a by-product of its existence.

One source of inspiration for the notion of the black god are
the Jirel of Joiry stories by C. L. Moore, published in *Weird
Tales* magazine in the 1930s. Jirel is a warrior with long red
hair and burning eyes of yellow fire. In the story 'Black God's
Kiss', she travels through a subterranean tunnel to a strange
alternative universe where she kisses the titular god in order to
transport the dark energy back to the conqueror of her people, a
warrior called Guillaume. He has already physically confronted
her and forcibly kissed her, so her return with this kiss of
death from the black god is an act of vengeance. The follow-up
story, 'Black God's Shadow', sees Jirel wrestle with conflicting
emotions about Guillaume and whether she actually loved him:
'She had taken the black god's kiss. Heavy and cold upon her
soul and she had carried it back, feeling the terrible weight
bearing down upon some intangible part of her that shuddered
and shrunk from the touch. She had fouled her very soul with
that burden, but she had not guessed what terrible potentialities
it bore within her, like some egg of hell's spawning to slay the
man she loved.'[63]

The black god is a torturous and deceptive deity – 'all death
and nothingness'[64]. For its believers it is a form of anti-salvation.

C. L. Moore's black god aligns closely with another dark agent of chaos from a different twentieth-century mythology in *Weird Tales* magazine we will encounter later.

Once the opening section of 'Supercoven' reaches its orgasmic climax at the seven-minute mark, we enter the ecstatic state of the bridge section taken from the 'Witchcoven (Live California Jam '74)' demo. 'You're mindless fucking slaves!' Jus barks through his distorted mic at this point – presumably to a listenership under the cosmo-sexual dictatorship of the band. From here, the lyrics shift focus and the threat of alien 'old ones' that form the coven is replaced by the more benevolent notion that they watch from the sun only because 'They want us to be free.' There are shades here again of Arthur C. Clarke's *Childhood's End*. Our lack of depth of perception – the narrowness of our worldview – is what impedes the human race from gaining a revolution in our consciousness.

The song's finale is the slaughter of hopeless innocents. Just as the song seems to have pulled into a cul-de-sac from which it can't escape, the last riff cleaves through it in the merciless fashion of Jirel's blade. Musically, it recalls the sleek brutality of Celtic Frost, a Swiss band formed by Thomas Gabriel Fischer, one of the originators of death metal with his previous band, Hellhammer. Visionary and experimental, Celtic Frost were already exploring the outer reaches of this new form of metal on their 1985 album *To Mega Therion*. The final riff of 'Supercoven' signals that Jus hadn't left death metal behind. It ends with Jus screaming 'Supercoven!', which the EP's lyric notes specify should be repeated 'until stoned'.

The EP was completed by a second track, Electric Wizard's sixteen-minute full-bore Hawkwind homage, 'Burnout'. It was recorded to please Hawkwind fan Dave Gedge, who ran the Bad Acid label that released the EP. Lee Dorrian had been happy for the small American label, Man's Ruin, to release the *Chrono.*

Naut EP, as he felt Rise Above benefited from the association. The band pushed their relationship with Rise Above a little further by putting 'Supercoven' out with Bad Acid. Loyalty to labels was purely functional. Jus regarded the Sex Pistols film *The Great Rock 'n' Roll Swindle* as his education in the music business and behaved accordingly.

Even by Electric Wizard's standards, 'Burnout' is a headfuck. It's a song for the mentally locked-in and totally fried, unable to escape their dried-out brain and negotiate reality at any level: 'Can't you see nothing is real/Transparent world I cannot feel'.

After the release of the EP, Gedge asked the band in his fanzine whether 'Supercoven' was the heaviest track they had recorded. 'No, 'cos it's just a saying, it's just categorising really, we want people to make up their own minds,' said Mark.

'We're not fast or sludge,' added Jus. 'But we've got the most depressingly heavy vibe, but that's probably just us, not the music we're trying to play. We just can't get away from it.'[65]

In their previous exchange in the first issue of the fanzine, Jus had been more adamant. He had described what to expect from the *Supercoven* EP as 'A thousand per cent MINDFUC-KERAMA. Doperiff crusher.' Adding as an afterthought: 'Maybe some experimental shit.'[66]

'Supercoven' is probably the most important Electric Wizard song. It says everything about the Wizard. When the band plays it live, for them it's like hearing it for the first time. It was so heavy and hypnotic they thought they could order people to go out and kill.[67] It is an audition piece to this day. Prospective members never get it fully right, but some do very well. It is the kind of epic to begin or end concerts. But back in 1998, Electric Wizard played it whenever they wanted in the set.

When reviewed in *Aural Innovations* magazine ('The global source for space rock exploration'), writer Jerry Kranitz applauded the way the EP drenched doom metal with the hallucinogenic qualities of space and psych rock. Electric Wizard created 'a lysergic satanic universe that will reward those who dare to venture with truly mind-blowing metallic acid rock'. He went on to single out Jus's performance, including one of numerous misspellings of his surname down the years: 'These guys can really jam and Osborn plays truly gut-wrenching acid guitar that in itself could turn a lot of more standard psych fans into metal fanatics.'[68] With Oborn as a second name, it's almost as if Jus wants to be called John 'Ozzy' Osbourne but can't quite make it.

Electric Wizard had upped the ante, that was beyond doubt. 'Remember that scene in [heavy-metal mockumentary] *Bad News* when Spider Webb jokes, "If we made a record it would be so heavy you couldn't get it off the turntable"?' *Terrorizer* wrote in their review of the EP. 'This is that record.'[69]

The insert of the *Supercoven* vinyl compared its sound to a 'dark, brooding Loop on downers'. Loop were one of a pantheon of bands that Electric Wizard thought sounded great whilst on acid. The feedback-drenched sound of 1988 album *Fade Out* spurred the Wizard on to make similar 'head music' for metalheads. The insert also declared the record a 'black magic trip to the darkest corners of bleeding consciousness.' A message on the back cover of the EP took an aggressive stance, inspired by the graffiti at the old mill in Wimborne: 'FUCK OFF WEAK DOOM! WE KANE HARDER!!'

'There ain't no fucking other band who smokes as much dope as us,' Jus said to *Bad Acid*. 'It's our curse, we're not showing off. We're cursed! Every band we've played with I've seen fall to the floor – weak. We've always got the best dope as well. They've always got soapbar and we've got fucking supremo fucking weed!'[70]

It set up a combative tone which persisted in the two years that followed. In that long-running arms race for heaviness,

Electric Wizard had the nuclear bomb of orgone energy at their disposal. If they could translate the awesome power of their jamming into live performance, they might start something: '. . . a revolution, guns and fucking in the streets . . .'[71]

The question was whether Electric Wizard could hold it together long enough to achieve that goal of either forming or defeating the Supercoven (it wasn't clear which). As important as orgone was, drugs fuelled the band – and like a spacecraft exploding on take-off, it could destroy them too.

Despite the acclaim the band were getting, they didn't play much live. Playing live didn't pay. They had to fork out for petrol, van hire, food and accommodation. If they had got offered more drugs, it might have been a different story.

When gigs did happen, chaos wasn't far away. Electric Wizard played at dangerous volumes. Amps blew up, leads malfunctioned and the band members were unpredictable: Mark might smash his drum kit to bits. They legged it from bouncers when things got out of hand. The band hadn't bothered with setlists before *Come My Fanatics* . . . and they weren't too bothered with them afterwards. On stage, they often argued about what to play. The songs were played differently at each gig. They jammed and they deviated, adding solos and extending sections. They made up songs on the spot. If the crowd was lacklustre, they doubled down, playing the songs as slowly and heavily as they could – or just let the guitars feedback from the amps and make weird screeching noises. If it was a good show, they were 'headbanging to fuck'.[72]

'I think most people who see us are totally blown away 'cos we are so aggressive and heavy live,' they told the *Serpent Eve* fanzine, 'plus we're usually staggering around madmen due to drugs and alcohol abuse. We always play in a hundred per cent fucked-up mental situation. I mean going to a gig is like a fuckin' party. So all the way in the van you're smokin' weed and when you get to the venue you start drinkin' and smoking more buds and then someone cuts up some lines or has some pills or something and by the time you hit the stage you're fuckin' gone! But your fuckin' rush on stage [is] better than any coke! We love it!'[73]

After the release of *Supercoven*, Electric Wizard toured with Lee Dorrian's Cathedral and the Liverpudlian death-doom band Anathema. Anathema were part of the 'Peaceville Three' – a trio of death-doom bands on the Peaceville Records label based in Bradford, alongside Paradise Lost and My Dying Bride. Cathedral had set a new bar for misery in the doom genre with 1991's *Forest of Equilibrium*, before loosening up, drastically improving their playing abilities and incorporating a more retro-progressive sound on their subsequent albums. The Wizard's touring relationship with Cathedral had been strained when Cathedral previously booked a short, four-date tour on which they were the only one of the two bands there was budget to feed. It was a strange way to treat a support band, particularly one signed to your label.

Electric Wizard opened the show on the Cathedral/Anathema tour. The *Terrorizer* review of their gig at London's LA2 was typical of the hyperbole used to describe the band live, likening the experience to the 'intriguing physical pelting of jagged rubble': 'Hulking and sullen, Electric Wizard's murky, muddy sludge 'Supercoven' stumbles through the air, slamming into bystanders without a flicker of conscience, it's [sic] bottom-heavy doom careening out of control in a hazy stupor. There are multiple bruises to tend to after they skulk off stage.'[74]

There is something apposite in describing 'Supercoven' as embodying the shambolic onstage persona of their creators.

Off stage, reports were that their behaviour was getting more erratic, even revolutionary. Word was out about how Jus had set fire to the Robin Reliant outside Wimborne police station, like an insurrectionist Rodney Trotter. He had argued with his girlfriend and wanted to destroy the world, starting with the car. When asked about this by the *Bad Acid* fanzine, Jus blurted out that he 'did a deal with the pigs'. Then he backtracked and explained that they promised to let him off for the arson, and reduce the charge to criminal damage, if he admitted to kicking off the wing mirror: 'You'll have to talk to my solicitor!!!'[75]

Jus might have imagined his lawyer was Horst Mahler, who represented members of the Baader–Meinhof terrorist gang in legal proceedings. The gang, otherwise known as the Red Army Faction (RAF), fascinated Jus from childhood. Main man Andreas Baader's arrest was covered by the British news in 1972 and the mythology around the group as an anti-establishment terror cell grew throughout the seventies and eighties, alongside that of the Manson Family and the Symbionese Liberation Army, who kidnapped Patty Hearst. Jus took a more serious interest in the Baader–Meinhof gang as time went on and read about their activities in the 1977 book *Hitler's Children* by Jillian Becker.

As the offspring of the war generation, the Baader–Meinhof gang crystallised the student and worker unrest that had swept across the divided Germany in the late sixties and early seventies. That unrest had been fomented in the communes of Berlin and other cities that sought to disrupt day-to-day life with artful protest, high on the critical theory of thinkers like Herbert Marcuse who characterised the students as potentially representing the 'most advanced consciousness of humanity'.[76] The communes were soundtracked by drug-addled krautrock collectives like Amon Düül II. This frenzied rock music itself might have set the tempo for the student unrest that followed.

Decades later, Electric Wizard saw themselves as both providing musical entertainment *and* violent societal upheaval.

One of the founders of Kommune I in Berlin, and later a terrorist himself, Dieter Kunzelmann brought Wilhelm Reich into the equation when he declared, 'I don't care about Vietnam, I care about my orgasm.'[77] *Konkret*, the paper which principal member Ulrike Meinhof contributed to, published articles on Reichian subjects such as 'sexuality and the class struggle' to growing sales.[78] Orgasmic energy and revolution were intertwined.

The fanatics of the Baader–Meinhof gang varied in their ideological passions. At the outset, Andreas Baader himself – according to Becker – hadn't read anything, had no interest in politics at all and 'liked to defy for the sake of defying'.[79] His girlfriend, Gudrun Ensslin, however, was a zealot from the beginning. Ulrike Meinhof herself was an increasingly polemical journalist who sought out an identity in any sort of collective.

'When Gudrun talked about the "fascist state" and rationalised her desire to attack it, he [Baader] replied that the state wasn't worth thinking about at all, it was just a "shat-in shithouse",' writes Becker. 'The police were "bulls" or "pigs". He showed her how to break into locked cars and start them without an ignition key. "Oh," she said, he was more "refreshingly close to reality" than anyone else she'd known. When she wondered what she should do about it all, he said, "Do anything, it doesn't matter what, everything's just shit anyway." Such was the pure simplicity of Baader.'[80]

At this stage, Electric Wizard were – or wanted you to think they were – a band of three Andreas Baaders. They expressed something of the attitude of the late sixties and early seventies – not the *Time* magazine memorialisation of the period, but the gritty underbelly of *Oz* magazine. The side history doesn't want you to see.

In the second interview with *Bad Acid*, Tim only managed a stoned mumble when asked about breaking into an off-licence and getting arrested afterwards. He got picked up by the police whilst slumped outside it, drinking the whiskey he'd stolen. It was also this period when Tim made his attempt to steal the cross from St John's Church, slipped, fell through a skylight below and sliced his arm open.

Mark also tangled with the police. In the second *Bad Acid* interview he spoke about getting nicked for being drunk and disorderly. He had shoved a copper who 'was coming on all arsey': 'My cell was all the way down the end, they were all the way down the other, and I kept on ringing the bell. They'd have to walk all the way down and say, "What's wrong with you?" and I'd say, "Nothing!" and just shout at them.'[81]

'We weren't very nice people, to be honest,' Jus reflected in 2009. 'We were feeding off that shit at the time. It made us feel like we were more of a heavy metal band.'[82] But over the next year their status as simply 'heavy metal' would be disputed by the band, not least by Jus.

In another, work-related incident, Jus sliced off the tip of the index finger on his fretting hand while fitting a carpet in one of his day jobs. It was a strange echo of what happened to Black Sabbath guitarist Tony Iommi, when he sliced off the tips of two of his fingers while operating the machine press in a factory in Aston in the late sixties. Whereas Iommi fashioned some plastic fingertips from melted-down washing-up liquid bottles to continue playing, Jus simply glued his fingertip back on.

This happened shortly before playing a gig at the Barfly venue in Camden, London, supported by Hangnail and Goatsnake. Hangnail were led by guitarist-vocalist Harry Armstrong, another figure from the Wimborne music scene – they released two excellent albums on Rise Above: *Ten Days Before Summer* (1999) and *Clouds in the Head* (2001). Goatsnake were

Poster for Electric Wizard's first gig.

The entrance to what was Cartoons snooker hall in Wimborne.

Horton Tower, outside Wimborne.

Badbury Rings on a June evening.

The NEL paperback cover of *Freewheelin Frank*.

Frank Reynolds presiding over the book's serialisation.

The Living Dead causing mayhem on location in Walton-on-Thames in *Psychomania*.

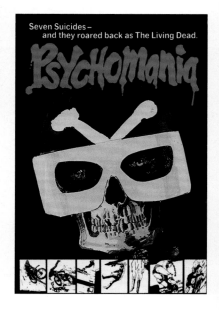

The VHS cover of *Psychomania*.

Electric Wizard at the time
of *Come My Fanatics* . . .
(L-R: Jus, Tim and Mark
standing)

The Sound City amp and cabinet used on
Come My Fanatics . . . and every album since.

'Classic is the only word
for it.' The *Kerrang!*
review of *Come My
Fanatics* . . .

ELECTRIC WIZARD
'Come My Fanatics...'
(Rise Above RISE14CD)
KKKKK
THE LUDICROUSLY named
Electric Wizard return with a second album
that isn't about to alleviate that nasty New Year
hangover. If anything, the Dorset doom blokes
have delivered one of the most punishingly
heavy albums in recent memory.
   Opener 'Return Trip' is the aural equivalent
of a herd of stampeding mammoths piling

down your headphones.
'Doom-Mantia' and 'Solarian
13' come on like Sabbath at
their trippiest, while 'Wizard
In Black' and 'Son Of Nothing'
are nothing short of crushing.
For maximum wig-out
potential, the neo-Eastern wail
of 'Ivixor B/Phase Inducer' is a
display of barking space doom.
   If you need reference points, take Kyuss,
New Orleans dischord merchants Eyehategod
and even early Monster Magnet, and you're
close to the brutal furrow ploughed by Electric
Wizard. Classic is the only word for it.
PHIL ALEXANDER

Promo photo for
the first album.

Early gig poster from
the mid-nineties.

Dorset Doom is born.

Playing live in 1995.

Passing the acid test – *Supercoven* promo photo.

Live in 1998.

The *Supercoven* EP insert.

Flattening the Camden Barfly with Goatsnake in 1999 (note Jus's elongated index finger after he glued his severed fingertip back on).

Germany's Most Wanted: The Baader-Meinhof gang.

'Yog-Sothoth is the gate': minds blasted by gods dwelling between the stars courtesy of H.P. Lovecraft.

US promo photo.

Three wizards crowned with weed.

Poster for a stop on the *Apocalypse Now* 2001 tour with Warhorse.

Playing Oklahoma City in March 2001.

Mark catches a nap in the cramped tour van.

The Wizard and Warhorse, all smiles in Worcester, Massachusetts.

The Wizard get a vehicle upgrade on the first US tour.

In Coney Island for the *Metal Maniacs* US tour in late 2001.

Jus in his element in 2002.

Aleister Crowley on a flyer for the band's third North American tour in 2002.

A disconsolate Electric Wizard around the release of *Let Us Prey*.

a Californian stoner-doom band with Sunn O)))'s Greg Anderson
on guitar. It was on the reverse side of a Goatsnake demo that
Anderson and Stephen O'Malley first experimented with the
drumless drone and feedback improvisations which would slowly
make them darlings of the avant-garde metal scene. That said,
Goatsnake was a much livelier band.

The gig was reviewed in *Kerrang!*, where Jus was given
another new variation on his name: 'Gus Osborn shows us
a recently reconstructed finger, then he has a bloody good
attempt at slicing the digit off again with "Supercoven".' If you
look closely at the blurred photograph on the back of 2000's
Dopethrone of Jus playing guitar live, you can just about make
out an unnaturally elongated digit on this fretting hand. It
didn't impede their performance. *Kerrang!* marvelled at the spectacle: 'How anything so lumbering and so close to grinding to a
complete halt can sound so awesome is beyond logic. It's akin to
the bells of doom put to music – and what a fantastic noise it
is.' The reviewer, *Kerrang!* cartoonist Ray Zell, even singled out
the quality of Mark's musicianship as 'of a class you just don't
usually witness at club level.'[83]

Electric Wizard walked the walk, there can be no doubt. Jus's
eardrum also got perforated on the Goatsnake tour. Surgery to
repair it was partially successful. He's dealt with his hearing
problems since by treating them with excessive volume.

But the band could also be found in a subdued, taciturn mood.
Prior to the gig, and probably because of the fact they were
consuming 'huge lungfuls of weed' backstage at the Falcon pub
at 32 Wilmot Place, Camden, where the Barfly club night took
place, one journalist found that Jus 'didn't say very much' and
Mark and Tim were 'friendly but quiet'.[84]

For all their bravado, as 1999 faded into winter, Electric
Wizard were drifting apart: 'I would safely say there was a
period where we split up. We just didn't tell anybody,' Jus

confided years later.[85] Mark, not drunk enough not to cycle but certainly drunk enough to crash into a tree, broke his collarbone. 'It's a good pain killer, vodka!' he later reflected.[86] It needed six months to heal. Then it was out of alignment and had to be snapped back into place. This excruciating process wasn't the cause of the malaise that cast a spell over the band, but rather a symptom of it.

The millennium was upon Electric Wizard. Jus and Tim lost their jobs. Mark tolerated his one. Perhaps they could get it together to make one last statement – a last pitch for greatness. To become the lords of all they surveyed and of all the drugs that passed through their fingers, like the sands of time.

Chapter Four
𝕴𝖓 𝖙𝖍𝖎𝖘 𝖑𝖆𝖓𝖉 𝖔𝖋 𝖘𝖔𝖗𝖈𝖊𝖗𝖞

𝕾omething different loomed in the lyrics of 'Supercoven'.
The song speaks of 'the old ones' and that 'Yog Sothoth is
the gate'. These were references from the story 'The Dunwich
Horror', written by H.P. Lovecraft, which first appeared in *Weird
Tales* in April 1929. Lovecraft is thanked for 'lyrical inspiration'
on the EP's sleeve.

'The Dunwich Horror' is about the attempts by Wilbur Whateley, a resident of Dunwich, Massachusetts, to summon the old
ones – ancient gods told of in the *Necronomicon*, written by 'the
mad Arab Abdul Alhazred'.[87] He is interested in doing so to allow
the passage of a monstrous creature that is growing larger by
the day in the farmhouse he lives in with his family. Pleasingly,
there is also a lodging house in Dunwich called Osborn's.

Wilbur is hunting for a certain incantation containing 'the
frightful name *Yog-Sothoth*', a being which has some connection
to him and the creature in his home. At the Miskatonic University of Arkham he is helped by the 'erudite Henry Armitage'
to translate a passage from the Latin version, which contains
'monstrous threats to the peace and sanity of the world':

'The Old Ones were, the Old Ones are, and the Old Ones shall be.
Not in the spaces we know, but *between* them. They walk serene
and primal, undimensioned and to us unseen. *Yog-Sothoth* knows

the gate. *Yog-Sothoth* is the gate. *Yog-Sothoth* is the key and guardian of the gate. Past, present, future, all are one in *Yog-Sothoth*. He knows where the Old Ones broke through of old, and where They shall break through again.'[88]

When Jus was at primary school, he began reading J.R.R. Tolkien. Tolkien convinced him that life would be an adventure: 'There'd be a big quest and I'd end up with a princess, but it doesn't happen!' he later reflected.[89] He read *The Hobbit* while other kids got their heads around *Jack and Jill*. He was so precocious in his reading that his teachers advised his parents that he should go to an advanced school. It didn't happen. Tolkien led him to Norse legend and then to classical mythology. He read Robert Anton Wilson's series of novels, the *Historical Illuminatus Chronicles*, when he was eleven years old. But around twelve or thirteen he discovered H.P. Lovecraft.

Lovecraft was raw. Not in terms of his prose: Lovecraft's writing is dense, allusive, almost overflowing at times. No, it was how he created other worlds that the reader was dragged into that fascinated Jus. Lovecraft's writing was about fear – cosmic fear and horror. There were other dimensions pressing against our own reality and Lovecraft held the key. But to what? For Jus, reading Lovecraft was to access a thrilling emptiness. The stories teemed with weirdness, but they conjured an ineffable dread. Lovecraft had been fascinated by astronomy as a boy – this equipped him to delineate the yawning void of space. To Jus, this felt the same as the appalling sense of the abyss he experienced on acid. Lovecraft wrote about minds blasted by gods dwelling in the spaces between the stars, unable to 'correlate all its contents'.[90] A sober person, Lovecraft wrote like a drug addict. Reading the stories prompted such vertiginous journeys in his imagination that Jus could only compare it to tripping out.[91]

The French writer Michel Houellebecq wrote an extensive essay about Lovecraft, first published in 1991, where he wrote that 'rejection of all forms of realism is a preliminary condition for entering his universe.'[92] According to Houellebecq, Lovecraft 'writes for an audience of fanatics'.[93] His mythology worked for Electric Wizard because their music was based on the same rejection – they spurned the quotidian. They embraced what Houellebecq calls Lovecraft's '[a]bsolute hatred of the world in general, aggravated by an aversion to the modern world in particular.'[94] The towering edifices of Lovecraft's architecturally impossible fictional cities teemed with unspeakable creatures in their lower regions. Houellebecq attributes this to the debasements of Lovecraft's time in New York, where he couldn't get a job and was near destitution.

In the early albums of Electric Wizard, Lovecraft's world is co-opted in the creation of the band's own imagery and dream-haunting archetypes. Lovecraft's mythology is partially defined, and his pantheon of gods is obscure and disturbing – it makes sense that they haunted Jus as they grazed our broader consciousness. He was compelled to give them a clearer shape in Electric Wizard's lyrics.

'I really got so many ideas from his stories,' Jus said in 2007. 'I'd sit there, out of my brain, reading his stuff, and extrapolating on what he'd written. It was amazing. The irony was that he wrote while straight, influencing someone like me, who certainly was not.'[95]

On *Dopethrone*, Electric Wizard's third album, they plunged into Lovecraft's world deeper than ever. For Jus, it stands as a 'megalithic abomination of drug excess'[96] in their discography. They pledged it would be 'beyond anything we've done before. Beyond anything anyone's done before, it's gonna be the final statement. When you smoke a bong and listen to it your heart will just stop. We'll try to kill everyone with this record.'[97] They promised that it 'will tear your mind like pure liquid LSD and stop your heart with inertial doom riffing.'[98] That's if the planet survived after the gig the band planned to play to usher in the year 2000: 'Electric Wizard will play a giant festival with black monoliths of amps clawing upwards. It will be the LOUDEST gig of all time and our heaviest riff ever will crack the fuckin' Earth, pouring molten lava death across the burning Earth.'[99]

All the pent-up frustration of the last few years – the arrests, unemployment, mental and physical self-abuses – was poured into *Dopethrone*: 'the whole "fuck you, fuck the world" attitude.'[100]

Speaking before its recording, Jus promised the following: 'It will be the heaviest/trippiest space doom mind feast ever recorded . . . some titles are "Lucifer's Children", "Mind Transferral", "Dope Throne", "Funeralopolis", "She Was Cruel", "Theme From 'Assmaster'", "We Have Contact".'[101]

There are a couple of candidates on the album for what they called their 'heaviest and slowest number ever with ultra-spaced-out shit'[102] but the Lovecraft-worshipping song 'Weird Tales' is probably the one. Like 'Supercoven', 'Weird Tales' was developed in three sections and eventually stretched to over fifteen minutes in length.

Jus had written the first section, subtitled 'Electric Frost', and Tim the second part, subtitled 'Golgotha'. That referred to the site of Christ's execution, a rare religious reference by the band, perhaps explained by Tim's strict Christian upbringing and interest in Martin Scorsese's *The Last Temptation of Christ*. 'Weird Tales' starts fast and hard, akin to the simplicity of hardcore punk. It feels faster than it actually is. Buried under the blanket of distortion that Jus used on his vocals throughout the album, he opens by singing, 'From ancient Yuggoth, black rays emit'.

Yuggoth is a Lovecraft creation which is described as 'a still undiscovered and almost lightless planet at the very edge of

our solar system'.[103] It is the home planet of an alien race called
the Mi-Go and plays an important role in the Lovecraft story
'The Whisperer in Darkness', which first appeared in *Weird
Tales* magazine in August 1931. Yuggoth has been associated
with Pluto, discovered the year before the story was written.
Told by Albert Wilmarth, another academic at the Miskatonic
University, the story is made up of his correspondence with a
resident of a remote farmhouse, Henry Akeley. The farmhouse
is in the hills of Vermont. Their letters concern evidence of an
alien race, washed up in the rivers following a flood. One of the
key bits of evidence is a phonograph recording of some kind
of ritual carried out by a human participant and a strange,
buzzing-voiced imitation of human speech, invoking something
called 'Nyarlathotep'.

During the correspondence, Akeley seems to have a change of
heart about the 'Outer Beings', seeing them not as a threat any
longer but as 'the most marvellous organic things in or beyond
all space and time'. Like the alien beings pulling the strings in
Childhood's End (written twenty years later), he claims that
Yuggoth will 'soon be the scene of a strange focusing of thought
upon our world in an effort to facilitate mental rapport.'[104]

'I would not be surprised if astronomers became sufficiently
sensitive to these thought-currents to discover Yuggoth when
the Outer Ones wish them to do so,' continues 'Akeley'. 'But
Yuggoth, of course, is only the stepping-stone. The main body of
the beings inhabits strangely organised abysses wholly beyond
the utmost reach of any human imagination. The space-time
globule which we recognise as the totality of the cosmic entity is
only an atom in the genuine infinity which is theirs.'[105]

Yuggoth is a stepping stone to cosmic oblivion. But there
is something fishy about Akeley's change of attitude and it
might have something to do with the nefarious entity called
Nyarlathotep.

The second verse of 'Weird Tales' introduces another desti-nation: 'unknown Kadath', a place in a 'Hyperborean continent entombed from time'. Kadath is the destination for the character Randolph Carter in 'The Dream-Quest of Unknown Kadath'. Carter is bewitched when he dreams of a 'golden and lovely' city. He resolves to find it in his sleep, by passing through the Gate of Deeper Slumber into the dreamworld.

Even by Lovecraft's standards, this novella is over the top. Aside from the multitude of 'Cyclopean' edifices, 'iridescent' colours and 'hellish' and 'foul' abominations such as gigs, ghasts and ghouls, it even contains a trip to the moon when Carter is captured by lunar slave traders: 'Carter felt the terrors of nightmare as Earth fell away and the great boat shot silent and comet-like into planetary space.'[106] Carter is rescued on the dark side of the moon by a clan of cats, of all things (who only fear the 'large and peculiar cats' of Saturn).

The story was never published in *Weird Tales* but emerged posthumously. In fact, Lovecraft worried that 'the very plethora of weird imagery may have destroyed the power of any one image to produce the desired impression of strangeness.'[107]

But this exotic fantasy has a terrific final encounter. Carter reaches unknown Kadath and the home of the Great Ones, on a mountain so large it defies the imagination, to be given the secret of the location of the sunset city he craves.

'There were towers on that titan mountain-top; horrible domed towers in noxious and incalculable tiers and clusters beyond any dreamable workmanship of man; battlements and terraces of wonder and menace, all limned tiny and black and distant against the starry pshent that glowed malevolently at the uppermost rim of sight.'[108]

There, Carter encounters a lone figure 'with the young face of an antique Pharaoh' who tells him in a voice with 'the mild music of Lethean streams' that he has dreamed '"too well"'.[109]

Carter is told it is out of his own boyhood dreams that he has conjured his marvellous city: "'Your gold and marble city of wonder is only the sum of what you have seen and loved in youth.'"[110] This is Boston, the city of his waking hours.

But at the end of his speech, Carter's addressor reveals himself as none other than Nyarlathotep, one of the Other Gods – the 'crawling chaos', whose plan it has been to taunt Carter all along. Carter is 'shot screamingly into space': 'The stars danced mockingly, almost shifting now and then to form pale signs of doom that one might wonder one had not seen and feared before; and ever the winds of aether howled of vague blackness and loneliness beyond the cosmos.'[111]

Carter is free to dream but those dreams can be manipulated and, ultimately, betrayed. But Carter also wakes at the end of the story in Boston, with the birds singing and the scent of trel-lised vines drifting into his bedroom window. Such a convoluted story leads to a deceptively simple conclusion: be careful what you wish for; be grateful for what you have. The story speaks to Electric Wizard's drive to escape Wimborne and Bournemouth, where Dorset stands in for Carter's dreamscape.

The key figure in both 'The Whisperer in Darkness' and 'The Dream-Quest of Unknown Kadath' is Nyarlathotep. He is not the evil centre, that is 'the mindless daemon-sultan'[112] Azathoth, but he is an envoy, a legate and a 'black messenger'[113] for power itself.

In the story Lovecraft wrote that was named after the char-acter, 'Nyarlathotep', he is even an Electric Wizard (like Nikola Tesla), who gathers to him restless crowds: 'Then the sparks played amazingly around the heads of the spectators, and hair stood up on end whilst shadows more grotesque than I can tell came out and squatted on the heads.'[114]

Nyarlathotep presides over *Dopethrone* – the vast shadow that hangs over it. If the album is about one thing, it is about delineating and opposing power and those who wield it – in our waking world, the dreamworld, and beyond.

Yet onward, onward the song goes, 'through the screaming, cackling and blackly populous gulfs'.[115] The song breaks and Jus leads the corkscrew descent downwards, following a giant spiral staircase to the monstrous 'caverns below'. The song is swept upwards, back on its original riff like Carter on the back of the huge flying shantak, a 'vast hippocephalic abomination'.[116]

Out in the vastness of the void, the song yawns open into the true doom of 'Golgotha' and then the droning synth finale of 'Altar of Melektaus': the sequence to stop your heart and send your stripped skeleton off into space. The liner notes of the album state that this sequence is based on the story '"The Altar of Melektaus" by G.G. Pendurues'. This is a typo courtesy of Rise Above. It is, in fact, 'The Altar of Melek Taos' by Gladys Gordon writing as G.G. Pendarves, published in *Weird Tales* in September 1932.

The story concerns a gentleman called Sir Hugh Willett, who is overseeing the excavation of an ancient temple in Baghdad. His wife, Evadne, is hypnotised by a devil-worshipping 'Yezidee' called Prince Dena ibn Zodh. Willett is aided by his Algerian manservant Hadur to rescue Evadne before she is sacrificed to bring about the return of Melek Taos, the Angel Peacock, the devil himself.

On the painting for the story, on the cover of *Weird Tales*, Evadne's breasts are exposed as she is held by the evil prince, with the devilish, anthropomorphised peacock looking on as it emerges from the flames. Jus didn't think that the story was that great but felt that Satan being represented by a peacock was a trippy image. Trippy enough that this final section of the song makes no mention of it in the lyrics – because there are no lyrics.

The story pits the rationalist West against the spiritualist East, and Pendarves chooses to support the away team. At one point, Willett tells Hadur, '"I did not realise clearly before that

I am a Westerner, and that you are of the East.'"[117] Willett's
wife is deemed the more 'intellectual' of the two by Pendarves
since she was 'more inclined to the mysticism of the East,
understanding much that lay outside the range of Sir Hugh's
strong, practical mind, more imaginative and receptive of the
older philosophies'.[118]

This, though, makes Evadne more credulous and susceptible
to Prince Dena's wiles. The prince has inherited the necessary
skills for handling the secret and occult force that governs fire
itself, from 'the true Zoroaster' and his Magi, who lived six
thousand years before Plato.

'"They learned,"' explains Hadur, '"through long discipline
and terrible ordeals of purification, to liberate the will entirely
from the senses, until they could hear the Very Voice of Fire,
until they could focus the universal fire – the Astral fluid that
radiates from every sphere in the universe – and direct it as a
weapon or a defence when they pleased."'[119]

Pendarves makes the same use of Lovecraft's cosmic powers
here but marries it to occult ceremony and to westerners' fear
of the unknowable Middle East. When, towards the story's
conclusion, Sir Hugh and Hadur venture to the Shining Tower
where this electric fluid is stored, Sir Hugh reasons it is a type
of super-heliograph.

'Hadur made no attempt to rob his companion of the comfort
of this logical explanation of the wonder before them,' writes
Pendarves. 'He knew that the light-rays from that infernal
Tower drew their power from every shining star and planet in
the universe, and that they sent out a force that touched people
and events as far removed as the poles. The Universal Agent
was concentrated and focused here, gathered up by means of the
Tower into a vast storehouse, in the identical manner in which
the true disciples of Zoroaster had learned to gather and store it
thousands of years ago.'[120]

The third section of 'Weird Tales', as it dissipates into strange echoes and vibrations, is like the Magi in Electric Wizard doing the same thing. After the ordeal is over, Sir Hugh and Evadne escape; 'They never returned to the East. Evadne's vague memories, and Sir Hugh's vivid ones . . . robbed the Orient of all its colour and romance for both of them, for ever.'[121]

Sir Hugh and Evadne are able to walk away. The Yazidis haven't been able to escape the persecution of their syncretic religious beliefs. They were hunted down, and many were enslaved and brutally murdered by Isis in 2014, acting on the reputation of the Yazidis as devil-worshippers as evident in Pendarves' tale.

'Weird Tales' was recorded in one take ('We got to the end and thought, "We can't do that again. It'll have to fucking do,"' Jus said in 2007).[122] It is the third track on *Dopethrone* and the first of four songs that were pulled together in the studio. They all leaned heavily into cult popular culture. The next song, 'Barbarian', was about the character created by another *Weird Tales* writer, Robert E. Howard: Conan the Barbarian. The lyrics speak of his 'black mane', 'steely blue gaze', guided by 'death lust', who comes to rule with 'an iron fist'.

Conan is another victim of power. The 1982 film, *Conan the Barbarian*, was directed by Hollywood tough guy John Milius, working from a script by Oliver Stone (and then revised by Milius). Famously, Conan is played by Arnold Schwarzenegger. His nemesis is Thulsa Doom, the leader of a snake cult. Doom is played by James Earl Jones in a remarkable performance. At the film's beginning, Doom raids Conan's village and kills his parents.

The sequence in which Doom beheads Conan's mother is extraordinary. He gazes into the camera, blue-eyed, and almost beatific. Just by looking at her, Doom gets Conan's mother to lower her sword. He has our complete attention, and we are left guessing his mindset – is he considering clemency for her? Almost imperceptibly, his unreadable expression changes. He turns his head slightly and he is all steel. Jus's lyrics could be about him rather than Conan. Fully turned away from the boy and his mother, Doom is now pure disdain, and we know he is not about to walk away. The camera is now on the face of Conan as a boy. We hear the swish of Doom's blade, see his mother's head tumble off her body and Conan's arm tugged as his mother collapses away from him, dead. He is left staring at the hand his mother was holding.

When Conan is captured and brought to Doom later in the film, in fully-grown Schwarzenegger form, Doom explains the 'Riddle of Steel' to him. The murder of Conan's mother was the making of Conan – such is the psychopathic logic of Doom's power: 'What is steel compared to the hand that wields it? Look at the strength in your body, the desire in your heart, I gave you this!'

Conan is sent to contemplate this conundrum on the Tree of Woe, where he is crucified. He is rescued by his comrades and brought to a wizard, who performs a ritual to revive him. This is not without its own costs. Conan's love interest (or should it just be sex interest?), Valeria, is mortally wounded by a snake shot as an arrow by Doom. After she is struck, she cries out, 'The wizard! I told him I would pay the gods.'

Valeria's cry of 'The wizard!' is sampled at the beginning of Electric Wizard's 'Barbarian'. The song describes Conan after his ascendancy to king, in a 'Hyborian Age' where 'battle prowess' is the true nature and measure of a man. Inevitably, bloodlust begets bloodlust.

Conan's crucifixion in the film echoes the story 'A Witch Shall Be Born', in which he is left hanging on a cross by his antagonist Constantius 'like a hare nailed to a tree'. It finds him at lowest ebb, kept alive by his 'red lust for vengeance'.[123]

'Curses ebbed fitfully from the man's lips,' Howard writes
in the story. 'All his universe contracted, focused, became
incorporated in the four iron spikes that held him from life and
freedom. His great muscles quivered, knotting like iron cables.
With the sweat starting out on his graying skin, he sought to
gain leverage, to tear the nails from the wood. It was useless.
They had been driven deep. Then he tried to tear his hands
off the spikes, and it was not the knifing, abysmal agony that
finally caused him to cease his efforts, but the futility of it. The
spike heads were broad and heavy; he could not drag them
through the wounds. A surge of helplessness shook the giant, for
the first time in his life. He hung motionless, his head resting
on his breast, shutting his eyes against the aching glare of the
sun.'[124]

In Howard's rich and lofty prose, the depiction of Conan's
bristling 'thews' (one of the author's favourite words) upon the
cross is far removed from the martyrdom of Jesus. He strains
every sinew to live and seek his vengeance, whereas Jesus,
forsaken, dies for the sins of his executors. As in Milius' film,
Conan even catches a taunting vulture in his jaws, breaking its
neck with his teeth.

Conan, as a Cimmerian from the Northern territories and a
mercenary barbarian, finds civilization perplexing: 'By Crom,
though I've spent a considerable time among you civilized
peoples, your ways are still beyond my comprehension,' he says
in another story.[125] This appealed to Electric Wizard, because it
addressed the lie at the heart of civilization itself. In 'Barbarian's final repeating refrain, 'You think you're civilised but you
will never understand', which Jus delivers in mounting frenzy,
it mocks the idea that we are anything but a blade-edge away
from a world of brutality and sorcery.

'Barbarian' was written in the studio. The grinding bass and
guitar tones have an unlikely resonance with 'The Barbarian',

the opening instrumental on the first Emerson, Lake & Palmer album from 1970. For a band associated with the convoluted excesses of mega-prog, it's strange to hear Greg Lake's heavily distorted bass tone reaching down the decades to Dorset's new-millennium musical progeny.

The locked grooves, particularly the first riff, of 'Barbarian' also reveal the impact of bass music on *Dopethrone*: drum 'n' bass, reggae and dub. At the time, Jus lived in a flat above a studio owned by a dance producer who had got lucky with a trance hit and spent the proceeds on cocaine and speccing out his own recording facility. When Jus wasn't threatening to kill the producer because of the incessant noise, they persuaded Jus to lay down some simple solo lines and rhythm playing over their dance tracks. The earth-shaking sub-bass and disruptive rhythms downstairs seeped into Jus's sonic consciousness.

The repetitive, trancelike groove of 'Barbarian' had absorbed a huge amount of the wider dance culture that gripped the UK during the nineties. The psychedelic nature of trance music, though not loved in and of itself by all the band, permeated the strata of *Dopethrone*. Tim was its biggest advocate in Electric Wizard. Jus was obsessed with layering the music with guitar tracks and effects. 'Barbarian' effectively stops, then builds back up again, like a piece of rave music. Electric Wizard went to raves and couldn't understand why the same wild abandon and communal, drug-fuelled atmosphere wasn't happening in rock music. It felt like that spirit had been hijacked: rock festivals were corporate affairs, nu metal was charting, and mainstream metal had lost its way. The Prodigy had smashed barriers between rock and rave culture, but they seemed to be erected swiftly again. Jus saw pictures of Richard James, aka Aphex Twin, posing with a shotgun and wondered where that spirit had gone in rock. Like Electric Wizard, James launched an assault on musical norms from a rural base, in his case Cornwall. To

Jus, Aphex Twin's 'Come to Daddy' was a black metal song written with synthesisers.

When Electric Wizard toured *Dopethrone*, they tried to create the feeling of a cross-genre underground scene. They played gigs with Jimi Tenor, the avant-garde saxophone player signed to Warp Records, also the home of Aphex Twin himself. Those gigs were eclectic and harked back to the experimentation of the German communes of the sixties and seventies as part of emergent krautrock.

'We like the idea of doing an unconventional gig,' Jus told *Terrorizer*. 'Everything's so stale, you don't just need the same three bands playing . . . I dunno it's cool, we just wanted something a bit different, a bit more exciting . . . It's about extremity of sound. I want anything that pushes the boundaries. I mean, I like extreme music, basically. Even extreme ambient, or extreme black metal . . . As long as it's on the fuckin' edge.'[126]

Extreme ambient black metal is a good way of describing *Dopethrone*'s next song, 'I, The Witchfinder'. It's the most oppressive song on the album. Its opening is so heavy and slow it verges on the appalling. It's sonic torture, but it feels great. The song roars and then it whispers, simulating the erratic tortures it describes. The band felt they needed subject matter as heavy as the song and turned to *Mark of The Devil*, a German-produced horror film made in 1970.

Mark of The Devil was one of the finds at Wimborne Market, a video nasty traded under the video stall. With the town's tuck-shop owner imprisoned, the market became the focus of the search for illicit culture. There was a co-op fund for friends interested in buying the marked-up VHS tapes. They were then circulated amongst the investors, getting increasingly worn out. After every band practice, the Wizard got high and watched ninth-generation copies of movies with titles like *Buried Alive*. *Mark of The Devil*'s poster described it as 'positively the most horrifying film ever made', 'guaranteed to upset your stomach', 'the first film rated V for violence': 'Due to the horrifying scenes no one admitted without a vomit bag'.

'It was a German rip-off of *Witchfinder General*, but it's loads more brutal, it's fucking horrific!' Jus said at the time. 'The character Albino was so cool I knew we had to dedicate a song to him. He's so evil! He is the epitome of the fucking twisted fuck!'[127]

Mark of The Devil has a serene, later jarring, main musical theme. Its opening sequence showcases the bucolic splendour of the German mountains filmed through a fish-eye lens, as the witchfinders capture their prey. After its opening conflagration of two witches, the film explains itself with gothic-font text over a burning background: 'In Europe, between the 15th and 19th centuries, it is estimated nearly eight million people were convicted of heresy and executed by fanatical witch-hunters, in order to save their souls. Their deaths on the scaffold or the funeral pile was for them the release from agonizing torture which often lasted for years. This motion picture shows three cases taken from the authentic documents from the time when witch-hunting had reached its peak and can only give a slight idea of the cruelties of one of the blackest pages in the history of Man.'

After asserting its historical and social conscience with this hugely exaggerated figure (the upper estimate today is a hundred thousand victims, still a very large number), the film goes on to show women jabbed by needles, raped, burned alive, stretched on the rack, branded, whipped, and, in the film's most graphic scene, one poor soul has her tongue torn out by an iron pincer.

The film differs from *Witchfinder General* in the way it focuses on the power struggles between incumbent witchfinder Albino and the incoming overseer Lord Cumberland. Count Christian

von Meruh, played by Udo Kier, embodies the selfish hypocrisy
of male desire, as he spurns his lover Vanessa Benedikt after
she is indicted. He eventually rescues her, but any moral
reprieve for the men in the film is wiped out by Cumberland's
rape of a noblewoman arrested for putting on a puppet show.

'We must never weaken in performing God's work,' Cumberland tells Christian as he tries to look away from the torture.
It's not all women. Baron Daumer is made to sit on spikes as
his feet are whipped; later they light a fire under his arse to
precipitate a confession to get him to forfeit his lands to the
church. When the tide turns, Cumberland eventually escapes,
but Christian suffers at the hands of mob justice, which proves
itself no fairer than the cruelty under the banner of justice
meted out by the witchfinders.

Albino (played by Reggie Nalder, himself disfigured by burns
on his face as a youth) introduces himself at the beginning of 'I,
The Witchfinder', in a sample from the film. The lyrics take the
first-person perspective, inhabiting his sadistic mind: 'I'll pierce
her flesh to find his mark'. Evadne from 'The Altar of Melek
Taos' was similarly marked by the devil before her attempted
sacrifice. Though there was clear glee in the transgressive
subject matter, Electric Wizard played it straight on the
witch-finding craze that spread through East Anglia during the
English Civil War. It was about incarcerating innocent people to
requisition their land by nefarious means. It was also misogyny
taken to its limits: 'I know she's guilty before I find her,' Jus
sings.

'Weird Tales', 'Barbarian' and 'I, The Witchfinder' form the spine
of *Dopethrone* and its thematic centre as a theatre of the cruel
and the oppressed. The album was the third in Electric Wizard's

'trilogy of terror', following *Come My Fanatics . . .* and *Superco-ven*: 'I look back with a lot of fondness on all three,' said Jus in 2007. 'With those albums, I believe we really found our mark as a band.'[128]

That didn't mean it was a happy time. The relationships within the band were strained throughout. It made for a productive, if abrasive, creative process. 'That was the lowest point, personally, as a band,' Jus recalled in 2009. 'Most of us were stuck in some drug addiction or alcoholism at the time, and it was just pure hate. It was us against the world and we just wanted to make the most disgusting, foul, putrid record that anyone has ever recorded.'[129]

Not that Jus wanted to believe that anything was wrong at the time. Then he denied that there were issues, but years later he admitted that there were 'constant death threats' in the studio between the members.[130] Electric Wizard were proud of the diversity of their influences and the different roles they played within the band. But they all wanted to lead, and that meant they pulled in different directions.

Jus was listening to classic doom metal like Penance and Dream Death; and death metal bands such as Celtic Frost, Bathory and Possessed. He singled out the Essex band Warning on the album's sleeve as 'true doom'. Warning was mournful in the same way Electric Wizard was hateful. Their 1999 album, *The Strength to Dream* (which shared its title with a book of 'existential literary criticism' by Colin Wilson, published in 1961), is held up as a classic. Its opening song, 'The Return', is a magnificent piece of Grand Guignol. A near twelve-minute story of madness and obsession in doom metal rent from grief, frontman Patrick Walker sings in doleful tones. He casts himself as a Dr Frankenstein, bringing back his dead lover, only for her to beg him to kill her once again. Warning are celebrated today. They were invited to play the album in full alongside 2006's

Watching From A Distance at the 2017 edition of the Roadburn Festival. Back in 2000, Jus remembers being one of only a handful of people at their gigs, alongside Will Palmer from Rise Above and Rich Walker from the band Solstice.

By contrast, Mark said in an interview that he liked The Doors, The Who, Super Furry Animals, Faith No More and Mr. Bungle.[131]

Dopethrone was recorded with Rolf Startin again, this time at Chuckalumba Studios. Jus was more involved in the production: he relayed his sonic concepts for the album and observed how Startin pulled it all together. 'There's a lot of intricacy and subtlety on the record,' Jus said in 2007. 'A number of sonic layers that had to be built up. If you listen carefully, there's more going on that [sic] perhaps we get credit for. I got a lot of ideas from watching Pink Floyd videos, especially the way they set up their microphones. I spent ages working out the best way to mic up my amps. It was very important to the way we sound on the record. The other two guys weren't as heavily involved as me, but that wasn't a problem at the time . . . '[132]

That didn't stop them later being dismissive of Startin. They complained bitterly in an interview with the *Vincebus Eruptum* fanzine after the album was released. Jus called him 'Rolf Fartsin'. He dismissed him as a 'twat' for not letting the band experiment in the studio. Jus felt that Rolf went out of his way to make *Dopethrone* sound like shit.

Tim said, 'He didn't let us do anything. After it was recorded, he wouldn't let us into the studio. He told us to go home, not letting us put any creativity into the album, on the production side of it.'[133]

Time plays tricks because Jus remembered in 2007 that the band wanted *Dopethrone* to sound 'horribly raw'. In the same retrospective on the album, Tim said they had wanted 'a heavy lo-fi sound, and that is what we got.'[134]

As the drummer, Mark's opinion on its sound is unsurprising: 'I wanted something with louder drums. I always regret all the Wizard releases, because the drums don't sound loud enough and the guitars are too loud. All the time was usually spent with Justin doing vocals and guitars. [*Dopethrone*] does not represent the sound I was trying to give off, as with all Electric Wizard releases.'[135]

The band spent decent stretches of time at the studio, its owner using the money they had paid to record there to buy equipment and fit it out. They commuted by train, or they 'camped out'. Mark slept with his head next to his bass drum. As Jus remembered, 'It was literally just: wake up, consume as much fucking drugs as possible and then just start jamming.'[136]

Jus scored a couple of ounces of weed for the first session. He made a point of getting twice as much as he usually would so that he could smoke through any temptation to nod off. The band was determined to get high, and stay high, hitting the bong before every take.[137]

Rolf recorded some of the sessions on a camcorder and uploaded them in VHS quality to YouTube in 2016 under the handle 'Rolphonse', with the following disclaimer in the descriptions: 'Not intended to amuse, excite, entertain or interest anybody'.[138]

They are remarkable fragments documenting the recording of a remarkable album. The band is seen tracking 'Barbarian' and 'We Hate You', listening back to mixes of 'Funeralopolis', and Jus shows how to pack the perfect bong. The studio looks like a cabin in the woods. As the band steps out into the leafy summer sunshine between takes, Jus smokes a joint and looks over a notebook of lyrics. They start capturing photos on the camcorder – freeze-frames of the band in their youth. A poster for *The Blair Witch Project* hangs on the wall next to Mark's drum kit. 'If we're gonna do it again, I need another line,' he says towards

the end of the footage. Rolf had got some very shitty cocaine
in for the sessions which gave everyone nosebleeds. This is
video evidence that Electric Wizard recorded at full volume.
Jus believed they must be 'the loudest recording band in the
world'.[139]

Startin must have tolerated some degree of experimentation
in the studio because the groovy, low-distortion, forty-seven-sec-
ond interlude 'The Hills Have Eyes' was a motif extracted from
one of the band's thirty-minute-plus instrumental jam sessions.
Tim – always in favour of dynamics in the band's sound –
enjoyed the contrast of this interlude track with the rest of the
material: 'A bit like Yin and Yang – light and extreme dark.'[140]

Another nearly ten-minute section of this jam, the protoplas-
mic 'Mind Transferral', was carved out and included as a bonus
track on the Japanese edition of *Dopethrone*. After the album
was remastered in 2006, it has since been included on every
version.

The process of mind transferral is central to the Lovecraft
story 'The Shadow Out of Time', about a 'Great Race' of ten-foot
tall conical life-forms with four-foot thick, flexible 'cylindrical
members' which protrude out from the apex of the body – on one
of them is their head.[141] Occupying earth 150 million years ago,
this Great Race had 'conquered the secret of time', and were
able to project themselves into the past and the future.[142]

When they cast their minds into the future, the Great Race
'would seize on the best discoverable representative of the highest of that period's life-forms; entering the organism's brain and
setting up therein its own vibrations while the displaced mind
would strike back to the period of the displacer, remaining in the
latter's body til a reverse process was set up.'[143] The protagonist
of the story, Nathaniel Wingate Peaslee, is tormented in his
dreams by pseudo-memories of his own mind transferral, affect-
ing him for five years: 'some background of black knowledge

106

which festered in the chasms of my subconscious.'[144]

In his monstrous form he reads 'horrible annals of other worlds'[145] and communes with other 'exiled intellects from every corner of the solar system'.[146] These include one from Valusia, a region created by Robert E. Howard and reigned over by King Kull. He also speaks with 'an Egyptian of the Fourteenth Dynasty who told me the hideous secret of Nyarlathotep.'[147]

Peaslee discovers that the Great Race themselves are terrified by subterranean horrors known as the Elder Things. The story's climax takes place as Peaslee discovers a 'terrible elder city of dreams' covered by the sands of the west Australia desert.[148] Electric Wizard's instrumental simulates the fungible nature of identity and consciousness without needing to say a word and is a powerful example of the band 'Gellering' their riffs to breaking point.

'The Hills Have Eyes' interlude is named after Wes Craven's 1977 film, in which the Carter family is terrorised by mutant cannibals in the desert after they crash their station wagon and caravan en route to California. They have just entered what the map describes as a nuclear testing site and the family's patriarch is a retired police detective from Cleveland. Their German shepherds, Beauty and The Beast, are agitated and aggressive. The family laughs when they recall how The Beast once killed a poodle and they had to foot the vet's bill for the dead animal.

We watch them from the perspective of the cannibal gang and its vantage points on craggy hilltops, a jumble of boulders and spiky extrusions. Sometimes we do so through binoculars. The family's radio signal is blocked by what they think is iron in the hills. The most striking antagonist is Pluto, with a large, bald, misshapen head and imposing stature. He is like the alien planet Yuggoth personified or one of the race of subterranean mutant humans in *Beneath the Planet of the Apes*, deformed by nuclear radiation, who has surfaced to wreak havoc on smug

107

civilisation. His brother, Mars, with his mass of dark curly hair, looks a little bit like Mark. It's a good thing that the Carters have a dog like The Beast, domesticated savagery in canine form, to bite back.

Craven partially based the film on the legend of Sawney Bean. In the sixteenth century, Bean was the head of a Scottish clan purported to have murdered and cannibalised over a thousand people during a twenty-five-year period. The clan was hung, drawn, quartered and burned for their crimes. Craven saw a parallel savagery in the punishment to that of the alleged crimes. He filmed *The Hills Have Eyes* with camera equipment borrowed from a pornographer, as if to up the exploitation levels. It was raw, horrifying cinema in a different sense to Lovecraft because it told its audience, *This could happen to you* and further still, *You too are capable of these savage acts*. Like the witch-finding craze depicted in *Mark of The Devil* or the bloody revenge of Conan, the film's shock factor had something to say about society's obsession with violence and punishment. Specifically, how we are all one step from each other's innately destructive natures.

'The Hills Have Eyes' interlude was a palate cleanser before *Dopethrone*'s response to the fist of power the band was being crushed under: 'We Hate You'. It was based on one of Tim's compositions. Tim wrote constantly, recording CDs of demos for various putative side projects – death metal, dub, space rock, you name it. Electric Wizard listened to these as a band to determine what might work for them. If something he had written sounded like Sisters of Mercy meets Roky Erickson (not unheard of), it needed to be transmuted into the Wizard sound by Jus. What that sounded like depended on which member you asked.

Tim's favourite bands at the time were Burning Witch and Nirvana. He can be seen playing the opening riff to the Burning Witch song 'Warning Signs' in footage of the Wizard's gig in San

Francisco when they toured the United States in 2001. He said
he thought Electric Wizard sounded like a combination of the
two bands.[149] This is actually true on 'We Hate You'.

Burning Witch was founded by Stephen O'Malley and Greg
Anderson, who later formed Sunn O))). In Burning Witch they
developed a harsh, stop-start, capture-and-release form of doom
metal. Appropriately, this was absorbed into 'I, The Witchfinder',
but 'We Hate You' made it catchier. The song is propelled on a
massive fuzz-bass riff and probably the album's best sample,
a piece of dialogue from the 1970 film version of *The Dunwich
Horror*. Wilbur Whateley, played by Dean Stockwell with
detached creepiness, is getting to know the pompous Dr Henry
Armitage over dinner.

'You see man as a rather dismal creature,' Armitage puts it to
him.

'Yes,' responds Whateley. 'Why not? Look around – you'll see
what's there. Fear, and frightened people who kill what they
cannot understand.'

The intolerant, mob-handed townspeople are perhaps
the film's true villains. They treat Whateley with disdain
throughout. They interrupt his attempt to bury his grandfather,
protesting that he cannot desecrate a Christian burial site with
the remains of a member of his family. They throw his ceremonial objects into the grave pit and jostle him about until the
town's biased sheriff intervenes. Not that Whateley's an innocent
man. He spears a security guard in procuring the *Necronomicon*
from the university library and prepares to sacrifice Sandra
Dee's Nancy to open the gate for Yog-Sothoth. The townspeople
also get what's coming to them.

'I've always thought this was a great adaptation and update of
the H.P. Lovecraft story,' Jus said of the film in 2017. 'I think the
use of psychedelic camera techniques and the 1960s' milieu really
work in its favour. The surrealistic tentacled "half-brother" in the

attic really works because it is only half-seen and then it's just a flash of psychedelic colours. It adds a real otherworldly feel that seems to really conjure up the cosmic horror vibe Lovecraft was trying to convey. Dean Stockwell as the almost "counter-culture" wizard Whateley is played really well and the drugged out erotic cult scenes are really enhanced by his intensity. I always wished that do-gooders Dr Armitage and [Dunwich physician] Dr Cory were zapped by Yog-Sothoth at the end though.'[150]

'We Hate You' is an anthem, but an uncomfortable one. It shows what happens when the 'black seed of hate' within a human being is allowed to grow – watered by contempt, oppression and ostracism: 'To be honest when I was quite young I had been exposed to some pretty disturbing scenes that illustrated the depths of vile human behaviour,' Jus told me in 2014 in an interview for *The Quietus*. 'So, yeah, maybe I am qualified enough to comment on these things. Somebody has to, and obviously it is challenging and personally dangerous sometimes, but that's what we believe. It doesn't mean we condone them or promote them. That would be taking a pretty narrow-minded view of a musician as an artist. Electric Wizard is heavy, man, we don't sing about love and flowers.'[151]

The song seethes with a self-righteous fury, though it was – as with all things with Electric Wizard – not wholly serious: '[T]hat was inspired in a way by Ozzy [Osbourne],' Jus told *Metal Hammer* in 2007. 'He was always going on about how much he fucking loved everyone, so we thought it would be great to go and do the opposite.'[152]

The song crosses a line, from hidden fury to public violence, in its second verse: 'So I'll take my father's gun and I walk down to the street/I'll have my vengeance now with everyone I meet, yeah!' (the 'yeah!' is another Ozzy-ism).

Dopethrone was released in October 2000, eighteen months after the Columbine high school massacre. In a period where

Marilyn Manson and heavy rock music were being blamed
for motivating the perpetrators of that attack, 'We Hate You'
embraced the idea of rock music having a dangerous influence.
It spoke to a generation who fantasised about walking into
school and killing everyone. The 'Trench Coat Mafia' of Columbine crossed that line for real.

Years later, the band was stranded for a time in Finland in
2011 following the massacre committed by Anders Breivik in
Norway, and subsequently missed their slot performing at the
High Voltage festival in London.

'All the stupid flights were cancelled then it was all backed
up for hours – we started the morning in Finland,' Jus told me
in an interview for *The Quietus*. 'Obviously I am not qualified
to comment on the shootings in Norway. But I am fascinated
by individuals who vent their frustration at the world through
random mass executions. And Norway too: it was tempting
to imagine he had Isengard [a black metal band] in his headphones. "We Hate You" was written directly after the Columbine
killings and inspired by them, but the lyrics reflected my own
experiences (my school/town had a similar shitty attitude
to "freaks" and the "physically inadequate") and long hours'
practice during school holidays with various illegal weaponry
stolen from my grandad's shed. I had a sawn-off, a pistol, a
long-barrelled ratgun and various incendiary devices I had
created that rarely worked! Some of the ammo was years old. I
couldn't believe someone actually did it.'[153]

If he didn't care much about the wider community, any fanta-
sies Jus had held as a teenager about murder-suicide were held
in check by a sense of responsibility towards his family. 'You
latch onto things that life's worth living for,' he told *Psychology
Today*, looking back in 2018. 'And there were certain people in
my life – they're going to be really upset. Why make my mother
upset? Just deal with it – at least for a bit.'[154]

'We Hate You' is a response to a society that doesn't seem to care. Its sentiment is self-pitying but sincere. In a perfect world, the song wouldn't need to exist. The fact its relevance keeps resurfacing is the problem. In the album's credits there was a slogan in block capitals that spoke to a similar sentiment: LEGALISE DRUGS AND MURDER. Again, Electric Wizard dared the listener to take them seriously.

'I was writing it ["Legalise Drugs And Murder"] on some bullshit job course I was on,' Jus told *Terrorizer* in 2000. 'It was like, "All I want to fucking do is kill everyone and get stoned." It would sort my fucking day out. There are some nasty people I could just murder y'know, there's nasty, shit, fucked people in the world, they deserve to die. On a bigger level there's politicians and whatever, and on a smaller level there's cunts who grass everyone up, liars, people who rip you off . . . I could happily kill the heads of corporations, and Tony Blair as well, that cunt can go down too!'[155]

Looking back in 2007, he described the phrase 'Legalise Drugs And Murder' as 'nonsense'. Nonetheless, the band ran with it: 'What we were after was a catchphrase that summed up *Dopethrone* – and this seemed to fit.'[156] It echoes the sentiments of Babs Johnson, played by Divine, in John Waters' 1972 film *Pink Flamingos*: 'Kill everyone now! Condone first degree murder! Advocate cannibalism! Eat shit! Filth is my politics! Filth is my life!'

'Legalise Drugs And Murder' became the band's trademark.

At the time we were walking around Wimborne and talking about the Uddens Cross slaughterhouse where his father worked, Jus began quoting the lyrics from 'Funeralopolis': 'Funerary cities, flesh press factories'. The second song on *Dopethrone*, 'Funeralopolis' is an indictment of our wage-slave culture and a compacted, redux version of *Come My Fanatics . . .* and its fears for a dead planet.

'Funeralopolis' works particularly well in the context of the album because it follows the album's shortest song proper, 'Vinum Sabbathi', which is only slightly over three minutes long. Written by Tim in about the time it took to play it, 'Vinum Sabbathi' was designed as a sucker-punch. The album begins with a sampled warning: 'When you get into one of these groups there's only a couple of ways you can get out: one is death, the other is mental institutions.' This is Dale Griffis, police chief of Tiffin, Ohio in the *20/20* documentary special about satanism from 1985 called *The Devil Worshippers*.

'Vinum Sabbathi' and 'Funeralopolis' are about huge cities and small towns, and their diseases. On 'Vinum Sabbathi' Jus sings of the 'black drug' and, again, 'the black god' – to one the narrator is enslaved, to the other a servant, all under the aegis of 'forbidden sorcery'.

The song's title refers to the wine of the sabbath. In Arthur Machen's story 'Novel of the White Powder', Francis Leicester is mistakenly dosed by a neighbourhood chemist with a powder from which this wine of the sabbath is prepared – for a month solid. The correct prescription is supposed to cure his languor and distemper. Instead, he undergoes a horrific physical transformation. A doctor who is consulted about Leicester's condition explains in a letter, 'The secrets of the true Sabbath were the secrets of the remote times surviving into the Middle Ages.' The wine formed part of a ceremony where 'this evil graal was poured forth and offered to the neophytes, and they partook of an infernal sacrament', before fornicating with the devil: 'the worm which never dies, that which lies sleeping within us all . . . clothed with a garment of flesh.'[157]

In an invocation of animism and even panpsychism, the doctor writes, 'The whole universe, my friend, is a tremendous sacrament; a mystic, ineffable force and energy, veiled by an outward form of matter; and man, and the sun and the other stars, and the flower of the grass, and the crystal in the test-tube, are each and every one as spiritual, as material, and subject to an inner working.'[158]

As 'Vinum Sabbathi' burns out, its last sustained, feedback-drenched note bleeds into the beginning of 'Funeralopolis'. The song harks back to Jus's first forays to visit Napalm Death and Carcass. He wrote to the bands and even travelled to visit them in the summer of 1988, when he was sixteen, impressing his schoolmates on his return about where he had spent his weekend. He had stayed with Mick Harris, Napalm's drummer, who took him to the studio where they were recording their second album, *From Enslavement To Obliteration*. It was also the first time Jus met their singer, Lee Dorrian, some time before Lee left to form Cathedral and started Rise Above Records, Electric Wizard's label for the best part of two decades.

The lyrics of 'Funeralopolis' could be from *Enslavement*, previous Napalm Death album *Scum* or Carcass' *Reek of Putrefaction*, in their depiction of the hamster wheel of capitalistic zombification: 'Death shroud existence, slave for a pittance' – people shuffling down the street with their 'staring blank faces'. The song is angry and momentous, connecting back to the condemnation of the 'mindless fucking slaves' of 'Supercoven'. It is almost stately in the way it unfurls with the cosmic dread of Lovecraft and *Childhood's End* (again), as Jus sings in desperation that 'Black clouds form to block out the sun'.

The impact of 'Funeralopolis' alone on doom metal is hard to overstate. It crystallised Electric Wizard's warnings about the enslaved masses as we entered the twenty-first century – keeping themselves busy but really sleepwalking to their oblivion. Its opening is underlaid with first Jus's hacking cough, then the sound of a drawn-out bubbling bong hit. Its main riff is black-age blues. The grinding verse section gives the song an imposing, titanic and lumbering presence – all held in precarious balance – until the song falls off a cliff in an act of wanton self-destruction at its peak.

The shock gear change of its finale recalls Black Sabbath's best turn-on-a-dime dynamics. It is pure eighties' hardcore punk: a pumping fist smashed into the guts or a boot stamping on a face – for ever. This final expression of rage is Electric Wizard at their most incandescent and uncompromising, wishing again for the world to burn away and take its inhabitants with it: 'Nuclear warheads ready to strike/This world is so fucked, let's end it tonight'.

The end is completely over the top, with its Broadway-style flourishes up and down the octave. Live, Jus and Tim would kick their legs out as if they were performing 'Springtime for Hitler' from the Mel Brooks satire *The Producers*. They had the image in mind of Cream on their 1969 *Goodbye Cream* album cover when they performed the song, all silver top hats and tails, bidding farewell to the planet. But they soon dropped the high kicks live.

'Funeralopolis' might be *Dopethrone*'s definitive statement, but Electric Wizard still needed a song to end the album to represent a fightback against the powers-that-be. The closing title track is both a celebration of their fuckedupness and a statement of their now incontestable dominance of the doom metal scene: 'Three wizards crowned with weed'. Electric Wizard had been proud to be known as a druggie band who played metal music, as opposed to a metal band who took drugs. But their thinking on the matter was growing hazier. A small part of them worried about whether it was a barrier to being taken seriously.

'We have been known as a druggie band and I will admit that without acid and vodka we'd have never made the "Supercoven" record. But we are cutting right back on the drugs,' Jus told *Metal Hammer* in October 2000 as they promoted *Dopethrone*.

This was either wishful thinking or an overstatement motivated by his then-girlfriend's father being a policeman. For one, Jus's kidneys failed from binge-drinking on vodka just before they entered the studio. It felt like he was 'pissing powdered glass', although he wondered whether it wasn't his use of speed that really contributed to his kidney issues.[159] Jus told *Terrorizer*, 'Just before we were about to go in for the recording I was staying over Mark's house, and it was fucking vodka again. I woke up in the morning and I was just fucked. My kidneys just stopped working basically, I was in agony. It was the week before we went in and I thought, Shit, the album's off *again* [Mark's collarbone injury had previously delayed it].'[160] Jus laid off the hard stuff for eight months following the hospitalisation.

'Without drugs we probably wouldn't exist,' Jus told *Kerrang!* in another interview from that October. 'When we formed we all started smoking weed together and jamming and writing songs together. As the band has gone along it's become a ritual that we always do drugs before we play, to the point where we don't play if we haven't got any drugs. But we see it as an important part of what we're doing. Pot is our magic potion.'[161]

'All good musicians are fucked-up on drugs,' Tim said on another occasion.

Mark was more diplomatic: 'I think it works both ways. Some bands don't do a lot [of drugs], and they're straight and they sound all right. It's just a way to categorise different bands. I don't think it matters that much. It helps us because we've gone along those lines for quite a while.'[162]

On 'Dopethrone', Electric Wizard united weed and power. In their case, the former led to the latter. The song described the power that flows in hidden streams throughout society, like the contraband that passed through the dope-smuggling routes in Dorset. It was time to kill or be killed – to get stoned and reign supreme.

'The concept of *Dopethrone* is that we're the kings of the fucking dope scene, and hopefully we'll control all the dope in the world one day,' Jus said at the time.[163] In 2007, he claimed the song title was 'based on a story that I'd heard, about someone who had a sofa completely made out of dope.'[164] He was probably still a little wary to say he had sat on that throne himself, in his own residence, at Thirteen. The album and song title were also a playful dig at Sleep's hour-long *Dopesmoker* (originally *Jerusalem*) from 1999 and Eyehategod's 1996 *Dopesick* album. *Dopethrone* completed this stoned trilogy – the best saved until last. In this musical era of the Puff Daddy/Damon Dash ascendancy, this was Electric Wizard's hip-hop-style claim to power.

'We had a reputation for smoking a lot of dope, so it was a nod to us being the kings of getting stoned. Sleep were the dope smokers, but we were on the dope throne!' said Tim looking back in 2007. Though Mark disputed that competitive edge in the same interview ('We were not trying to beat anyone or to be anything'). Jus, like Tim, was comfortable to say that they were 'fucking wasted' and accordingly 'arrogant shits'.[165]

The lyrics of 'Dopethrone' bring back previous motifs of monoliths, black towers and stoned prophecy. 'Black amps tear the sky' in 'this land of sorcery'. Jus came to introduce it onstage as a song about where they lived.[166] The song demanded a riff as anthemic as its message and the opening, ushered in by the evil laugh of Albino from *Mark of The Devil*, is one of the simplest and most powerful in the band's whole catalogue. Like the great songs of this ilk – 'Enter Sandman', 'Highway Star', 'Paranoid' – it was written in a matter of minutes. When it comes back – slowed down and super-heavy – towards the end of the song for one long, last go around, it truly feels like they have fulfilled their Millennium Eve wish to crack open the Earth. And is that Jus reading from the 'Novel of the White Powder' faintly under the song's denouement?

The band wanted an album cover with a nightmarish, Lovecraftian quality. It was drafted by Jus and the final version illustrated by Tim's brother, Tom. Black structures reach skywards in the background like the towers of unknown Kadath. Sinister hooded figures look on as Satan takes a bong hit. The cover might have been briefed by Lovecraft himself, based on the visions of Robert Blake in the story 'The Haunter of the Dark', as he stares into a polyhedron stone which contains, or summons, Nyarlathotep: 'He saw processions of robed, hooded figures whose outlines were not human, and looked on endless leagues of desert lined with carved, sky-reaching monoliths.'[167] *Dopethrone*'s cover encapsulates all the seedy, hashish-dream, pulp-horror atmosphere of the album.

By the time of the album's release, Electric Wizard's antics had become something approaching mythology. *Kerrang!* was already calling them 'doom legends'.[168] All the interviews at the time talked up the gap between releases as if the *Supercoven* EP hadn't been put out only two years previously.

The band, who barely had access to the internet, weren't sure how the album was being received. They were too stoned to care most of the time. But Electric Wizard did something to music journalists, like a parasite invading a host, turning them inside out. The *Metal Hammer* review of the album is so gonzoid that it's worth including in full. For some reason, they call the album *The Dopethrone* throughout:

'Slimier than the Democrats' convention, heavier than a sumo wrestler in a chainmail jockstrap, more cosmically "out there" than a psychic fed on a diet of ketamine-laced LSD. Yep, Electric Wizard are back. Back to confound and dumbfound the masses with perhaps the most ludicrously enigmatic doom-esque sludge-monstrous album since Sleep loosed *Jerusalem* onto an unsuspecting general public.

'The masters of trudge, sludge and bludgeon, the Wizard hotwire you into a bleak world of contradictions, where the melody is enslaved to the riff and the passage of time is measured not in bogus rap-metal affectation but rather in the deliverance of an aural swamp-beast rampaging with a bedeviled [sic] touch of supreme lightness. You want big selling pop-rock? You're on the wrong wavelength, baby. You want easy listening? Retune that dial. Because what the Wizard offer is a sublime, subliminal, subsuming, re-energising of the cosmic. Material like "Vinum Sabbathi", "Weird Tales" and "We Hate You" see a morphing of all characteristics of the doom genre into something altogether more contemporary – so cutting edge you'll need a transfusion from blood loss. This is challenging music that refreshes you by draining you of all resistance to the extreme metal disease. A monster that dwarfs Godzilla, *The Dopethrone* is arguably the finest musical triumph of the year so far. It dares to break all the rules, consigning them to the incinerator of behemoth rhythms and polydecibelic plagues. Each song is a carefully constructed monolith of monotones, replete with riffage built from the ashes of Saint Vitus and early Cathedral – every utterance a sonically somnambulant shriek.

'*The Dopethrone* will doubtless go on to sell about as many copies as a book on "suntanning for goths" would. But it is a stroke of genius – in fact, six strokes of genius, ripping into the skin, the soul and the spirit.'[169]

Looking back at the year 2000 twenty years later, *Metal Hammer* still thought it merited a spot in the top twenty albums of the year, alongside nu metal's worst excesses, such as Disturbed's *The Sickness*: 'Although their reputation had been simmering by the time their third album was released, *Dopethrone* quickly became epochal. In the likes of Cathedral and Sleep, doom wasn't short of lysergic visions and transcendent Sabbath worship, but Wizard's straddling of raw, parochial discontent and slowly percolating Lovecraftian horror opened up vast portals where lived experience became infected with writhing, cosmic dread.'[170]

From the start, most right-(and wrong-)minded heavy-music heads thought that *Dopethrone* was a masterpiece. Not, though, for the band themselves — the conditions of its birth were strained and painful to recall. Nonetheless, it was going to take them to places a band of their nature had never been before.

In 2009, *Terrorizer* named *Dopethrone* the album of the decade: 'The fact an album released at the turn of the century has found itself in the position of album of the decade is testament to the impact of this doom metal masterpiece, the memory of that first listening experience lingering like the scent of marijuana in a well-used festival tent . . . the album utterly crushes with the weight of *peine forte et dure* using the moon as the starting stone. It's a journey through the mouth of madness, a vision through THC and an album of such misanthropic depression that it heralded the beginning of the end for the original line-up.'[171]

It was true: *Dopethrone* sowed the seeds of the band's destruction. The energy expended in crafting the album left the band enervated, especially because the source of that energy had been extraordinary amounts of drink and drugs. The band might have conjured the black god one too many times. The 'crawling chaos' was perilously close to unleashing itself on Electric Wizard.

It was one thing to usurp the throne, quite another to rule.

Chapter Five
I am now an outsider

After the release of *Dopethrone* in the autumn of 2000, Electric Wizard were summoned to tour the United States. At home, their reputation preceded them – unfairly, perhaps – as a haphazard and unreliable live entity. But the quality of their recorded output was not in question: they were sitting atop the Dopethrone.

In the USA, Electric Wizard were seen as kings across the water by the small but committed contingent of musicians making a similar noise. The Wizard's 'Dorset Doom' was impressive, strange and culturally alien. The three US tours they embarked on – in the spring of 2001, winter of 2001 and summer of 2002 – were tours of duty in a literal sense. America was Electric Wizard's Vietnam. The tours enshrined the original line-up's legacy and, ultimately, sealed its fate.

Greg Anderson – guitarist of Goatsnake, Sunn O))) and formerly Burning Witch – owned and ran a label called Southern Lord. He was instrumental in financing and promoting (alongside Tone Deaf Touring) a tour of thirty-three dates for Electric Wizard alongside Southern Lord band Warhorse. From Boston, Warhorse were a perfect foil to the Wizard. Their 2001 album, *As Heaven Turns to Ash . . .*, if not as genre-defining, was as titanic as *Dopethrone* – it was the sound of being ground to powder in a ginormous pestle and mortar. Rise Above had also been keen to sign them.

On *As Heaven Turns to Ash . . .*, Warhorse resolved to 'slow the fuck down'. They blended the 'soul of the sixties and seventies' with the 'nuts heaviness' of early death metal. Ultimately, it sounded great to the 'fucking fucked up'. 'Totally straight it sounds one way and fucked it sounds another way,' Warhorse bassist/vocalist Jerry Orne told *Rock Sound*. 'If you wanna smoke weed we'd encourage it, but if not – whatever! I just think that if you add that narcotic element, it adds another level.'[172]

The tour started at the Khyber Pass venue in Philadelphia on 4 March 2001 and concluded at The Middle East in Cambridge, Massachusetts on 8 April. The names of these clubs seemed portentous of the war that was to explode after the 9/11 atrocities that year.

The two bands shared transport, a 1990 Chevrolet G20 Mark III (with the gear towed behind), for the month they toured the club-sized venues together. Judging from the photograph of their vehicle, it's a miracle they didn't kill each other in something so confined. Naturally, there were blow-ups: on one occasion Mark threw a mic stand at Warhorse guitarist Todd Laskowski, but they had been drunk and soon smoothed it over. Neither eating nor sleeping right, drugs were a necessary pacifier for the bands. Warhorse pushed Electric Wizard in a good way. They were excellent live performers and held the Wizard to a standard that had rarely been demanded of them.

The tour was supposed to begin in Boston, but the gig was never confirmed, with Electric Wizard laid over at Jerry's house. Ahead of meeting, Warhorse had been nervous about the members of the Wizard. They had heard the stories about them, which had gathered steam and became more elaborate as they travelled across the Atlantic. Warhorse drummer Mike Hubbard phoned Jerry to see if everything was OK: 'When they first got here, I called over to Jerry's house to ask him how it was going.

Then I told him to hold on for a second, pretending I had a call on the other line. Really, I was just listening, expecting the Wizard guys to be smashing dishes and terrorising him in the background.'[173]

With the band embarking on a serious US tour, Electric Wizard knew the stakes were high. They had put everything into *Dopethrone* and this was their chance to capitalise on it. Their druggie reputation was beginning to chafe. Jus struggled to disentangle the disposition of the band from its drug use: 'Well the mood of the band, even when it's not fucked up, is just totally fucked up, ya know? Life totally gets in the way of being in the band, doing gigs and recording and then you've got to do shit to pay the rent. So a lot of the times [sic] life's a bit too much, but it's never the band itself.'[174]

Procuring good weed and smoking were struggles in the US. The band thought the American way of smoking joints, with no tobacco and often no roach, was also an abomination. It led to joints burning up one side and other unacceptable outcomes. Things weren't helped when the band was busted just before the fourth gig of the tour, at the Twister's venue in Richmond, Virginia. They had followed a local drug dealer into the back of their van when they were suddenly surrounded by police. They had already paid an exorbitant hundred dollars for an eighth of weed and the bust was an unnecessary indignity after being ripped off.

They were terrified of being arrested, charged and deported. Erik Larsen, guitarist of Alabama Thunderpussy (supporting them that night), intervened and talked the police down. The cops decided the band wasn't a front for a drug cartel, so chose to toy with them instead. The police declared they wouldn't arrest them: 'You're like The Beatles on tour,' they taunted.[175] They singled out Mark for special attention, calling him 'Ringo'. They threatened him with their guns and what might happen to him in prison. Appearing to think they had scared him enough, the cops laughed and backed off. Mark seemed to have a special relationship with the police and his skill for attracting their attention travelled well.

'They put the shits up us and told us we could go to jail, but we smoothed it over,' Mark told *Rock Sound*, clearly baffled but putting on a brave face. 'Because we didn't go "Fuck off, you dirty pigs," the police were cool – we don't want to get into trouble on the third show!'[176]

The incident was perfect fodder to promote the tour. Rise Above wrote on their website under the headline, ELECTRIC WIZARD EXPERIENCE THE US'S WAR ON DRUGS FIRST HAND! The Music Cartel, the band's US label, put out a more po-faced statement: 'With a band like Electric Wizard, something like this happening isn't very far off the mark. I just hope nothing worse happens before the tour is completed.'

Jus wasn't impressed with southern hospitality in general. He seemed a little hurt that people would find Electric Wizard intimidating. 'In the south, nobody spoke to us but in the north, everybody would be like, "Yeah, baby, yeah! Let's shag!" like Austin Powers, you know? But I think people in the south were frightened. Everybody thinks we're going to be trouble. It's not like we're Oasis, most English people are quiet.'[177]

They certainly weren't Oasis, but the Wizard respected the Mancunians as an awkward band who resisted playing the music industry game and ultimately succeeded. Oasis were also a British band in the ascendance after years of American dominance in music. They played loud and didn't give a fuck. They might have struggled to make inroads in the States, but their attitude rubbed off on Tim in particular. He held himself like Liam Gallagher on all the US tours, keeping trouble close at hand.

In mid-March, the tour reached the South By Southwest (SXSW) music festival in Austin, Texas. What better place to show off this weird, appallingly heavy English band? Electric Wizard played back-to-back nights: at the Backroom on 15 March for the Tee Pee Records showcase and Emo's on the 16 March at the Man's Ruin label showcase. Man's Ruin had released the 'Chrono.Naut' single. The band took to the stage after 1 a.m. and Jus declared, 'We are the KINGS of the fucking stone age'. This was a little dig at Queens of the Stone Age, founded by former Kyuss guitarist Joshua Homme, who were getting serious recognition on both sides of the Atlantic for their 1998 self-titled debut album and its 2000 follow-up, *Rated R*. Jus's onstage proclamation seemingly missed the point of QOT-SA's name and its deliberate subversion of atavistic heavy rock.

The set was chaotic. Warhorse's Jerry helped Mark replace a misfiring hi-hat and Jus broke two guitar strings during 'Chrono.Naut' itself – their primary reason for being there. The previous night he broke a string playing a cover of 'Interstellar Overdrive' by Pink Floyd. These incidents didn't amount to much in the eyes of the band. Technical glitches and fuck-ups *were* the Electric Wizard live experience. During the tour they were often on fire during at least three-quarters of the duration of their sets, and otherwise scrabbling around and improvising when things went wrong.

After the Man's Ruin showcase, label owner Frank Kozik invited the band to meet the 'Man's Ruin girls' who were ensconced in another hotel room. Mark and Tim were otherwise preoccupied, but Jus went to find the room full of semi-naked women.

Jus told the *Midwest Metal* fanzine that Tim had lost his job and that he himself had broken up with his girlfriend to do the tour. In fact, at SXSW Tim had to put down rumours circulating on internet forums that he was about to quit the band itself.

Prior to leaving for the tour, the band hadn't been where they wanted to be in terms of playing standards. They had to work (relatively) hard to get there. The tour is remarkable for the number of decent recordings and footage that came out of it, showcasing the band in all their dishevelled glory.[178] Fuck-ups got swept up in the rolling thunder of the gigs, and that intuitive understanding of each other born from years of jamming. A triangle of power, the Wizard was greater than the sum of its members. A large part of the tour's success was the band's setlist rotation and spur-of-the-moment adaptations during gigs. They were a long way from the days of arguing onstage about what to play next. By this point, they also really knew how to talk up what they were doing. Jus warned that the gigs were going to be 'like having rats thrown in your face'.[179]

'It's going to be pretty varied,' Jus told *Midwest Metal*. 'We've got four different sets, each one lasts an hour. We're doing a little off every album, we're going to be doing "Electric Wizard" off the debut! Loads of stuff off *Come My Fanatics* . . . and loads off *Dopethrone*. We're not sure if we're going to get an hour a night, I mean if people think we're gonna play for an hour and a half they'll be dead, then we'd die (laughing)! We're just an assault of fucking feedback, the feedback of death and it doesn't stop. People think we're gonna be mellow or something, ya know chilled out or whatever. But we start and the chaos doesn't stop.'[180]

The tour arrived at the Troubadour, Los Angeles, on 19 March 2001. The two touring partners were joined by Acid King and Goatsnake for the show, the latter on home turf with most of their members from the city. The gig was typical of the bills on the tour in that it included the best of the millennial stoner-doom scene. Support slots across the tour were occupied by 5ive, Witch Mountain and, on multiple dates, the mighty Bongzilla.

During the LA gig, Mark once again had hi-hat issues, but otherwise the set was a success. However, they found it offputting

126

when former Misfits frontman and goth-punk legend Glenn Danzig appeared in front of the stage, disappeared, then reappeared again, several times. Even so, for a Monday night with a few hundred people in attendance, Electric Wizard brought out the celebrity fans: Josh Homme and Nick Oliveri from Queens of the Stone Age themselves[181], Jello Biafra from Dead Kennedys, H.R. from Bad Brains and John Garcia (then of Unida, but previously singer of Kyuss alongside Homme and Oliveri). Bizarrely, Anthony Kiedis of Red Hot Chili Peppers showed up – at the height of his band's popularity off their 1999 album *Californication*. Less than two years previously, Red Hot Chili Peppers had presided over the conflagration of the disastrous Woodstock '99 festival in Rome, New York. With the revival of the hippie dream dead, Kiedis had come to watch Electric Wizard bury it.

The Wizard were most impressed to meet Dave Chandler, the guitarist of Saint Vitus. The band had drawn comparisons with Saint Vitus from day one. They rated 1986's *Born Too Late* as one of their favourite albums. That album's buzzy, super-slo-mo plod was the sound of hardcore punk on downer drugs. The title track introduced the idea of being born out of one's time, and of doom metallers as the keepers of arcane knowledge.

Every time I'm on the street
People laugh and point at me
They talk about my length of hair
And the out of date clothes I wear

They say I look like the living dead
They say I can't have much in my head
They say my songs are much too slow
But they don't know the things I know

Southern Lord rented out the Magic Castle hotel in Hollywood for the bands to celebrate the show. It was the kind of place where you could jump into the swimming pool from the balconies. Electric Wizard chatted to Josh Homme and, despite their dig at his band's name at SXSW, found him gentlemanly and free of the brashness that often marked American musicians in their eyes. It was in LA that the full force of the dissonance of their English and American existence hit Electric Wizard. In the States, they were being treated like Led Zeppelin, and behaved accordingly. To Jus, it confirmed a truism that American bands tour the UK for professional affirmation but British bands tour America to cement their dissolute reputations.

One band who was desperate to play with Electric Wizard was Sourvein. Former 13 guitarist Liz Buckingham had joined the band and moved to New Orleans after failed attempts to get new projects going in New York. She had been intending to reform 13 with its singer, Alicia Morgan, when she was invited by Sourvein vocalist T-Roy (Troy Medlin) to play guitar with him. T-Roy played Liz some live recordings demonstrating his new vocal approach, moving away from a punk sound and in a sludge direction. Liz agreed to join Sourvein and the band relocated to North Carolina for a period. She ended up writing all the music on their 1999 self-titled album and 2002 record *Will To Mangle*.

In particular, *Will To Mangle* is one of the most underrated pieces of Sabbathian doom. Opener 'Bangleaf' exudes the power of Liz's guitar playing, leaning back into the seat of the muscle car as she presses on the gas pedal, with moments of more subtle, exploratory riffing. T-Roy's rasp keeps the album knee-deep in the bayou, but the music is insouciantly colossal. When Jus heard the track, he immediately wanted to re-record it with his vocals, because it was so in keeping with his approach to riffs.

'I went to New Orleans with a romantic view of something but reality is sometimes a bit different,' Liz recalled in 2009. 'It wasn't the same feeling as the early days in NY, because back at that time the bands were just forming; it wasn't even called sludge then. In NOLA [New Orleans] there were lots of bands going for the same sound, getting competitive and it wasn't as fun any more. But it was inspiring to write music there and much easier to do things. You need to work all the time in NY to make rent and you can't take off to go on tour. For me, it offered a different way to look at a band, so Sourvein was when I really started to tour.'[182]

Sourvein got themselves on the Electric Wizard/Warhorse bill at Seattle's Breakroom on 23 March and gigged their way up the country from New Orleans. Sleep's Matt Pike, a good friend of the band (and even then something of a legend of the scene), came along and they jokingly introduced him as their 'roadie' on the trip. After years of mutual admiration, including a poster of Liz having hung on Jus's wall since 1992, it was the first time they had met in person. Jus had previously written to Alicia, the singer of 13, but Liz didn't play penpals.

'When I met him at the gig, we both said how we'd rather be at home watching some particular movie,' Liz said in 2011. 'It was like meeting someone and feeling like you instantly knew them well.'[183]

They spoke at length that evening, mostly about films. The band had played well that night and were in high spirits. Jus and Liz were largely oblivious to the backstage antics around them. Consumed in their conversation, they realised they had a lot of shared interests and a similar outlook on life.

'Sometimes I think we were separated at birth,' Jus said in 2008. 'We're very much on the same wavelength; we like all the same shit. I don't wanna get romantic and stuff, but we were kind of born to be together, I think.'[184]

'I had a special feeling, it was really weird. I saw him from behind and thought, I know this guy!' Liz remembered in 2012.[185]

As the tour moved into the end of March, the existing live recordings of the band show Electric Wizard on fire. At the 15th Street Tavern in Denver, someone in the front row managed to place a joint in Jus's mouth mid-song – a lungful of weed powering the band into the groove. With all the adrenaline in the air, they often played at a higher tempo. The set at the Double Door in Chicago on 30 March begins with Jus declaring the audience to be 'mindless fucking slaves', before beginning with a devastating 'Supercoven'.

What stands out from all these performances, apart from the fantastic, unpredictable spontaneity of the band, is the sonic force of Tim's bass. At the Double Door, he let it feed back with the resonance of a guitar while Jus chugged out the opening of 'Son Of Nothing'. Rich, insanely distorted and dredging the lower frequencies, Tim's bass playing was the melodic pit and the rhythmic pendulum that enabled Jus to embark on solos on a whim and Mark to restlessly rattle around his kit.

At the same show in Chicago, Jus recited the copper's speech from *The Living Dead at the Manchester Morgue* which precedes 'Wizard In Black' from *Come My Fanatics* . . . The Virginia run-in and numerous other close calls with the law were fresh in his mind: 'You're all the same, the lot of ya, with your long hair and faggot clothes. Drugs, sex, every sort of filth. And you hate the police, don't ya?' The songs from *Dopethrone* were dominant in the set, with 'We Hate You', 'Dopethrone' and 'Weird Tales' regular features. The gig at the Velvet Lounge in Washington DC on 6 April even included a very rare outing of 'Vinum Sabbathi' as an encore. Weirdly, 'Funeralopolis' – perhaps *the* classic song from *Dopethrone* – was never played on this tour.

At the second-to-last gig at New Jersey Metal Meltdown at the Convention Hall in Asbury Park, they were interviewed by *Rock Sound* magazine. Writer Darren Sadler bemoaned how the band's headline set was 'scuppered' by the 'pure shite' of

Raven, Anvil and Unholy – old-school metal acts who were out
in the cold in 2001. Sadler had been warned the band was on
the verge of killing each other, but he found them in a pleasant,
if stoned, state. They delighted in telling him they had stayed
with Ron Holzner, bassist of Trouble, a founding doom band who
were labelled as 'white metal' at one point due to their Christian
lyrical themes. His house was purportedly full of black magic
artefacts.[186]

'Doom', as a concept, is inherently Christian. It means judgement before God. Some of the genre's best musicians struggled
with their faith. Victor Griffin, the guitarist of Pentagram, used
his music in solo project Place of Skulls to confess his sins and
to explore his attempts to live a better life. Doom was long
the battleground for vulnerable souls. Where Electric Wizard
differed was that they didn't care enough about what people
thought to worry about being judged – by God, or anyone else.

Apart from complaining about the quality of the weed, how
America was a 'police state', how Americans made tea badly
and how the processed food was making their gums bleed, it
was clear from this *Rock Sound* interview that Electric Wizard
relished the tour. They inspired devotion and not a little fear
everywhere they went. Jus recounted being called a 'lime' in
a bar and throwing a chair in mock anger, to stunned silence.
Mark, misnamed 'Martin' throughout the interview, explained
how difficult the early days of the tour had been. 'I was thinking
about splitting up and telling everyone we're leaving it, but I
think that was just an off day. There was a time at the start
when I was like, "Fuck this shit – I've had enough of this crap
already," but you just shut your mind and just get out and do it.'

'If the gigs had been shit, we'd probably have quit, but this
has been so successful it would be stupid to throw it all away
now,' added Jus. 'Ninety-nine per cent of the shows have been
outstanding. I can't believe we have a following. I had no idea!

We're doing better here than in Europe, and there's bigger turnouts. We're treated like a cult over here – you know what I mean? In England we're just scummy Electric Wizard.'[187]

Their imminent return to England was playing on their minds. With it came unemployment and an uncertain future. Mark openly speculated that the band probably wouldn't rehearse for a year and would inevitably return to 'back to where we were before the tour anyway': 'I can't believe we did it, it seems like a dream world. It seems like we're going to [go] back to England and no one's going to believe us, everyone will just think we've been locked up in a mental home for a month!'[188]

The final date of the *Apocalypse Now* tour took place at The Middle East in Cambridge, Massachusetts. The bands were supported, surprisingly, by explosive future hardcore legends Converge, who went on to release their genre-shattering album *Jane Doe* in September 2001. Converge joining the bill was typical of the more agnostic state of the American metal underground at the time.

The Wizard ended their set with the title track from their self-titled debut album. Jus signed it off: 'We are Electric Wizard. This is "Electric Wizard". Goodbye, America.'

That final gig at The Middle East began with a six-minute instrumental jam that settled Electric Wizard into the set. Its coiling, unfurling and slithering nature went well with its title, 'Mother Of Serpents'. The Wizard laid the song down in the studio during the sessions for their fourth album, *Let Us Prey*, which took place over a six-week period in September and October 2001, back at Chuckalumba Studios. Rolf Startin was not involved. Instead, they worked with *Dopethrone*

engineer John Stephens and Jus took on more of a producer's role.

As Mark warned, the band had fallen back into their old,
disillusioned patterns. They were nearer implosion than ever.
They were all pulling in different directions, both to the benefit
and detriment of the record's sound. After *Dopethrone*, which
already stood out like a gigantic black monolith in the band's
discography, Jus wanted to try and expand their music, and
maybe even transcend it.

But any experimentation needed to be within the self-defined
limitations of their sound. Mark and Tim wanted to bring in
newer textures. At this point, Linkin Park and Slipknot ruled
the nu metal roost and they suggested hip-hop scratching on
one song. Jus was having none of it.[189] Instead of focusing on
each other, they consumed themselves with the studio itself. No
longer a gateway to other imaginative realms, it became their
refuge from the crumbling edifice of reality.

As with *Dopethrone*, they camped out at the studio. This time,
they didn't have any songs ready. They jammed the whole thing.
The process was to wake up, smoke some bongs, take a walk in
the forest and record whatever came out.[190]

'I think that was our Genesis record,' Jus told *Kerrang!* in
2009. 'We were all just about the studio, and we wanted to
make music using the studio. We were really into the *idea* of
recording then, this pretty technical album. We wanted to be
experimental, like trying out some horror movie-type stuff, just
to see how it works. Each song was like an idea, we didn't write
it. We just got an idea, and went with that for how we wanted it
to sound.'[191]

The key to the album, and to understanding Electric Wizard
during this time, is its song 'The Outsider'. It is an instrumental
in principle, though Jus recites a mantra under its many layers:
'Always watching/Never screaming/Forever watching/Always

133

feeling/Never dreaming/Always dreaming'. He shied away from including lyrics to the album, uncomfortable that they might expose his emotions at the time.

'The Outsider' is named after a short story by H.P. Lovecraft, published in *Weird Tales* magazine in April 1926. The narrator of the story lives in a castle which is 'infinitely old and infinitely horrible'.[192] The inhabitant is self-taught, learning about life outside the castle walls by studying mouldy books with no teacher to guide them. Bereft of light, the castle is dominated by a black tower 'which reached above the trees into the unknown outer sky'.[193] The narrator decides to climb the tower and, once reaching its highest point via a 'capacious observation chamber', goes through a door and meets an 'abysmally unexpected and grotesquely unbelievable sight' – not of the starry sky and treetops, but the solid ground stretching away from them.[194] Determined to still reach light, the narrator proceeds: 'I neither knew nor cared whether my experience was insanity, dreaming or magic.'[195]

After two hours of journeying, they reach a castle which seems 'maddingly familiar, yet full of perplexing strangeness'.[196] They observe open windows ablaze with light through which can be heard the sounds of revelry. Looking through the window, they observe a company making merry and speaking excitedly to one another, some of whose faces 'brought up incredibly remote recollections'.[197]

When the narrator crosses the sill, the mood changes, and upon the company descends 'a sudden and unheralded fear of hideous intensity, distorting every face and evoking the most horrible screams from nearly every throat.'[198] Soon after, the narrator is confronted with their reflection and with it 'the putrid, dripping eidolon of unwholesome revelation' and 'in its eaten-away and bone-revealing outlines a leering, abhorrent travesty on the human shape'.[199]

Electric Wizard were trapped in a nightmarish castle of their own making. The leaden downwards trudge of 'The Outsider' simulates the journey of this 'unholy abomination'.[200] Once 'free', they dragged their mouldering corpse to look upon their half-remembered former glories. The song's freeform soloing, relentless, repetitive drum breaks and bass excavations sometimes sound like the band satirising itself – baulking in horror at their own, inexplicably fast, deterioration. But even when Electric Wizard sound like they are running out of ideas, they lather them in lysergic ointments that preserve the songs and keep them moving forward.

In another sense, if the partygoers seen through the window of Lovecraft's story represent mainstream metal, or even mainstream music, then Electric Wizard were the perennial outsiders. It was their outsiderdom that thrust the band into the pages of magazines and launched them on a US tour, guided by a force beyond their will. They were cursed, and they were blessed. Cursed to crawl unbidden through the sill of culture as a thing to be horrified by and condemned. Blessed to be noticed, and to recognise something of themselves in these successful people on the inside, staring back at them in horror. The crucial difference between Lovecraft's story and the Wizard's is that this glory didn't reside in the band's past, but in its future.

At the end of Lovecraft's story, the ghoulish narrator resorts to 'nepenthe', a type of cosmic balm which erases memory 'in a chaos of echoing images'.[201] The narrator resides in the catacombs of Nephren-Ka and rides with the ghouls on the night wind, not unlike the Lovecraftian demon touched by the occult glamour of ancient Egypt: Nyarlathotep – the Crawling Chaos.

The ghouls of the night wind seem to be rushing through 'We, The Undead'. The second song on *Let Us Prey*, it isn't played so much as spat out by the band. Jus's screaming vocals are warped and distorted under wah and phaser effects. The song is as fast and filthy as the underside of a neglected chopper motor-cycle. As an expression of disgust at the state of themselves, it is the rawest and blackest metal the band had produced.

The hypnotic, spellbound first section of third song 'Master Of Alchemy', subtitled 'House Of Whipcord', feels like being bound up in a nightmarish LSD trip. The riff is a noose being wound and tightened around your neck.

House of Whipcord was the name of a 1974 film directed by the exploitation king of Soho's film industry, Pete Walker. It begins with the following title card: 'This film is dedicated to those who are disturbed by today's lax moral codes and who eagerly await the return of corporal and capital punishment . . . ' We are entering a grubby world, but one made in a sophisticated fashion – from the well-composed framing of the credit sequence against the silhouette of a noose onwards.

Most of the film was shot at Littledean jail in Gloucestershire (now a strange private museum of the bizarre and bad taste). The trip begins when the comically named Mark E. DeSade seduces nineteen-year-old glamour model Ann-Marie. She is played by Penny Irving, a real-life Page 3 girl who graced numerous *Top of the Pops* album covers. After only one date he tells her he is taking her to meet his parents. This is true, except his parents run a private jail – his mother is the sadistic Barbara Markham, a former corrections officer, and his father a blind ex-judge, Bailey.

When Ann-Marie arrives at the prison she is taken into the charge of the female wardens, Walker and Bates. She is one of several women held there in terrible conditions. On sentencing her in a makeshift courtroom with the slogan 'The world for Christ' emblazoned on a banner, Bailey states that the court exists 'to pass what we regard as proper sentences on depraved females of every category, with whom the effete and misguided laws of Great Britain today have been too lenient.'

For the prisoners' first infraction, or attempt at escape, the punishment is two weeks' solitary confinement; for the second, a lashing; and the third is death by hanging. It is a nasty, effective film and a jet-black satire on moralism and authoritarianism.

House Of Whipcord has a grim, mischievous character that marks it out as part of a particularly British form of exploitation cinema. Markham is haunted by the ghosts of her former career, and she is tinged by a creeping insanity – she embodies the justice system collapsing in on itself. As a director, Pete Walker doesn't pull his punches, but chooses potent imagery over cheap gore and shocks. It has a bleak, pyrrhic victory of a resolution. For 'Master Of Alchemy', the film's morally perilous world, cruelty and suffocating ambience, gives the song guiding purpose.

As if passing through a gateway, the song shifts into long drawn-out chord changes and lashings of wah pedal soloing. Mark's drumming is practically all breaks and time is kept only by the regularity of the chord sequence. Subtitled 'The Black Drug', this part of the song creates a queasy trip to the heart of the problem, a mythical substance with a terrifying real-world analogue that was destroying lives and had killed loved ones. Underneath the music, an indiscernible voice (processed through an effect that makes it sound like a drugged-out mechanoid) worms further into our brain stems. Jus had been working on a novella called *The Black Drug* since his late teens (it remains in a half-finished state).

Mark had wanted to sing on *Let Us Prey*, but was informed that Electric Wizard wasn't the fucking Monkees. Or even KISS, for that matter. But Mark did play piano, and his standout contribution to *Let Us Prey* is 'Night Of The Shape', which saw the band's vision around studio experimentation fully realised.

Mark's bare-bones piano motif and the panning violin which is processed to sound like a saxophone (indeed played by someone called Paul Sax), amounted to the opening musical sequence of an unmade horror movie. At the time, Mark fancied recording an entire album on Hammond organ ('Like a Hammer Horror movie or something cheesy').[202] The problem was that the low-budget snuff film was indeed about to be made, and its unwitting stars were to be Electric Wizard.

'So how does it feel to be sat with the most miserable band in the world?'

It was 7 December 2001 and Electric Wizard were back in America. *Kerrang!* journalist Catherine Yates was trying her best to get an interview out of them before they played the North Six venue in Williamsburg, New York. They were on a fourteen-date tour as part of a package put together by *Metal Maniacs* magazine.

It was a strange package bill which featured Norwegian black metallers Enslaved, touring their stoner-groove-inflected album *Monumension* (an album that divided members of Enslaved itself, as well as fans). Another of the bands was Macabre, who had written a death-metal rock-opera about serial killer Jeffrey Dahmer, called *Dahmer*.

The full-page photo of the Wizard in the *Kerrang!* article depicts them walking down the street in Manhattan. It resembles the scene in *A Clockwork Orange* where the droogs are walking down the Flat Block Marina in Thamesmead. In the scene, their leader Alex hits them in the yarbles and throws them into Southmere Lake to the strains of Rossini's overture to *La Gazza Ladra* (*The Thieving Magpie*).

Mark is walking in the centre of the picture, looking somewhere off camera (as he often did in photographs). With his hair grown out and prominent sideburns, he looks like X-Men's

Wolverine. He sometimes wore a T-shirt of the Marvel character
to drive the association home. Both Tim and Jus are staring at
the camera – Tim in the voluminous trousers that marked him
as a hip-hop head with a buttoned-down shirt, Jus in a cut-off
denim jacket with a Sons of OTIS shirt underneath.

The mere request for an interview had prompted them to
throw bottles and scream at each other before Jus eventually
agreed to do it. It was on tours like this one, with the opportunity to go up a level, that caused bands to buckle, and he knew
it: 'It's *exactly* why bands break up. That and the fact that they
work their arses off, then never get paid for it. I'm thirty years
old. I want to be able to pay my own rent for once in my life,
give myself some self-respect.'[203]

Around this time, Jus spoke more frequently about bucking
his ideas up and taking the band more seriously. That day, he
was particularly pissed off about having no weed to smoke. He
was also tired of the usual Sabbath comparisons, whilst having
to cope with being out of place on a death and black metal bill:
'That's the thing, Sabbath have influenced us, but it's 2002, not
1970 any more. I don't want to be retro. I'm not trying to recreate the past, and in their time, Sabbath weren't trying to be the
past, either. They were influenced by blues and jazz but wanted
to play heavy . . . I mean, take [death metal band] Deicide – it's
nineties' music, man. *Last* century. It's time we invented some
new music.'[204]

The gig at the North Six was opened by Khanate, another
band involving Sunn O))) guitarist Stephen O'Malley. Khanate
were the kind of band Jus was talking about – a forward-facing,
challenging, even frightening, band. O'Malley played a Travis
Bean guitar – made with an aluminium neck – and it tore
through venues like a machine through sheet metal. O'Malley
designed the cover of *Let Us Prey* – a cross-faded king cobra in
reds and gold.

When their previous tour passed through New York in early March, Electric Wizard played at the infamous Continental venue, where Joey Ramone used to prop up the bar. Then, the Wizard were supported by a band featuring members of Sir Lord Baltimore, one of the proto-metal bands that constituted the heavy underground of the early seventies, with their 1970 album *Kingdom Come*. Liz had had her own memorable evening at the Continental when she had performed at a Motörhead tribute show with Lemmy himself in attendance.

Backstage at the North Six, Mark, described as 'friendly, almost bashful' by Yates, seemed in a better mood, despite the fact he had supposedly ingested a bottle of bleach the night before. He was happy with his new drum stands ('I whack 'em as hard as I can') but perplexed at the tour's line-up. He would have preferred to be touring with his hero Mike Patton: 'We should be supporting [Patton-fronted experimentalists] Fantômas, not this lot!' Later, just before the gig, Yates was not sure Mark would be able to stand up, let alone play drums. Tim refused to cooperate at all: 'I have nothing to say.'[205]

But when chaos reigns, nothing can be taken for granted. Yates describes how 'when the set ruptures out of the PA with near atomic force, it all falls into place.' Will Palmer, who ran Rise Above alongside Lee Dorrian at the time, watched the band alongside Yates: 'The thing about Electric Wizard is when they get it right, nothing can touch 'em,' he told her.[206]

Two nights later, the Wizard delivered a superb set at the Jaxx nightclub further south in Springfield, Virginia. In the footage of the performance, you can hear the audience members reeling between songs. It was so good that the band played an encore – which Jus claimed onstage they never usually did – 'Wizard In Black'. He told the audience it was 'a song about ourselves'. Later in the tour they played a sketchier gig at Foufounes Electriques in Montreal, Canada. Jus opened the

set complaining about their start time: 'We're Electric Wizard
from England. We've come a long way to play at eight-thirty.'
Throughout the North American tours Jus speaks onstage in
what the *Midwest Metal* fanzine called a 'vague English accent'
with a transatlantic twang.[207] In Montreal, Mark messed up
a drum break before the solo section of 'Return Trip' and then
seemed uncertain how to end it. Tim snuck in a cheeky bit of
'Love Buzz' by Nirvana at the end of
'Weird Tales'.

Let Us Prey was released at the end of April in 2002 by Rise
Above in the UK and the Music Cartel in the US. Rise Above's
press release described it as a 'marijuana-induced minefield
of riffs, alchemy and screams of the undead': 'It is the cloud of
black chaos that seems to guide their every move, upon which
they seem to thrive, dragging them deeper and deeper into the
psychedelic nadir of apocalyptic sludge.'

It received very good reviews. Dave Ling in *Metal Hammer*
said the band 'mined a stream of black gold' (presumably he
meant 'seam') and stated that the album was being favourably
compared to *Come My Fanatics* . . . Rise Above were responsible
for this, citing in their press release a 'return to the more
tripped-out hypnotic mantras' of *Come My Fanatics* . . . Really
though, *Let Us Prey* was more the blackened chemical stain
after *Dopethrone*. It sounded like the band were on nastier drugs
than they had been at the time of *Come My Fanatics* . . . and
the trip was commensurately gnarlier. Dom Lawson in *Kerrang!*
noted 'a strong whiff of Black Flag adding extra poison to "We,
The Undead"'.[208] Indie rock revivalists The Strokes were on
the cover of *Kerrang!* for that issue – typical of heavy music's
identity struggles at the time.

The 10/10 review for the album in *Terrorizer* magazine was remarkable. Writer Jim Martin prefaced it with a quotation from William Blake's 'Proverbs of Hell' ('The road of excess leads to the palace of wisdom') and later extracted a line from Baudelaire's 'The Dancing Serpent'. He wrote that Electric Wizard 'manage to bridge centuries in forming an invocation of the spirit of Coleridge far more vividly than any other band in metal's history'. He went further into the comparison with the drug-addled Romantic poet: 'Wizard's primitive, intoxicated transcendence, as on the alternately blissed-out and blinded-by-fear riff-submission of "Priestess of Mars" is nonetheless oft-times reminiscent to this acolyte of the opiated fever dream of "Kubla Khan", with Jus Oborn's behemothic guitar-wrath journeying down those caverns measureless to man to that very sunless sea.'[209]

Martin went all out to underline the timelessness of the album and say something truly original and ambitious about the artistic lineage of which the band deserved to be considered a part. Whereas on *Come My Fanatics . . .* the Wizard were willingly lost in space, Martin's review compounded the feeling that the band now seemed (unwillingly?) frozen outside their own time. The album carried a quote from the final paragraph of Lovecraft's 'The Outsider' on its back cover, involving the opiate-like substance 'nepenthe': 'For although nepenthe has calmed me, I know always that I am an outsider; a stranger in this century and among those who are still men.'[210]

Warhorse flew over to join Electric Wizard for a European tour lasting three-and-a-half weeks. Once again, the two bands were crammed into a box van, where they negotiated who got to sleep on the floor amidst continual searches for the bong and pipe. They often sat in the van together in total darkness to save battery power.

In Hamburg, Germany, the promoter threatened to call the police because of how loudly Warhorse played. He pulled the plug during their second song, but begged them to come back on when they left the stage in disgust. Back on home turf, in Camden, London, someone pulled a gun (well, it looked like a gun but was concealed beneath a jumper) on Mark: 'I don't even know if he had one or not – I just wanted to get the fuck out of it. He reckoned he was going to jail and had a stash he needed to get rid of. He wanted to sell it to me and give the money to his wife – it wasn't really that bad, it was the fact that we couldn't get rid of him.'[211]

Asked by *Rock Sound* whether they were impressed to be playing gigs in England, the home of Black Sabbath and metal in general, Warhorse drummer Mike Hubbard not only demurred but got a shot off at Saxon, another old-school metal band out of favour at the time: 'It's a world market now and for every Black Sabbath, you have Saxon, so I guess it evens out.'

Asked whether he thought Warhorse or the Wizard rocked harder, Jus used it as an opportunity to highlight the heritage of the band: 'We're the Wizard, aren't we? If I thought they were better I'd go and join Warhorse. We're better because we are British, we're playing English music and it's the loudest and heaviest shit around.' In the same interview, Jus also said he put the band's staying power down to the fact the band was, in a way, splitting up all the time. As a result, they were constantly playing reunion gigs ('It's like being married!'). Mark was more concise: 'We are a disaster on tour.'[212]

But something ran deeper in what Jus was saying. Two months earlier he had spoken openly to the same magazine about what he saw as Mark and Tim's lack of ambition. In that comment, Wimborne loomed large: 'They've got in the habit of being there – and even moving to Bournemouth [where Jus was living] is hard from someone from a town like that. Tim and Mark are badass in Wimborne, everyone knows them and respects them. If they moved, no one would know who the fuck they were! I think they're stuck in [a] small town and they just use drugs to escape the pissless reality of the shitty town they live in as there's nothing to do.'[213]

Still, when the circumstances demanded it, Jus was still happy to declare that their ultimate ambition was to build a huge warehouse, fill it with marijuana plants, and 'play to a fucking forest of weed'.[214] But that mask of bravado was slipping in public more often to reveal a more sober, ground-down realist.

After completing the European tour with Warhorse, Jus returned to Wimborne for his sister's wedding and then set off for Electric Wizard's third, fateful, US tour at 5 a.m. the following morning. The band was exhausted. When they arrived back in the States, they saw a huge tour bus waiting for them and support acts Unearthly Trance and Sons of OTIS. They were not yet playing bigger venues than they had the previous year and the band felt as if they were watching the proceeds of the tour waiting to fill up the gas tank.

The first show was an unmitigated disaster. Once again in ill-starred Richmond, Virginia – the location of their earlier run-in with the police – at a venue called Alley Katz on 29 May, they managed (almost) two songs before the wheels fell off. After a miscue on opening track 'Dopethrone', Jus tossed two sheets of paper onto the stage, presumably the setlists. Tim was hammered, stumbling about the stage and risking damage to his (pretty valuable) Kramer XL-9 bass. He kept playing the chorus riff in the wrong place.

The band attempted 'Supercoven', where the bass made a resonant lowing sound like a dying whale. Something happened to Mark's snare because he started fucking around with it before punching it into place out of sheer frustration. By this point, Tim had wandered off-stage. Jus left his guitar propped against the amp feedbacking as Mark took a self-flagellating drum solo. The remaining twenty-plus minutes of the gig was a jam with

Sons of OTIS bassist Frank Sargeant standing in. At points during the camcorder footage of this car crash, it zooms in on the '13' sticker below the bridge of Jus's guitar, like a beacon from the future.

Jus took the mic at the end of the improvisation: 'That's it. If anyone sees our bass player out on the streets, please kick his fuckin' ass.'

From the footage, it wouldn't have been a surprise had Electric Wizard broken up that night. Tim walking off was a spectacular strop, but the tour carried on. The band was drinking a lot and the gig didn't seem enough of an aberration for drastic action, especially not one date into the tour.

Reflecting on the tour ten years later – when this incident was being discussed on an internet forum – Ryan Aubin, drummer of Sons of OTIS, wrote of Electric Wizard: 'Even on their absolute worst nights they had this awesome presence; one that denoted destruction, desperation, depression, and DOOM. No one can ever claim that they were the best musicians, or even an original band for that matter . . . but anyone lucky enough to have witnessed the Mark, Tim, and Jus version of the Wizard maybe saw something as close to seeing Black Flag and Black Sabbath tearing at each other onstage as you're going to find.'[215] For Aubin, it was also a question of maturity – an older and wiser version of this Electric Wizard might have handled things better.

Two nights later, at the Star Bar, Atlanta, Electric Wizard were back to their erratic best. They added 'Funeralopolis' to the setlist, playing it second. They enjoyed stretching the song to nine minutes by warping its raging final section into new shapes. Mark dropped a stick, recovered it in two beats, and the runaway nuclear train was off again – he almost lost the song again during a fill but the energy of the finale was relentless. Jus broke a string and Tim saw the tune out. After a brief jam interlude to repair the string, they played the two songs from *Let Us Prey* that graced the tour: '. . . A Chosen Few' and 'Priestess of Mars'.

'. . . A Chosen Few' has one of the best riffs Electric Wizard had written up to that point. Despite the disunity in the band, it feels like a pledge of allegiance: 'Our coven is only three/The chosen few, masters of sorcery'. That designation of a worthy chosen few would later evolve to have a life of its own.

'Priestess of Mars' played on the Princess of Mars of the science-fiction of Edgar Rice Burroughs. It was a song of devotion. Sounding like slow-curling flames lapping the cosmos, it is a seduction by the universe itself: 'The stars reached out and they drugged me.'

The song describes a quest, and a possible future for the Wizard:

I have searched three worlds to find
Climbed black mountains in my mind
Serene and primal you are
My priestess of mars

It was also unusually lustful for the band: 'Perfect in thy nakedness/Enchanted flesh beneath the moon'.

Some of this can be attributed to the stories of C.L. Moore, one of the writers noted as 'lyrical inspiration' in the *Let Us Prey* liner notes. Moore wrote the Jirel of Joiry stories in *Weird Tales* and invented the Northwest Smith character, a spaceship pilot and smuggler. Her vision of our solar system at some point in an indeterminate future was sleazy and populated with exotic drugs and hard-boiled characters like the leather-clad Smith. The stories partially fuelled Jus's vision of a band that was a grottier version of Hawkwind.

In one Northwest Smith story, 'Shambleau', published in *Weird Tales* in November 1933, he is seduced by a humanoid alien creature called Shambleau – with wormlike appendages instead of hair. They wrap around Smith in its embrace. Moore posits that Shambleau might be the alien entity that inspired the Medusa myth when it was encountered by the ancient Greeks. Smith is attracted to Shambleau despite himself, with a 'perverted revulsion that clasped what it loathed'.[216]

In another story, 'The Tree of Life' (published in *Weird Tales* in October 1936), Smith encounters a priestess in the ruins of a Martian temple. Moore goes on to describe her in similar terms to Electric Wizard's priestess of mars: 'A blaze of luminous white had appeared among the trees across the clearing. The priestess had returned. He watched her pacing slowly toward the Tree, walking with a precise and delicate grace as liquidly lovely as the motion of the Tree. Her fabulous hair swung down about her in a swaying robe that rippled at every step away from the moon-white beauty of her body.'[217]

What follows is a disturbing embrace between this sacred tree – 'all the blossoms glowed more vividly at her nearness, the branches stretching toward her, rippling with eagerness' – and the priestess: 'And the Tree's tremor ran unbroken through the body of the girl it clasped.' Smith has to choke down his terror and cover his eyes 'to blot out the sight of the lovely horror behind him whose vividness was burnt upon his very brain.'[218]

The alien acts of lust in both stories are intoxicating and undeniable. They are also profoundly disturbing – they set the tone for the song: of something transgressive and inevitable.

'Priestess of Mars' felt like a confession and an ode. Who was this Priestess of Mars who was the object of such yearning? Live, the song bewitched and bedazzled. Considering the band's name, Electric Wizard had rarely cast this kind of spell. It felt like a glimpse of some larger ritual to come.

Despite these moments of greatness on stage, the band continued to deteriorate as the tour continued. Tim seemed to have drunk himself into another world. He was frequently arrested and returned to the band by the cops. One night, according to Ryan Aubin, Tim was beaten up by Sons of OTIS guitarist and vocalist Ken Baluke after Tim tried to stab Ryan with a knife while he slept. Another time, Tim and Mark had a fist-fight on the bus and the driver threw them off in New Jersey.[219] They both found moments to conspire with Jus about ejecting the other.

Liz came to see them return to the North Six in Brooklyn. She was disgusted to find Mark and Tim smirking at each other on stage, seeming to want to sabotage the songs. It was as if they were trying to cast Jus into the water like the droogs from *A Clockwork Orange*. It struck her that the band needed something to make it more cohesive – a second guitarist to add stability, help hold the riffs down and support the layering of the music.

Jus and Liz were getting closer. They discussed starting a side project, if not yet speaking directly about her joining Electric Wizard. Liz had brought Jus a mixtape of movies he could watch on tour. One was 1970's *The Dunwich Horror*, already one of his favourites. Another, which he hadn't seen but Liz had told him about during their first meeting in Seattle, was *Werewolves On Wheels* (1971). In it, a biker gang is turned into lycanthropes by a hooded, satanic cult.

Liz was an authority on biker flicks – she reckoned she had seen them all and was even writing a book about them. She started the project in 2000. There was only one book available at the time on the subject: *Races, Chases and Crashes: A Complete Guide to Car Movies and Biker Flicks* by David Mann and Ron Main. In Liz's mind it was far from complete and full of mistakes. She resolved to track down every single biker movie ever made, focusing on the exploitation movies of the 1960s and 1970s. Liz's music endeavours have taken precedence over completing the project, although she still reckons she has more rare movies than the books that have come on the market since and says she might yet finish her 'ultimate guide'.

Her interest in biker culture started with her cousin. When she was five years old, he used to pull up outside her grandma's house with his friends, all straddling choppers. Later, she was attracted to biker movies by the badass women on the cover artwork. She soon learned that the movies often didn't feature those women and a lot of them were populated by crap bikes and dweeby men. Wanting to track down the good entries was the beginning of her obsession and a lifelong hobby.

In exchange for the video mixtape, Jus told Liz about the Euro horror she had not seen. A book had recently been published called *Ten Years of Terror: British Films of the 1970s*, by Harvey Fenton and David Flint, which later became a bible of sorts for Liz and Jus, along with *Immoral Tales: Sex & Horror Cinema in Europe 1956–1984* by Cathal Tohill and Pete Tombs. There were many synchronicities in their interests in horror cinema, but they homed in on films involving hooded satanic ritual in particular. Their conversations revolved around movies and atmospheric visuals, rather than playing guitar. There was a tacit understanding that they agreed on how music should sound.

Jus was quietly asking around about possible replacements for Tim. Stephen O'Malley showed up at one gig and blurted out to Tim in surprise: 'You're here! Everyone said you'd been kicked out of the band!' Stephen and Tim had previously 'bonded' after Tim threw Stephen down some stairs during a fight in England around the time the Wizard recorded 'Supercoven'.

The band trailed the final gig of the tour as the last Electric Wizard show ever – most of it was filmed for posterity on camcorder. The gig took place at the Khyber Pass venue in Philadelphia on 27 June. This meant that the Wizard entered America in 2001 and left it in 2002 via the Khyber Pass.

Electric Wizard had made it through the tour – just. But, like the Baader–Meinhof gang that fascinated them, the band was dissolving in acrimony. Jus waited until they dropped Mark off at home from the airport, then sucker-punched him as he bade farewell. The ensuing fight was Mark's final contribution to the original line-up of the band.

A drummer was waiting in the wings, ready for his chance to pounce on the opportunity. Justin Greaves had made his name in Iron Monkey from Nottingham, who released two albums: *Iron Monkey* in 1996 and *Our Problem* in 1998. They had formed in 1994 and chartered a similar course to Electric Wizard in the late nineties with a viscous hybrid of sludge, doom and hardcore. Like the Wizard, they smoked a prodigious amount of weed, as evidenced by the final song '9 Joint Spiritual Whip' from *Our Problem*. The album's artwork – a drawing of a crucified ape with an enormous erection – was by Mike Diana, an artist imprisoned for obscenity for his comic book *Boiled Angel*. Iron Monkey's self-titled debut featured a fold-out of a simian crea- ture which was originally a depiction of Grendel from *Beowulf*, nicked from the Usborne *The World of the Unknown* children's book about monsters.

Iron Monkey's albums were released by Earache Records, who had previously propelled capitalism's premier grindcore antag- onists Napalm Death into mainstream consciousness, featuring Lee Dorrian before he set up Rise Above. Earache partnered with American wrestling federation ECW (Extreme Champion- ship Wrestling) to use footage of burly men hurtling through tables in the music video for *Our Problem* song 'Supagorgonizer'. It worked well.

Like Electric Wizard, Iron Monkey had also released an EP with Man's Ruin to spite their label: *We've Learned Nothing*, in 1999. But unlike the Wizard, they never toured the US or broke through outside England. They spent the time after their set at

Holland's Dynamo Festival in 1999 looking for loose change and lighters in the mud. Iron Monkey split up that year but managed a posthumous odds-and-sods album bluntly titled *Ruined By Idiots*.

Even after they split, in the early 2000s, Iron Monkey had built a mythology around themselves. A rumour circulated widely that they had formed in prison. Other stories were largely based on the real-life activities of lead singer Johnny Morrow during the time of the band. Johnny was a wailing banshee. His vocals were gargled acid and his lyrics were fractured, Burroughsian cut ups with little semblance of coherency: 'Sneak the drag from/The piss on a crow rope/Slayer of a burred man' ('Boss Keloid'). If his recordings didn't leave your jaw on the floor, his live antics would. He burst on the stage straight from work, wearing a backpack and glasses, and began shrieking his head off; he hung off exposed pipes in the ceiling of venues and one time he even flung an open bag of flour he had found backstage at a ceiling fan, obliterating the front rows of the gig. Iron Monkey's audience interaction had often got out of hand. Johnny took acid one time in Bristol and started throwing the support band's cymbals at the crowd like frisbees. He dropped his mic in one punter's pint of beer and walked out.

In June 2002, Johnny Morrow died at the age of twenty-eight. He had been hooked up to his kidney dialysis machine and suffered a heart attack, a result of rising blood pressure that hadn't been caught – something that could have been prevented. Justin Greaves knew that without Johnny, Iron Monkey could never come back (though a reunion was attempted many years later by a bastardised line-up of the band).

Jus Oborn knew Greaves better from his other hardcore band, Hard To Swallow. He was a powerful and disciplined drummer. He hit the drums fucking hard and he knew how to keep time and how many beats were in each bar – musical practices which had sometimes seemed to mystify Mark. When Greaves arrived, he changed the way Electric Wizard sounded, for better and for worse. 'Dopethrone' took on even more immense proportions in his huge, scarred hands. But he struggled more with fluid, intuitive pieces like 'Supercoven', as if he was trying to make a square out of a triangle.

With Greaves on drums, Electric Wizard set off in November 2002 on a tour supporting Cathedral. The new three-piece enjoyed jamming on 'Supercoven' interminably. At a gig at the Islington Academy, London (then the short-lived Marquee N1), they ingested a decent portion of the mountain of Valium they had procured from a teenage kid in Wales earlier in the tour. They got lost in the (relatively small) venue, taking fifteen minutes to find the stage. 'Supercoven' was particularly attenuated that evening thanks to the 'blues'.

However, Jus and Tim struggled to regain their equilibrium after Mark's departure. Tim spoke about starting a side project called Ramesses. Jus even designed a logo for their demo. Before a gig in Sweden Tim took ecstasy and, after he had come up, confided in Jus that he couldn't carry on and needed to sort himself out. Jus agreed with him. Tim left at the end of the tour.

With that second fracture of the original band, the Crawling Chaos was satisfied. Electric Wizard was no more.

Chapter Six
Coffin womb for rebirth

The dissolution of the original line-up of Electric Wizard was sobering. Well, not literally. It did ask questions of whether Jus could continue under the name, or if he should start something new. He seriously considered formulating a new project, but Rise Above, for one, insisted that Electric Wizard continue.

There was also the fact that any music Jus wrote sounded like Electric Wizard. He couldn't not write for the band. Any attempts to move away soon resulted in being clawed back – as if Electric Wizard was an entity that had outgrown the members who spawned it and was dangerously in control. Perhaps Jus was dispensable too?

'It doesn't matter who's in the band, there's just me left from the original line-up, Electric Wizard is Electric Wizard,' Jus said in 2009, a few years after this quandary. 'If I leave Electric Wizard, there'll still be Electric Wizard. It's off on its own now, it's its own thing.'[220]

Jus toyed with some adjustments to signify that this was a new era, a splintering, in the same way that Amon Düül II split from the more political original incarnation of their band in the 1970s. One of these changes was using the definite article in the name for a time and on the cover of the band's fifth album, *We Live*: The Electric Wizard. It never really stuck seriously. This wasn't Cream, referred to as The Cream interchangeably. But 'The Electric Wizard' is what it says on the bass drum to this day.

Jus also felt pressure because Mark and Tim had by now formed Ramesses as a serious entity. They had enlisted Adam Richardson, who years previously had played with Jus in Lord Of Putrefaction in Wimborne. Adam played bass and sang in Ramesses while Tim moved to guitar. Jus was concerned about being sidelined in the doom wars, so he moved fast. He asked Rob Al-Issa, a friend and sometime roadie of Electric Wizard (who also played in a deathcore band in Bournemouth), to join. Jus started demoing material with Rob and Greaves and sent the material over to Liz back in the US for feedback – Jus was harbouring plans to get her involved in what came next.

Liz had expected to tour Europe with Sourvein in summer 2003, but the plans fell apart. Being in the band had been feeling like an uphill struggle for a little too long and she decided to quit. But she still had a plane ticket booked to the UK.

Jus asked whether she wanted to jam when she flew over. That fast evolved into requests for her to try out for the band, then join the band, and then record a new Electric Wizard album. Liz was nervous – there was pressure for her too: she would be the envy of her peers back in the States and there were lots of questions around the logistics of joining, not least the fact she was resident in the US. She had wanted to move to England when she was small because her father was English; as an adult, she was attracted to the birthplace of Tony Iommi and the unholy land of doom. Her greatest concern was stepping into the still-smoking wreckage of a band.

'It felt a bit like winning the lottery! I was pretty psyched when Justin asked,' Liz remembered in 2012. 'Especially since I had already quit Sourvein and was wondering, What the fuck am I gonna do now? I was really a fan of Electric Wizard, Jus and I had talked about doing a side project for years and when he was just like, "Why don't you just join Wizard?", I was pretty surprised. When I saw them live, I did secretly think they could do with another guitarist – I never imagined that guitarist being me.'[221]

Liz was raised in a classical music household, surrounded by opera and singers because of her father who was himself an opera singer and vocal coach. 'I still consider what is commonly known as Beethoven's "Moonlight Sonata" as one of my favourite heavy pieces of music,' she told NPR in 2011. 'It stirs your emotions in all the right ways of a truly heavy piece of music, and it was the first piece of music to teach me to really feel music and play it with passion.'[222]

Liz first picked up a guitar when she was fifteen but found it too frustrating to learn and didn't re-engage with it until she was nineteen. Then she was shown the basics of power chords and downtuning. Dave Chandler, guitarist of Saint Vitus (who the Wizard excitedly met at their LA gig in spring 2001) was an early guitar hero – as was Sonic Youth's Thurston Moore and Black Flag's Greg Ginn. Liz learned about Saint Vitus from an insert in a Black Flag album. Saint Vitus's *Mournful Cries* from 1988 is one of her favourite albums.[223] Ginn released Saint Vitus's early albums on his SST label and toured with them as well. Saint Vitus are seen as an influence on Black Flag slowing down on the dirges that populate the second side of their 1984 *My War* album. With these discoveries it dawned on Liz that 'I only really liked the slow bits in all the music I listened to.'[224]

Liz started a band in New York in the early nineties called Thunderpussy 13 with drummer Ellen Mieczkowski. It had a grimy, Motörhead-meets-The Obsessed, beefed-up biker rock sound. Based in Maryland, The Obsessed was led by Scott 'Wino' Weinrich on vocals and guitar before he left to join Saint Vitus in the mid-eighties. He subsequently returned to the band and released three classic doom albums: *The Obsessed* (1990), *Lunar Womb* (1991) and *The Church Within* (1994). Wino is another (somewhat flawed) forefather of the doom metal scene.

Thunderpussy 13 had a rotating cast of singers and bassists. Liz met Alicia Morgan, the singer in a crust-grind metal band called Insurgence, through Danny Lilker, who played bass at the time in the similarly disposed Brutal Truth. Liz, Alicia and Ellen formed a new band, called simply '13', with the intention, in Liz's words, 'to be as heavy as humanly possible'.[225] Danny filled in on bass a few times for 13, including playing on one of their demos. The name '13' was chosen as a statement against organised religion. The Catholic Church had designated thirteen an 'unlucky' number, since it was associated with many pagan beliefs in which it is perceived as lucky and powerful. The name also referred to Judas Iscariot's position as the thirteenth disciple and Loki, Norse God of mischief, as the thirteenth guest at the party at which he killed Baldur, triggering Ragnarök. In biker culture, the numeral thirteen symbolises marijuana; 'M' being the thirteenth letter of the alphabet. Thirteen is also considered a feminine number.

13 were obsessed with the nauseating, cavernous doom of local New York bands and friends Winter and Nausea. They also liked the guttural metal of Celtic Frost, Hellhammer (Celtic Frost frontman Tom G. Warrior's proto-death metal band) and Birmingham's Bolt Thrower. Alicia described the defining characteristics of their music as 'crushing oppression, claustrophobia, and uneasiness'.[226]

The scene was small and they traded tapes with other bands who produced sickly slow, heavy music, such as Eyehategod and Grief, before the subgenre was named 'sludge'. Eyehategod sent 13 the rough mixes of their 1993 breakthrough album *Take as Needed for Pain*, as they worked on it. 13 went on to contribute to splits with Eyehategod. Liz and Alicia even recorded two songs with Eyehategod members under the moniker Never. The DAT of the session was thrown out of Eyehategod's bus by an unstable 'friend' of the band.

'I started 13 because I wanted to play in a really heavy band, and there weren't any guys around wanting to start a band with me, so it just so happened to end up being a "girl band",' Liz said in 2012. 'The term sludge hadn't been invented yet. Back then we considered it all doom. It was outsider music. All these bands came together that had a common love of the slow and heavy. None of us really fit into our respective scenes; we were all too slow for whatever punk, hardcore, metal, alternative scene we would usually play in. We all came together under the black cloud of doom. Everyone supported each other. The love of doom was unique . . . the one per cent.'[227]

13 recorded a demo in 1992 (where Jus first heard the main riff to 'Whore', which he pilfered for the opening of 'Return Trip'), a live session for New York radio station WFMU and did some week-long tours of the East Coast. But 13 never got comfortable enough with bigger label interest to record an album proper, because of their DIY ethic and concerns over loss of control of their publishing rights. They also never had enough money to do it on their own. Alicia said Liz always had 'some super-heavy riffs rattling around her head' but that wasn't enough to keep their relationship going. As for 13, the band ended for various reasons. It was around this time that Liz's friend Arik Roper played her 'Supercoven'. She couldn't believe how heavy Electric Wizard sounded. After a few different musical projects, Liz eventually left New York and joined Sourvein.

'There's injustice in how women are seen in heavy music and I've felt quite frustrated and annoyed that I've never been taken seriously because of it – it's a passion for me to prove I can do it,' Liz said in 2009. 'And that is what comes out when I am purely playing with aggression, it's like, "Fuck you. How about that?" But there's far more sexism at metal shows in NY than there ever was in the sludge scene [in New Orleans], because even if some of them were redneck, they were more punk rock in the way they thought, and so they were more accepting.'[228] Live, Liz often observed preconceptions of her as a woman in a band dissolve on the faces of men in the audience the moment she started playing.

When asked, after the release of *Dopethrone*, whether they would ever consider augmenting Electric Wizard with a second guitarist, Jus insisted that the power trio was 'the best format ever. We wouldn't want another guitarist, would we?'

'We wouldn't want a guitarist. Maybe just a Hammond organ. It gets too messy otherwise,' added Mark, 'We wouldn't get as much money either if we had another person in the band. There'd be more arguments as well. It would be more hassle.'[229]

Interviewed in 2008 for *Decibel* magazine, with Liz long established in the band, Jus changed his story: 'I've always wanted two guitars in Electric Wizard – it was just a matter of finding someone who could do it, who could step up to the mark. Liz is the only person I've found who's good enough. Everything she does is spot-on doom. The first time I saw her play, I was bowled over, I thought, I gotta get this chick in my band. That worked out.'[230]

Liz came to it from the opposite direction: 'The only hesitation I really had is that I never really wanted to play with another guitarist,' she said in 2011. 'In my other bands, I was the primary writer of the music, too. And I'd definitely fucking lose a lot of that, because Electric Wizard is Justin's baby, obviously. So, I thought it might be difficult. But it turned out not to be, because I really respected the band and the music a lot. It was kind of a relief to let go of being in control of so much stuff. And after the kind of destruction I had witnessed with the old members, I felt almost a duty to do it. I didn't want Electric Wizard to fall apart and become shit.'[231]

Bringing in Liz on rhythm guitar raised a fascinating prospect for Electric Wizard. Twin guitars, which harmonised and thickened the sound, were the hallmark of a more 'traditional' doom sound. It can be heard in the early albums of Illinois band Trouble in the mid-eighties – *Psalm 9* (1984) and *The Skull* (1985) – and Cathedral's debut album in 1991, *Forest of Equilibrium*. Electric Wizard had helped smash that blueprint with their return to Iommic, single lead guitar heaviness – what would the band sound like with two guitars and a powerful, disciplined drummer like Greaves? How would it change their songwriting?

These questions were partially answered by *We Live*, which was recorded in the summer of 2003, and produced by Jus and Mathias Schneeberger. All the material was wholly written by Jus and demoed before Liz joined. The demo was 'filthy as fuck' in Jus's opinion, in a way the album failed to achieve, even though he believed 'the songs are wicked'.[232]

As a transitional album, *We Live* is the problem child of the Electric Wizard back catalogue. It carries a lot of baggage: it was born from a period of tumult, although the songwriting is often better than its reputation within, and outside, the band dictates. There are both stark differences from and defiant continuity with what came before in the title track. It starts with a sample from *Psychomania* and two police officers bemoaning the undead biker gang The Living Dead after a road accident. It was old ground and reflected some of Jus's lack of inspiration at the time. The break-up of Electric Wizard had sent him into a spin and he leant more into 'party drugs' than old favourites like weed and LSD.

'Something must have forced him over. Did you get anything out of the witnesses?'

'Yes, sir. Exactly the same story from all of them. Two motor-cyclists jabbing at his tire with a knife.'

'Any identification?'

'Yeah, the living dead again'.

Out of the context of the film, the lugubrious resignation of the last line makes it the funniest sample deployed by Electric Wizard. But for those in the know, it symbolises a return to first principles and the defiance that follows – the song is wholly lacking in humour: 'Can't fucking die/Can't fucking win/Got something to prove/Got nothing to lose'.

Hinged around the subject matter of *Psychomania*, 'We Live' is pummelling. Jus wrote it, like most of the album, to play to his new drummer's strengths. The introductory section sounds like the cracking open of undead biker coffins. Under the chorus – 'We live/We kill' – Jus meanders on a lead line as Liz scrapes the earth off the sarcophagus. They had clearly done some work to make the two guitars count. The song's series of false endings showcase Greaves's control and power, restraining the guitars as if he is taming wild horses. There was also something reminiscent of Greaves's past here too: the false endings of Iron Monkey song 'Bad Year' from their album *Our Problem*.

Compared to *Let Us Prey*, *We Live* is a muscular, almost brutal recording. But what stands out most is the nakedness of Jus's voice. Since *Come My Fanatics* . . . he had filtered it through all manner of effects and distortion, but on *We Live* he expressed himself clearly as a singer in a way that pushed the band towards somewhere new. This was even more the case on 'Flower of Evil a.k.a. Malfiore' where he reaches a higher register in a clean voice, something he had only managed before by screaming his head off. That song's soaring vocals glide across the full-chord, chiming washes of guitar and evince the new band at its fullest. Where it suffers, like other parts of the album, is the tendency to indulge staying in this new sonic territory just a little too long – its seven and a half minutes could comfortably be five.

The album was an experiment concerning Electric Wizard's future. It was an attempt to create an updated monster from constituent parts – a doom supergroup from three bands that had collapsed for their own reasons. It resonates with one of the films that obsessed Jus and Liz at the time – *The Erotic Rites of Frankenstein*, made in 1973 by Jesús 'Jess' Franco under the French title *La Malediction de Frankenstein*.

The Erotic Rites of Frankenstein is a deeply weird film, what Jus has described as a 'demented LSD-drenched tale' which served as a literal kind of 'acid test' for the Wizard's inner circle.[233] In it, Dr Frankenstein is fatally injured at the beginning by a strange bird woman called Melisa, while he is working on his gigantic monster. His creation boasts a Boris Karloff-style prosthetic forehead, and for some reason is painted silver, giving him a budget iron-man quality.

The plot is paper thin but involves the monster falling into the clutches of madman wizard/mesmerist Cagliostro, an entity that died thousands of years ago but which has transmuted into human form. Cagliostro is pitted against Frankenstein's daughter, Vera, as he attempts (through mind control he exerts via 'magnetic waves') to get the monster to copulate with the perfect woman, assembled from parts of other women – in order to breed a master race.

The whole thing is elliptical, badly dubbed and shot in an erratic, shaky-cam style. Like the attempts to piece together the perfect being, it falls way short of its mark. But the patchwork of images stay with you – particularly the chrome monster flogging a naked couple and the sonic disturbances of the soundtrack and audio design, including the bird woman's electronic screeches. Cagliostro is a particularly deranged and debauched performance by Howard Vernon. When Jus and Liz showed the film to Greaves, he was deeply disturbed.

'This is one of my absolute favourite Jess Franco movies,' Jus said in 2017, about the way the relentlessness of Franco's film-making mirrored touring life. 'He had a period in the mid-1970s where he essentially made movies that were like the Italian horror comics – the *fumettis*. He churned the movies out in the same way: he wanted to recreate that feeling. It's happening in front of your eyes. Franco lived like a nomad. He had no life outside of his films. It was relentless: making films, going on sets, travelling to the next set, cheap hotels.'[234]

After recording *We Live* in July 2003, Jus flew to America and stayed with Liz while she waited to receive her British passport. 'Even though I'm entitled to it, they make you go through hell to get it,' Liz remarked in 2011.[235]

They decamped to Los Angeles, where Jus tried remixing the album ('like a tosser'[236]). They had booked Billy Anderson (producer of Sleep's *Dopesmoker* album), but a last-minute scheduling conflict meant he couldn't make it to LA in time. Jus collaborated with Mathias Schneeberger instead. To Jus's ears *We Live* had ended up sounding neutered by comparison with the rough mixes. At the same time, Jus and Liz half-considered what Electric Wizard might look and feel like if the band was based in the city. The couple also married during this period.

As much as Jus was tempted to recast himself as a Lemmy-type figure, hanging out at the Rainbow Bar and Grill during the week, the couple weren't convinced. Even some time spent with Tim Herrman, an ex-member of schlock-rock legends GWAR, helping him make a documentary about 'ponygirls' (a BDSM practice in which submissive women dress up as ponies), failed to tip the balance. Herrman also directed a trippy-as-hell psychedelic video collage for *We Live* song 'The Sun Has Turned to Black'.

'I didn't get on with being American,' Jus reflected in 2008. 'It's not that I didn't like it – it's just not what I was born to.

It's a very different culture, a different world with different food. The food was a big thing, actually. There's too much salt in American food. Your taste buds have been raped before you get to taste the real shit.'[237]

They spent the remainder of their time together in the States in Long Island. After they drove from Los Angeles, they made a road trip to pick up Liz's possessions from storage units in different parts of the south. One mission to get her stuff resulted in them being chased out of a remote town in Tennessee by a gang of feral children, like something out of *Gummo* meets *Mad Max 2*.

Once in Long Island, they took the opportunity to visit Northport, the scene of the infamous 1984 'Acid King' Ricky Kasso murder of Gary Lauwers – a key episode in the 'satanic panic' of the eighties that fascinated the couple and would re-emerge in their music down the line. They even bought knives at the same shop used by Kasso, run by the same owner. They visited the crime scene in Aztakea woods. They also went to the nearby house where the Amityville murders took place in 1974. There, a family's twenty-three-year-old son, Ronald 'Butch' DeFeo Jr, shot his parents and four siblings in bed in the early hours. The real-life horror inspired a 1977 book and then film, both called *The Amityville Horror*, claiming the house at 112 Ocean Avenue was possessed by malevolent spirits after the murders. Liz's dad even viewed the house when it went up for sale, but didn't make an offer. He was disappointed (having a serious interest in the occult and the supernatural) not to sense any genuine 'malevolent forces'.

Jus periodically ventured out to jam with 2002 support act Unearthly Trance, based on Long Island, who kept him supplied with weed. It wasn't necessarily a sedate time. Jus managed to have a run-in with a local biker gang during a family BBQ. They also continued the painful process of Liz emigrating to England.

'It was a bit surreal, really, trying to do band stuff and not knowing when I was going to get this passport and not being able to tell the record label when we were coming back. Because we didn't know,' Liz said in 2011.[238]

From the States, Jus was able to start preparing the ground with the media for the next album. He used it as an opportunity to describe how recruiting Liz helped 'open out' the sound of the band. Jus and Liz played in a similar way – from the rhythm of their downstroke to the sculpting of riffs, and the way they managed the sustain emitting from their amps.

It was also Jus's first opportunity to discuss the dissolution of the original line-up publicly. Before, he had compared the band to being in a marriage. The last US tour in summer 2002 was 'like watching a family break up' slowly and tortuously over the length of a long tour: 'I didn't enjoy it. I used to, but that last tour just drove me into the ground. I just don't wanna do such long tours. I mean we play heavy, hateful music, we're heavy, intense people, and staying on the bus with someone trying to be all la-di-dah for so long, it's too much.'

Surprisingly perhaps, there wasn't much residual acrimony in the air between Jus, Tim and Mark. Electric Wizard even shared a rehearsal space when Ramesses was formed and things were civil enough: 'We're friends, but we don't sleep together anymore,' said Jus.[239]

The stresses of the 2001/2002 tour cycle seeded the idea of Electric Wizard touring less and playing more impactfully when they did. The much-improved, solid musicianship of the new line-up meant they could be more forceful at driving the songs home. Electric Wizard could be as devastating as Warhorse and some of the other bands they had played with, in a more dependable manner.

'It feels like I can do anything I want to do, I've got the right people about to create the best music I've ever done,' Jus told

The *We Live* lineup: (L-R) Jus,
Greaves, Rob and Liz.

In Australia with Andrew McKenzie.

Backstage at the ICA
supporting Mogwai in
2006. 'Turgid, deafening,
dully repetitive,' *Metro*
sneered in its review.

Liz (far left) in
her 13 days.

An obligatory whipping in
Jess Franco's *The Erotic
Rites of Frankenstein*.

Rehearsing *Witchcult Today* with whiteboard.

'His behaviour is out of control, his drumming is out of control': Shaun aka The Beast.

'Can you turn it down a bit?' Liam Watson meets Jus.

Jus at Toe Rag studios.

That's not the control room at Chernobyl, that's Toe Rag studios.

Jus and Shaun recording *Witchcult Today*.

Liz doing some research at Toe Rag.

Jean Rollin's *Le Frisson des Vampires* (*Shiver of the Vampires*).

The *Witchcult Today* lineup taking some gatefold inspiration from Pink Floyd.

Promo photo in a room at Shaun's place doubling as a satanic temple.

Two sources of inspiration from the *Witchcult Today* period.

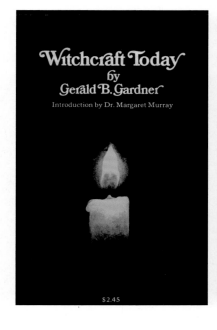

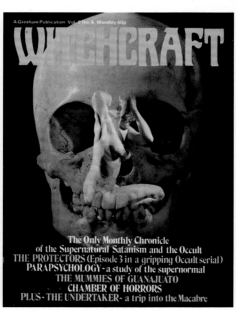

Concept art by Jus for a *Witchcult Today* video promo.

Poster for the 2007 tour with serial killer-themed Japanese doomers Church of Misery.

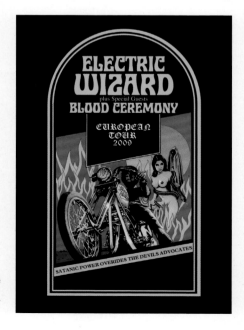

The Devils Ride Out: poster for the 2009 tour with Blood Ceremony.

The *Black Masses* lineup in the graveyard of the Holy Trinity church in Buckfastleigh, now including Tas.

Liz summoning the hounds of hell in the graveyard.

Feedback, death and destruction: *Black Masses* promo poster.

An 'outlaw biker gang from a seventies' exploitation movie'.

Cover of the *Crypt of Drugula*
comic included with the deluxe
'die hard' edition of *Black Masses*.

Poster for the 2011 *Black
Masses* European tour.

Electric Wizard in Bergen, Norway.

Backstage at Hellfest, France, in 2011.

Prepare the sacrifice: poster for the 2012 show at the Kentish Town Forum in London.

Making a momentous return to the US after a decade at 2012's Maryland Deathfest (with Simon on drums).

Terrorizer. 'I still want to write the best Electric Wizard songs I can, and I think they are getting better. Much more brutal all round!'[240]

His dreams of Martian landscapes and meteors crashing into the Earth, as well as the band's break-up seeping into his subconscious, gave *We Live* its post-apocalyptic feel. But even Jus was laughing at himself when he reiterated tried-and-tested lines in the *Terrorizer* interview about getting loaded and killing everyone in sight.

His discussions of drugs had also become more reasoned, describing how smoking weed helped with music and artwork, but was not an end objective in itself. He had enough self-reflection to be able to point to how 'addictive' personalities behaved on stimulants. Heroin had touched enough people around him to merit a po-faced declamation ('That's for weak people who haven't got the guts to do anything with their lives'). But he sounded focused and promoted a long view for the calibre of band that he considered Electric Wizard to be: 'Every classic band runs aground sooner or later; hopefully I'll be able to keep this one going!'[241]

Electric Wizard spent eighteen months existing and yet not really existing. The album was recorded but remained unreleased while Jus and Liz were in America. They returned to England – or in Liz's case, properly arrived – just before Christmas in 2004. Their first business as a four-piece was to record a session for BBC Radio 1. They were originally invited to record a session by John Peel, but his death in October that year threw some doubt over whether it would go ahead.

After some lobbying of the BBC by Rise Above, the session was recorded on 25 January 2005 and broadcast during the *Radio 1 Rock Show*, which back then aired in the early hours of the morning. The *Rock Show* was presented by Mike Davies, who originally presented a punk and hardcore show called *The*

Lock Up on the same station. He is all over the place during the broadcast, saying that Electric Wizard had three albums out (*We Live* was their fifth), one of which was called *Deepthrone*. As he struggled to make his links, Burning Witch's song 'Warning Signs' reared its ugly head again as the soundbed.

The session consisted of 'We Live', 'Dopethrone' and 'Another Perfect Day?' (also from *We Live*). 'Dopethrone' sounds colossal. Greaves slows the song right down, digging deeper than ever, before the final, seismic rolling out of the main riff. Jus's soloing is as ecstatic as it is erratic, with Liz pinioning the song with her rhythm playing until it finally collapses in an exhausted heap with a screech of the guitars' amp signals cutting out.

'Another Perfect Day?' is another beast entirely. It's irrepressible and rolls along on Greaves's high-tempo drumming, firing out rim shots left, right and centre. When it slows to a mid-paced juggernaut groove, it is, in fact, shifting down gears to the *really* slow bit, where Greaves delineates the song's cyclopean architecture in his flams, hi-hat accents and pounding of the toms. Again, Jus has the freedom to take off on guitar solos as Liz cycles the loping riff over and over. The song opens a fissure in a musical process akin to that described by its lyrics: 'A chasm black and wide/Between me and mankind'. Another of *We Live*'s protracted outros becomes a bitter incantation: 'Pack the pain away/Until another day . . . Another perfect day.' The band burned a hundred CDs of the session. They were sold on eBay with a sticker and an illustration of a whip-toting, hooded torturer silhouetted against the entrance of a dungeon as a near-naked woman, head hanging low, crawls towards the viewer.

Midway through the broadcast Davies flagged the band's appearance at the Roadburn Festival in Holland. The line-up that year was particularly strong, with Sunn O))), High On Fire (led by Sleep's guitarist Matt Pike) and Alabama Thunderpussy (with guitarist Erik Larson, who saved Wizard from the police in

Virginia in 2001) all showing up.

Electric Wizard played a triumphant set. True to their word, the sloppiness was gone. They played 'Eko Eko Azarak' and 'We Live', the first two tracks from the new album, followed by 'Dopethrone' (dedicated to Holland, naturally), 'Return Trip' and a spectacular, seventeen-minute-plus version of 'Supercoven'. The heft of two guitars truly made itself felt when the supernova of the song's main riff kicked in, even though Greaves seemed determined to add an extra beat just before the explosion, almost throwing the band off course.

A short UK tour followed, in which everyone was struck that this heaviest of bands seemed, impossibly, to have got even heavier. The dates were accompanied by instrumentalists Capricorns. The gig at the Fiddlers in Bristol on 1 May was heralded in a five-K review in *Kerrang!* as 'an oppressively heavy return from the UK's masters of doom': 'There's heavy, and then there's *heavy*. Massive, lumbering chunks of elephantine riffs that stomp their way into your ears and shake your bones, music of such sheer rumbling force that it should be measured not with Ks [*Kerrang!*'s rating system], but with a seisometer,' Nick Ruskell gasped.[242]

I saw the band for the first time on this tour, at the Garage venue in London's Highbury. High on mushrooms, I was pulverised by the performance. I spent ages trying to get it together to leave the venue as the indie club night began afterwards – wrecking my head further with the terrible new bands of the period, such as The Killers and The Kaiser Chiefs. My friend, who managed to leave the venue promptly, was spun out enough to get lost walking home through the north London streets he had grown up on.

Electric Wizard toured again at the beginning of 2006 supporting Cathedral with Swedes Grand Magus. Again, the potency of the new line-up was acclaimed, this time by Dom

Lawson in *Kerrang!* In a review of the show at the Concorde 2
in Brighton on 25 February, he wrote: 'The mighty Wizard are in
their element . . . and not just because they're palpably the most
stoned people in the room. The fact is, they're the heaviest band
on Earth, and this relatively new line-up of the band is even more
skull-flatteningly monstrous than past incarnations. Each riff
pounds and drones for what feels like hours, but far from being
boring the incalculable intensity generated by those bowel-rattling
low frequencies coalesces in mid-air, messing with our brains
until we all rock gently on our heels in a soporific trance.'[243]

The band also played a short European tour with Reverend
Bizarre and Thee Plague of Gentlemen. They stayed with the
latter's front man, Steve McMillan (aka Steven Wackenier).
There was an odd vibe in his house. He had two dogs that were
trained to hold people down. Downstairs was a children's comic
shop. In retrospect, Electric Wizard's unease was understand-
able. Thee Plague of Gentlemen was disbanded in 2006, with
the band issuing the following statement: 'Frontman Steve has
been arrested and imprisoned for criminal acts that none of the
members could ever imagine to happen and which are totally
unacceptable. Therefore we all disassociate ourselves from all
his acts, deeds and comments.'[244]

In the autumn of 2005 Electric Wizard went further afield, on
a nine-date tour of Australia, hosted and supported by the band
Pod People. There were good gigs there but odd ones too – they
played a Chinese restaurant and the lobby of the Excelsior hotel
in Sydney. They found Australia a strange place. It felt like a
giant council estate near the Antarctic, where British people
were lured by how great it looked on glossy tourism adverts and
in its soap operas. Travelling up the Gold Coast to Brisbane was
a surreal experience – it felt like travelling back fifty years into
the American Midwest with its diners populated by fat cowboys
and characters that could have stepped out of *The Waltons*.

There was also something unnerving, near psychedelic, about the countryside. Purple jacaranda trees stood on rolling green hills as alien creatures hopped about. When their leaves fell the landscape was shrouded in an LSD-like haze. Then there was the brutality of the vast, empty outback and the way its wildlife was splattered along its roads – an eviscerated kangaroo, or a koala with half its face missing. They were woken at night by giant spiders descending on them and heard strange noises crashing through the jungle – like Conan the Barbarian alerted to a pursuing dragon in the jungle of Robert E. Howard's story 'Red Nails'.

There is a stomach-churning kangaroo hunt in Ted Kotcheff's 1971 film *Wake in Fright*.[245] The director filmed it by accompanying a real-life kangaroo hunt – a nightly ritual in the outback at the time. Frozen by electric spotlights, hundreds of kangaroos would be slaughtered. After a dozen or so were killed, they were skinned and taken to a refrigerator truck. The skins ere used to make cuddly toys and the carcasses were used as pet food.

Determined not to have any unnecessary cruelty inflicted on the animals for the sake of the film, Kotcheff invited representatives from the Royal Australian Society for the Prevention of Cruelty to Animals to accompany him. They pushed him to include more of the footage he had shot to educate Australians about the barbarity of the kangaroo hunts. He didn't use three-quarters of it because he felt it was 'too bloody and horrifying'. The kangaroos are hunted as vengeful night spirits, but they are the real victims – of crazed hunters.

In the film, the kangaroo-hunting scene is the climatic degradation of John Grant, its central schoolteacher character. Grant has been stranded in Bundanyabba – the 'Yabba' for short – after he fell asleep on his train. He makes his way to a pub and his descent into alcoholic madness begins.

'Have a drink, mate? Have a fight, mate? Have a taste of dust and sweat, mate? There's nothing else out here,' reads the film's tagline.

The opening shots of the outback show what Adrian Martin, professor of film studies at the Goethe University in Frankfurt, calls 'less a wilderness than a pure void'. The outback is a 'haunted, menacing place suggesting a vacuous, existential abyss', barely held in check by this outpost of humanity where its rough, white inhabitants are beast-like and also fragile, unaware of their wrongdoings.

'[Y]ou come away with a sense of epic horror,' the critic Pauline Kael said in her review of *Wake in Fright* in the *New Yorker*. 'You come out with the perception that this master race is retarded.'

Jus and Liz had not seen the film, but the imagery of Australia burnt into their minds and chimed with the pitiless view of humanity expressed in their music – not in the yawning emptiness of space but at the heart of a country. Kenneth Cook wrote the novel on which the film was based in 1961. Its one-line foreword reads: 'May you dream of the devil and wake in fright'. Cook had grown up in Broken Hill, an industrial centre of thirty thousand people in a desert region over a thousand kilometres from Sydney, where it rained only five inches a year. He was revulsed by emotional indifference, which might have clashed with Electric Wizard's worldview, but they would have found common ground in their distaste for what he called Broken Hill's 'brash and aggressive friendliness'.

In Australia, problems began to emerge with Greaves. He was so dominant in the live mix that the cymbals could drown out the guitars. He was a larger-than-life character – flipping the bird to the audience between crashes. By contrast, Rob had almost no stage presence at all. Off stage, people felt Greaves sucked the oxygen out of the room and dominated conversations with his tales of life in Iron Monkey. He got taken to see Mad Max's car and was treated as if he was a minor celebrity. It sometimes felt that the band was playing support to him. More generally, he had issues with money – he once tapped the band for the cost of their breakfast when they stayed over at his house during one of the UK tours. He was forever cadging money for cymbals and other equipment from Rise Above, depleting the band's income.

Then there were his musical ideas. He was forceful in wanting to include acoustic parts in the Wizard's songs, although he had overly complicated compositional ideas that didn't fit. He wanted to push the band in a more Americana-like direction. It was useful in a way, because it confirmed to Liz and Jus where they didn't want to take the band, as their vision crystallised about what Electric Wizard could become.

What if Electric Wizard was more than a band, but a world to step into? They were visual people, with their heads continually in films, art and design. Jus had written a screenplay called *House Of Sadism* and was conceiving of the next album as the soundtrack to two twenty-minute movies.

He imagined a cross between *The Dunwich Horror* and *The Texas Chainsaw Massacre*, where the soundtrack and movies were locked in tightly together. They recorded a song called 'The Living Dead At Manchester Morgue' during the *We Live* sessions (released on subsequent reissues as a bonus track). It was based on the Jorge Grau movie sampled at the beginning of 'Wizard In Black', which partially set a zombie film in the Peak District. The song's demo was produced like a piece of music from a Giallo film, such as Goblin's soundtrack to 1975 film *Profondo Rosso*, one of Liz's favourites. What if Electric Wizard became the horror movie themselves?

We Live was the unloved child of the band, spurned at birth. But 'The Sun Has Turned to Black' got close to their vision – its

171

funereal riff plunges the album into darkness for the Old Ones to
return, with a harmonised bridge that sounds like supplication.

In particular, the fifteen-minute album closer, 'Saturn's
Children', stood as a beacon on the horizon. It has a Janus-face
quality since it looks back to their most awe-inspiring cosmic
doom and forward to the step they were about to take. The CD
carried a symbol of Saturn from *Key of Solomon* (an occultist
favourite) – a symbol also tattooed on Jus's forearm. The planet
has a baleful reputation. The song explores that hinterland
where the occult and the extreme right merged 'in the shadow
of the iron cross'. For the children of the sun it is time to 'invoke
the supercoven' and 'turn off your mind, there's nothing to
find . . . Find out here . . . '

Saturn is the Romanised name for the Titan Cronus, who
– fearing his children will overthrow him – eats each one at
birth. It is the subject of paintings by Rubens and, particularly
strikingly, by Goya, who depicts Saturn as a huge, dirty-haired,
wild-eyed monster, biting down on the left arm of his child's
bloody corpse, having already eaten the right arm and head.
The artwork was used on the cover of The Obsessed's *Lunar
Womb* album. Invoking the myth of Saturn asked a question
about whether Electric Wizard would allow itself to continue and
overthrow its original incarnation or devour itself out of spite.

Electric Wizard had broken through into wider consciousness
with an injunction: *Come My Fanatics* . . . They returned to it
on *We Live* opener 'Eko Eko Azarak: I. Invocation II. Ritual':
'Come my fanatics come to the sabbat . . . ' Jus sings. The song
is a collision of classic Electric Wizard tropes and images, fuelled
by Jus's recent dreaming – black pyramids, a dying land and
Martian landscape, thirteen years in the depth of space and
subjugation by an ancient, alien race. 'Earthbound send by
sorcerous flight' invokes perhaps one archetypal trickster figure
in Lucifer.

The phrase 'Eko Eko Azarak' is a Wiccan chant, popularised in an occult work of fantasy fiction called *High Magic's Aid* by Gerald Gardner, published in the late 1940s. As part of the New Forest Coven, Gardner claimed he tried to ward off the Nazis in 1940, using a magical attack on the mind of Adolf Hitler known as the 'Operational Cone of Power'.

But 'Eko Eko Azarak' can also be traced back to an essay called 'The Black Arts' by Major General J.F.C. Fuller, which originally appeared in the journal *Form* in 1921, published by the artist, occultist, and erstwhile associate of Aleister Crowley, Austin Osman Spare.[246]

Fuller himself was an acquaintance of Crowley. He wrote a critical essay-cum-panegyric of Crowley's work called *The Star in the West* (Crowley being the star), after Crowley announced a competition for the best critical essay of his work (with a hundred pounds in prize money) in 1904. Back then, Fuller was a regular army officer of the First Oxfordshire Light Infantry. By the time the heavy-going, 327-page entry was submitted in 1907, Crowley struggled to make good on the prize money, if he paid it at all. The pair later fell out and Fuller concentrated instead on writing books about the military.[247]

In 'The Black Arts', Fuller makes an eloquent argument for black magic's role in unlocking the secrets of unconsciousness:

'Man is human and a mystery; herein is to be sought all our sorrows, all our joys, all our desires, all our activities. Man is a troublesome creature, inwardly troubled by his consciousness, outwardly troubled by the unconscious, the things which surround him, the "why" and "wherefore" of which fascinate his mind and perplex his heart. We cannot fathom the origin of life nor can we state its purpose; we can but judge of it by inference, and inferences, if we probe them deeply, dissolve into an unknowable ether, an all-pervading miracle. Yet, such as these shadows are, we follow them, and as day creeps out of night so does the conscious emanate from out of the vast and formless body of that unconsciousness which softly enfolds us in its gloom.'

In the essay, Fuller decries the sheep who inhabit the 'coffin of existence' and applauds those who 'hammer at the lid, and with bleeding brow loosen the nails of oblivion, and, through the chinks between mind and soul, peer into the beyond.'

Those in power or authority – king, lawyer, priest or physician – lead the unquestioning flock onwards. But, he argues, our innate curiosity is impelled to go further, to go beyond, following that impulse which is 'the ultimate source of that ancient and yet ever youthful magic'.

For Fuller, the black arts are a war against received wisdom and the acceptable, only because we have been forced to accept it. They separate the goat from the sheep: 'They are black because they are unknown, evil because they unfrock the commonplace and take the bread from the mouths of mumbling priests. Sometimes these arts are terrible and infernal, sometimes they are sublime and celestial, but always they are powerful, compelling hostility or allegiance.'

For Fuller, the figure of the wizard and the witch seek out evil, dwell in dark places and turn to the spirits of the night only because what is deemed 'good' is enchained by religious institutions. 'Eko Eko Azarak' is a cry for freedom.

'In the middle ages of Christian rule did once again the spirit of man break the shackles which bound him, and it broke them by an alliance with Satan. Mad, if not insane, would the sorcerer creep forth to some heath or grove, far away from monastery or church, and, bereft of his senses through the gloom of those desolate places, would he shriek to the stars:

174

COFFIN WOMB FOR REBIRTH

Eko! eko! Azarak. Eko! eko! Zomelak!
Zod-ru-kod e Zod-ru-koo
Zod-ru-koz e Goo-ru-moo!
Eo! Eo! Oo . . . Oo . . . Oo!

    Though the words be different, it is the same chant of the Assyrian seer, for it is the conjuration of freedom, freedom which was to beget the arts and sciences of today, that consciousness which, though latent, was unconsciousness when these words were uttered. They were the love murmurings of a new betrothal.'

In order to gain its full freedom from the tyranny of reality, Electric Wizard needed to marry with the darkness completely. To embrace that vast, formless body of unconsciousness they needed to institute their own black faith. It was time to step into the mirror, to traverse the gate. It was time to form the witchcult.

Chapter Seven
Hail covens this is it

*T*he *Devil Rides Out* is a Hammer horror film released in
the UK in the summer of 1968 – just as Europe and the
US erupted in a fury of countercultural revolution. Christopher
Lee plays Nicholas, Duc de Richleau, a bastion of the ruling
class. He pledges to save Simon, the son of a friend, from 'the
most dangerous game known to mankind': black magic.

At the beginning of the film, when Nicholas and his associate
Rex arrive unexpectedly at Simon's house, they find a gathering
of strange, exotic people, purporting to be a meeting of an
astronomy society. Simon, like Swithin in Hardy's *Two on a
Tower*, claims he is a budding stargazer, but Nicholas soon
discovers a black cockerel and a white hen hidden away, ready
for slaughter in a black magic ceremony.

Simon has fallen under the spell of Mocata, the nefarious
group leader who uses mind control to his ends, not unlike Prince
Dena ibn Zodh from 'The Altar of Melek Taos' and Cagliostro in
The Erotic Rites of Frankenstein. Mocata praises black magic as
'the science of causing change to occur by means of one's will.' In
the film's most famous scene he summons Baphomet at a night-
time ceremony in the woods, at which a hidden-away Nicholas
cries out, 'The goat of Mendes! The devil himself!'

On one of the posters of the film (also known as *The Devil's
Bride* in the US), Baphomet is depicted standing upright,

wearing Mocata's purple ceremonial robe. Baphomet is carrying Tanith (one of the female initiates) – she is clad in a diaphanous night dress, unconscious in his arms. It is an image of a demonic priest taking his satanic mistress to bed.

For the cover of *Witchcult Today*, released in 2007, Electric Wizard adapted this poster. Baphomet and Tanith (now fully naked) are rendered in a shadowy black outline against a silver background. For the first pressings of the album, the silver had a mirror finish. The devil may have ridden out, but on the album cover he is receding. He is luring the onlooker through that mirror, and into Electric Wizard's world.

The album title was a composite of the titles of two books about witchcraft: *Witchcraft Today* by Gerald Gardner (the author of *High Magic's Aid* which popularised the 'Eko Eko Azarak' chant), published in 1954; and Margaret Murray's 1921 book, *The Witch-Cult in Western Europe*. The latter explained how the witch hunts of the sixteenth and seventeenth century were a way for Christianity to wipe out ancient symbols of matriarchy.[248]

The opening, title track of *Witchcult Today* is an invitation and an incantation. The stately progress of its descending riff exerts an alluring self-control. The wild excesses of Electric Wizard's first incarnation were being, if not extinguished, then channelled into a ceremonial fervour, where fanatics group together in the witchcult, and worship the 'black goat' as it 'forms from dopesmoke'. The guitars sear and buzz, and the song grows in power, like the cult it depicts, accentuated by small shifts in the tones and harmonies, all underlaid by a strange soundbed of backwards chanting. The Wizard had been initiates of their own rites on *Come My Fanatics . . .* Like Conan, they had ascended to become barbarian kings on *Dopethrone*. Now, on *Witchcult Today*, the band was a rejuvenated coven.

Witchcult Today is the centre point of Electric Wizard. Before, the three-piece had absorbed their cultural influences amidst their daily lives in Dorset and puked them out in uncontrollable paroxysms on their early records. *Witchcult Today* mythologised the band itself – evolving what Electric Wizard was and what it represented.

'It is a way of life that I'm espousing to people. I feel that this is the way. For us it is a cult,' Jus said in 2009. 'The cult of the riff. The mindless worship of the riff. It's fucking doom. This is everything. This band is for real. I don't know what else to say. It's not an image. People can read it how they want. They can read it in any way that they choose. But they should dig deeper. I'm not going to spell it out for anyone but people who listen to us really can understand what we mean. Most of the time.'[249]

With *We Live* released, Liz, firmly established in one of her favourite bands, was able to properly advance her musical and aesthetic ideas for Electric Wizard. She was driven to make it as good as it could be. Liz was (and still is) a killer when it came to writing and touring. She put herself in the centre of the vortex – be it a swirling riff cycle, or the full-blown carnage of life on the road. To this day she struggles to catch up with friends or take in cities when travelling because she finds touring and performance so all-consuming. Liz was tough to begin with, but hardened by her experiences in 13 and Sourvein, now the gloves could come off for good. Being in Electric Wizard was an opportunity to build a life of heavy music fully under her control, in partnership with Jus.

It felt like the beginning of a new band, but also like they were returning to the source and extracting its essence. This time everything was premeditated – concept, music, production and art. Liz had seen how others had purported to know better than the band, particularly the record label. She was very enthusiastic to bring back to Electric Wizard what she thought had slipped away: to reignite Jus's passion for the cult-like denizens of songs like 'Doom-Mantia' and 'Supercoven'. She saw herself as his partner in crime – in a position to galvanise Jus and keep them both focused on their vision. The elements of the movies they had first discussed on Electric Wizard's US tours were brought to the fore: cloaked satanists, occult gatherings, sexy and dominant vampire women, biker gangs and the 1970s' witchcraft revival.

'Everything we do in Electric Wizard is a reflection of what we like. It's not just the music. We're fanatical about being able to convey our vision/message,' Liz said in 2012. 'So that includes what you see as well as hear. Personally, when I like a band, I want the artwork and everything to be an expression of the music; better still, I want to know that the band is really the living embodiment of what the music is creating in my imagination. The way we dress and the artwork we produce is all part of our vision of Electric Wizard, and we really live our everyday lives in the same way. We dress like it's 1971, we live in a Hammer house of horror filled with weird stuff and we usually wake up each morning with an unrelenting hatred for modern society – it's why we create this alternate world of our own. I don't like phoney bands or people. I think you should practise what you preach. We certainly do!'[250]

The 'immoral insanity'[251] (Jus's words) of the early 1970s had long influenced the band, but now they devoured occult books, magazines and music from the time. The seventies were the cynical shadow left by the idealistic sixties. Electric Wizard wanted to live and breathe the period after the Age of Aquarius ended in catastrophe at the feet of the Rolling Stones at Altamont Raceway and Charles Manson's 'family' at 10050 Cielo Drive. They wanted to create music that expressed itself with the force of occult magician Aleister Crowley's edict to 'do what thou wilt': consequences be damned! – to recreate the acid-damaged hangover following the sixties with renewed force.

Liz had been on a 'lifelong quest' to recreate the feeling she got from the cover of Black Sabbath's 1971 album, *Master of Reality*: 'It's so simple, yet it just says it all; it says seventies' doom. The black and purple and the ghostly lettering are so ominous and perfect and also very of their era.'[252] Black Sabbath's label, Vertigo, had a swirling logo – entrancing listeners who stared at their records going around on a turntable like skyclad dancers around a fire performing the rites of Lucifer.

Nineteen-seventy-one was undoubtedly a heavy year – *Master of Reality* was released and, after that, Jus was born. Black Sabbath's third album was the blueprint for the entire doom genre. It was downtuned and slovenly. In it, the lingering revolutionary sentiment of 'Children of the Grave' vied with the insularity of 'Solitude', druggy obsession ('Sweet Leaf') and the urge to leave the Earth behind entirely ('Into the Void'). Electric Wizard loved Black Sabbath, but it was the twenty-first century and they wanted to be regarded as on the same level.

'Ninety per cent of the bands I meet, their ambition is to be as good as their idols. That's not why I formed a band,' Jus explained to *Terrorizer* in December 2007, not long after *Witch-cult Today*'s release. 'I wanna be better than Black Sabbath, not as good as. I may not be, but that's my aspiration. I've always said if you put on an Electric Wizard album, I want people to say, "That's Electric Wizard" not, "That's a doom band." That's what every band should strive for and if they don't they should stick to fucking cover versions.'[253]

Jus and Liz struggled to find many other bands from the early seventies who were as heavy as they promised to be – who sounded as good as they looked. The reality of many bands (and films) of the era was they were never quite what the pair hoped for – it was often just bits and pieces that were truly electrifying. They wanted to create the ultimate fantasy vision – an amalgamation of the choice cuts. The band that never existed in

1971 but they were desperate to find. They resolved to become
that band themselves, through total immersion.

'I'm into all that shit, anything like that,' Jus said of the
era. 'I'm into poppy, occult weird shit. I collect seventies' porno
with witchcraft in it. I collect weird movies, fucking goat heads,
black fucking mass shit, really old, weird shit, statues of Pan
and all from Victorian times. I love that whole vibe, I love that
era. I like what they were trying to evoke, the horror movies. It
seemed like, right around '71, people went fucking heavy. It was
cool to be fucking doom.'[254]

After he had returned to England after his time in the US,
Jus had one job driving a forklift truck in a warehouse. The
radio in the warehouse was tuned to BBC Radio 1 and that was
what he listened to all day. With the dull routine of a regular
job, he started to get his drive back after the strain of moving
the band forward after the disastrous US tour of 2002. Building
up to and after the release of *We Live*, Jus had been desperate
to keep the show on the road and had found himself becoming
someone he didn't want to be – a typical musician, hustling and
chasing a vanishing dream. Now, he was with normal people,
had a boss and everything was shit again. His original desire to
play music returned. He began fantasising about being on *Top of
the Pops* – the heaviest band to ever play it!

'Looking back, *We Live* was a reaction against the old line-up,'
Jus told *Metal Hammer* after the release of *Witchcult Today*.
'We'd just done some touring and everything had been a fucking
disaster and in my head at the time I just thought, We're going
to make a really tight record, to prove to people that this band
wasn't a bunch of shit. Those feelings have subsided since then.
I'd probably turned my back on what we're all about, and so that
album wasn't really *us*. It seemed for a moment that we were
getting too fucking clichéd. We were touring, too much hanging
out at gigs with people in bands. People moan that bands lose

their edge after a while, and I think that's how you lose it. You become part of the rock world, not part of the real world anymore, and it's all bullshit.'[255]

Two songs were being played on Radio 1 which sounded different and hit him harder than the rest of the station's playlist at the time: 'Empire' by Kasabian (with its striking Charge of the Light Brigade-themed music video) and 'Seven Nation Army' by The White Stripes. The White Stripes single was massive: a mainstay of festival crowds and football stadiums for years afterwards. It sprung from The White Stripes' 2003 album *Elephant*, recorded in Toe Rag studios in Hackney, London, by producer Liam Watson. Phil Alexander, the former editor of *Kerrang!*, who had originally given *Come My Fanatics . . .* its glowing 5K review, suggested to Electric Wizard the studio might suit them.

The band needed the right kind of facility to create the atmosphere for the new material they were writing. A place where they could push back hard against any impulse to make them sound more slick, modern and commercial. If they wanted a studio that Black Sabbath might have walked into in the early seventies, this was it. There wasn't a computer in sight. The all-analogue recording room was full of equipment from the fifties and sixties – everything was grey and laboratory-like with weird devices covered in dials. There didn't seem to be anything there from a more recent time than the mid-seventies. When something broke down, you either persisted with it malfunctioning (recalling the *Come My Fanatics . . .* days of amps burning to death in the studio) or waited for it to be repaired. Liam cut the two-inch tape he used to record bands with a razor blade. The approach was tactile and handmade. Liam was also a seventies horror buff, sported a twirling moustache and smoked a pipe. He made the studio technicians wear lab coats for the full impression of an ageing Soviet-era nuclear power station.

Liam was initially wary of Electric Wizard's reputation and
their (lack of) professionalism. Likewise, Jus told Liam he didn't
want overbearing producer bullshit. He wanted Liam to record
the band exactly as they sounded – fuzzy, crunchy and crackly.
Liam was into jazz and sixties' beat groups more than anything
else, so he brought few to no preconceptions of what a doom
metal band should sound like. He suggested they have a trial
run with one of the new songs and go from there.

Jus and Liz focused on a song they had called 'The Chosen
Few', harking back to the musical eulogy sung to Tom, the
leader of The Living Dead biker gang from *Psychomania*:
'And the world never knew his name/But the chosen few
knew of his fame'. The Chosen Few was a name they had
also seriously considered for the new incarnation of Electric
Wizard.

Whereas 'Witchcult Today' is a descent into the band's world,
'The Chosen Few' is an ascension – it could even be the mirror
image of the opening track. It reaches towards the light before
the coffin lid of the sky closes on it completely. Liam left Jus's
voice in the distance in the mix, but otherwise his singing is raw
and surprisingly soulful, as he invokes a collage of the symbols
and motifs the band had amassed over the years: from the one
thousand amps that 'toll the end time riff' to 'Satan's Slaves',
pledged to die 'in the shadow of the pentagram'.

The song is a sinister call to arms in which the 'children of
the grave' are urged to take up a knife and repeats the band's
dictum to 'legalise drugs and murder'. It prompted a fan to
make their own video, using the song over footage from the 2004
film *Zero Hour: Massacre at Columbine High*, which dramatised
Dylan Klebold and Eric Harris's killing spree in April 1999. The
phlegmatic and methodical killers make their way through class-
rooms and the library. Each shooting is marked by a photo of the
victim, their age and whether they were injured or murdered.

It is a harrowing video and reframes the song's lyrics in an ominous light, recalling the nihilism of 'We Hate You'. What if a generation was galvanised by the massacre to unite together in the service of hate and murder, rather than compassion and love? The video proves that the imagery and metaphor of Electric Wizard's music manifests in a shadow world with real-world analogues. 'The Chosen Few' ends in a fading Hammond organ, played by Liz (who studied piano from age seven until she was a teenager), repeating a doom-laden refrain.

Liam delivered on his promise. He only commented when Jus went out of tune and otherwise left him to it, with the result that one writer noted that he sounded great, albeit like he was stuck in Professor Edward Jessup's isolation tank from the film *Altered States*.[256]

'I'm not a singer that can plan what I'm gonna do. The song's in my headphones, it's time to go, and this is what comes out. Maybe the riffs are more melodic on this album, but it's not something I plan. My mouth opens and hopefully whatever I do won't sound shit!' Jus told *Metal Hammer* after the album was released.[257] To *Terrorizer*, he was more succinct: 'I'm actually singing for a change.'[258]

If the Wizard wanted to invoke The Chosen Few and live out what they depicted in their songs, the band got more than they bargained for with their new drummer, Shaun Rutter. Greaves had left Electric Wizard in 2006 to pursue his own music in Crippled Black Phoenix. Aside from musical differences, Greaves had lived too far away (Reading was a two-hour drive from Bournemouth), which was an inconvenience, and in general he was too miserly to continue to be in the band. In any case, Greaves was frankly too metronomic, some might say too *good*, to be in Electric Wizard. They needed, according to Jus, more 'danger in the drums'.[259]

After the release of *We Live*, Jus had also worked for a company doing conservatory telesales. His boss was known as 'Mad Mark' and had wild, unkempt ginger dreadlocks. He badgered Jus to come and jam with him and a drummer he knew called Shaun. Jus eventually relented and went around to Shaun's house with Mark. Shaun was watching an obscure 1976 biker film called *Northville Cemetery Massacre*. Jus remembered him from Wimborne, when Shaun used to roar into town on his chopper. Back then, Jus was convinced Shaun was a wrong 'un who might knife a kitten.

Northville Cemetery Massacre cast a real-life biker gang from Detroit called The Scorpions. In the film, they are framed for a violent rape of a young woman by the cop who perpetrated it. The cop joins the girl's father and a gun-happy hunter in a three-man vigilante group going after the bikers. The Scorpions themselves are wild and brash but also innocent and bright-eyed. That is, until the scene at the club house where two of the bikers are assassinated while taking a piss outside. At the funeral for their two colleagues, one of the bikers eulogises, 'Nothing in our life is rehearsed. It's all real. We take it like it comes and give it back twice as hard.' After their destruction in the graveyard massacre at the film's conclusion, a title card reads: 'Freedom: RIP'.

Shaun proved to be a true animal on the drums. After a few jams, Jus realised he had written dozens of riffs with Mark and Shaun and hardly any for Electric Wizard. Shaun gave it back twice as hard as it was given and Jus loved his 'raw, fucking ritual' style – he was a 'dirty-ass drummer' in the best sense.[260] He was invited to join the cult.

Shaun, whose father had worked for Dallas Arbiter, the makers of the popular 1960s' Fuzz Face distortion pedal, was scary. He was obsessed with Gary Glitter and The Glitter Band, in a deliberate, somewhat obnoxious way. He barely used the phone and when he did, he emitted terse grunts. His taciturn approach extended to rehearsals and the stage, where he also refused to communicate. He left it to other – presumably occult – forces to keep the show going. He lived around the corner from Jus and Liz in Bournemouth and whenever Jus and Liz invited Shaun over for a drink, they heard the roar of Shaun's motorbike as he left home, then idling while he picked up his preferred brand of white cider from the off-licence, before completing the journey. He had a room at home mocked up as a satanic temple with red-painted windows, handy for *Witchcult Today* publicity photos. On the sleeve of the album, in their group photo, the band recalled Pink Floyd for their 1971 album *Meddle*, when they were shot separately but composited together, wearing black and staring balefully at the camera. Electric Wizard wanted a similar composition but with a psyche-delic, Bram Stoker-ish vibe. Jus convinced Shaun to wear a fur coat, so he looked like Attila the Hun.

With his bald head and beard, Shaun also resembled Anton LaVey, founder of the Church of Satan, or maybe he was more like Ming the Merciless from *Flash Gordon*, who some think LaVey might have modelled his look after. LaVey's biographer wrote that shaving one's head was an ancient ritual practice linked to the Yezidees – the devil-worshipping cult of 'The Altar of Melek Taos'. A razor washed in the waters beneath the Seven Towers of Satan, used to shave the magician's head, was supposed to set him apart from the sons of Adam.[261] The bald look was also in the tradition of Aleister Crowley, aka 'The Beast 666'.

'He's like a fucking ape. We call him "The Beast",' Jus said of Shaun in 2009. 'I don't think any other band would put up with him. I'll get in trouble if I say too much, but it always involves drinking too much and pissing somebody off or breaking something or getting us kicked out of somewhere and practically getting arrested half the time. He just attracts bad luck. His behaviour is out of control, his drumming is out of control – it's everything, really. But if you want a real drummer you've got to take the bad side. I don't want some pussy who's mincing around the drums.'[262]

Shaun refused to participate in what most people in a band would consider a normal way. He made a living stitching sails by hand. He was the only specialist in his company who could hand-stitch body bags. He later developed tendonitis in his arms, which his doctor said meant he was ruled out of playing drums for life. But within three months, he was back pounding the kit. He had a growing reputation to uphold.

'Our old drummer [Greaves] knew what he was doing and he did it, but there was no fucking about, and I *like* fucking about,' Jus told *Metal Hammer*. 'Sean [sic – the curse of misspelling Electric Wizard members' names strikes again] jams a lot more. He's a lot freer around the kit. He tries stuff, and if it doesn't work, it doesn't work. Now it feels like a real band again. We're all living in the same town again, so it's like the old line-up, brothers living together. It feels like Electric Wizard to me. There has to be a social reason why you're in a band together. All good music comes from a social background. All good black metal comes from right-wing Christian countries, those areas where people are reacting against something and not just trying to pose. I started this band because we were stuck in a tiny town, and the only way out was to play music. People would write to us from foreign countries and it blew our minds. It still does.'[263]

Shaun's flailing presence drives 'Dunwich', the second song
on *Witchcult Today*. He gets a solid four bars to lay down the
foundation of the song on the drums. 'Dunwich' was written
by Liz, and its loping, up-tempo riff has the immediacy of the
kind of song written in minutes that just *works*. Like Sabbath's
'Paranoid' or Deep Purple's 'Highway Star', it is accessible, and
in a way, pop – very heavy pop. If someone had demanded that
Electric Wizard enter a song for the *Eurovision Song Contest* at
gunpoint, it would be this instead of 'We Hate You'.

The fact Liz had written all the music of 'Dunwich' was in
itself significant. Throughout Electric Wizard's existence Jus had
been the lead songwriter, and something of a control freak at
that. Accepting the whole song showed his respect for Liz as a
songwriter and created a strong bond of trust between them as
bandmates. It also allayed Liz's fears about relinquishing her
role as the main songwriter in her previous bands. Songwriting
was her first love and the reason she played guitar. Perhaps it
was the fact that the music of 'Dunwich' was all Liz's work that
freed Jus up to write one of his best lyrics for the song.

Jus filters H.P. Lovecraft's 'The Dunwich Horror' (originally
published in *Weird Tales* in April 1929) through the prism of his
youth in Wimborne. It mythologises his own birthplace through
the story of the son of Yog-Sothoth: 'Child of Dunwich rise/You
have your father's eyes'. The song combines the long-established
vitriol of Electric Wizard ('End the world that you despise') and
cosmic hopelessness ('"Why was I born at all?"') with the ceremonial taking of control that marked out this new era: 'Our time
has come/The end has begun'. No longer were Electric Wizard
subject to these otherworldly forces, they were themselves the
subjects that wielded them.

There are oblique references to the topography of Wimborne
and its surrounding area. The Dunwich Child and Jus (casting
himself as Wimborne Son) 'ascend dark wooded hills to Kane'.

'High on the hill' in the case of 'The Dunwich Horror' refers to
Sentinel Hill, site of the rape that resulted in the conception of
the story's monstrous child. In Wimborne, it is the hill where
Horton Tower stands. From this promontory, Jus is free to wail
at the stars and end the world for good, something which fails to
transpire in 'The Dunwich Horror'.

Jus took lyric-writing seriously and he needed the conditions to
be right – particularly for this album, which represented a grand
new conceptual phase for Electric Wizard. He wrote in his hotel
room in the early hours of the morning during the period that
the band was recording at Toe Rag. They kept a tight schedule of
three recording days at a time and sessions took place between
midday and 6 p.m. – no camping out at the studio this time.
The hotel room was a good place to stay up or get up early (ish),
and let the lyrical ideas come to him, unburdened of the cultural
inputs – posters, books and objects – around him at home. As long
as he had enough weed, he was fine. *Witchcult Today* is the sum of
the lyrical themes and imagery that Electric Wizard had amassed
over the previous decade – of black arts wreathed in weed smoke.

'The lyrics are really important,' Jus said at the time. 'I
think the lyrics weren't so good on the last album. Kind of
directionless. I don't know what I was thinking of. Every fucking
reference, every fucking lyric in there [*Witchcult Today*] means
something. You could sit down with each line and fucking start
researching everything and there's so many references; horror
movies, occult shit, my own, personal, fucked-up theories on
how these things correlate. There's everything in there. There's
the whole guide to Electric Wizard's world in the lyrics of this
record, definitely. And that's important, you know? People like
that. I wanna get a cool record and I like to think that there's a
depth to it. "There's a secret in here somewhere." "What the fuck
are they trying to tell me?" I like that feeling. We're not Blink-
182 for fuck's sake. We're fucking heavy, man.'[264]

The gloomiest mindset of Electric Wizard is encapsulated in the album's closing song, 'Saturnine'. I've always thought of 'Saturnine' and 'Dunwich' together, as different as they are. I think of how W.G. Sebald's narrator has an exhaustion-induced breakdown when he gets lost on Dunwich Heath as he makes a journey along the Suffolk coastline in the 1995 book *The Rings of Saturn*. The nature writer Roger Deakin said the Suffolk landscape was transformed by 'a particular state of mind, gloomy but compelling.' In the book, wandering lost amongst the gorse thickets of Dunwich Heath in the relentless sun, the narrator believes he is dreaming and sees a labyrinth of hedgerows 'which I knew in my dream, with absolute certainty, represented a cross-section of my brain.'[265]

'Saturnine' expresses the internal state of being in Electric Wizard. It is a personal black hymn: 'I hear a death bell tolling out my life'. It's hard not to think of the church bells of Dunwich village, which were claimed by the sea along with most of the mediaeval coastal village in the thirteenth century, and supposedly ring out when the tide is high.

Under the black sun that dominates the landscape of much of their catalogue, 'Saturnine' depicts someone unable to escape the shadows that cross their path, until, too late, it's 'time to die' (it wasn't quite time to die for Electric Wizard . . . yet). The only hope seems to be in the song's final line, where 'my priestess of mars' might set the subject free.

The song begins with another of Shaun's voodoo drum, rolling introductions. Though it doesn't gradually hove into view like the colossal 'Saturn's Children' from *We Live*, the song progresses in an insidious motif. It swells to an untrammelled bridge section. Then, as if the song's third verse takes up the part of the chorus, the drums phase out and solos strafe through the melange, then fold back on themselves.

It sounds like the song is being absorbed into the debris-strewn rings of Saturn themselves. 'Saturnine' dissolves towards its ending like the moon which Sebald writes was disintegrated when it got too close to Saturn's tidal, gravitational pull.

> Saturnine for all time the only way I've ever been
> Saturnine in my mind high I sail the astral sea
> Saturnine for all time I'll never find a way to be free
> Saturnine in my mind load another hit of weed

'It's about the same thing,' Jus said when he was asked about the connection between 'Saturn's Children' and 'Saturnine'. 'It's a personal thing. It's a planet I associate with on a personal level. The lyrics definitely have the same resonance; well, it seems at first. Saturn's a savvy planet. It's the wizard's planet. It's a planet of black magic. It's the planet that protects against black magic. Protects against people who try to fuck with you. It's an important planet. It's the feminine side on some levels but . . . it's a planet of secrets, and it's a planet to protect against outside forces, which everybody has to suffer from time to time. People trying to fuck with you, people trying to wish bad shit would happen to you. It's good to have a bit of protection.'[266]

Sometimes Saturn felt like an overbearing presence. In one of their homes, the planet seemed to shine continuously through whichever window they were near. In the same way as 'Saturnine' contemplated inner and outer space, *Witchcult Today* as a whole polarised the chaotic vibrations of the wider universe. Electric Wizard harnessed those energies in the architecture of the album. It was a house of their own making. The Crawling Chaos still stalked the band, but in another, spectral form.

In 'The Dreams in the Witch House' by H.P. Lovecraft, Walter Gilman occupies the 'unhallowed garret gable' of a boarding house. The room was previously occupied by Keziah Mason, a witch: 'Old Keziah, he reflected, might have had excellent reasons for living in a room with peculiar angles; for was it not through certain angles that she claimed to have gone outside the boundaries of the world of space we know?'[267] Indeed, Keziah had mastered the art of passing through dimensional gates, just as Electric Wizard staked their claim to wrench open the gate of Yog-Sothoth in 'Dunwich'.

In the story, as May Eve Walpurgis Night approaches (30 April – the Witches' Sabbath), Gilman is troubled by atrocious dreams of Keziah; a horrible, furry, fanged creature with a human face called Brown Jenkin and the figure of 'the "Black Man" of the witch-cult'[268], a materialisation of Nyarlathotep, who has Keziah under his control and insists they all venture 'to the throne of Azathoth at the centre of ultimate Chaos.'[269]

On May Eve itself, Gilman is transported through the kaleidoscopic abysses of the churning void: 'He seemed to know what was coming – the monstrous burst of Walpurgis-rhythm in whose cosmic timbre would be concentrated all the primal, ultimate space-time seething which lie behind the massed spheres of matter and sometimes break forth in measured reverberations that penetrate faintly to every layer of entity and give hideous significance throughout the worlds to certain dreaded periods.'[270]

Witchcult Today is the harnessing of this 'Walpurgis-rhythm'. 'The Dreams in the Witch House' helps explain why Electric Wizard focused on occult ritual on this album, because the pulsing of the cosmos is what mounts and summons, in Lovecraft's words, 'the initiates to nameless rites'.[271] The witches' sabbaths were patterned on this faint pulsing 'which no earthly ear could endure in its unveiled spatial fulness.'[272] Electric Wizard had long been the conduit but not in control of such a force – performing this Sabbath ritual gave them full control over it.

'It's hypnotising, you know? I mean, imagine in a ritual,' Jus said after the album's release, speaking to this point. 'You need to be in a hypnotic state, out of your mind on the night of the Sabbath. That droning sound puts you in a hypnotised mood. I see people at gigs, nodding like zombies. It's like fucking hymns of doom, and that's what puts people in a ritualised state. People are open to suggestion, the ones in a hypnotic trance. The heavy riffs do it. I mean, "Supercoven" – we could've ordered people to go out and kill. Oh yeah, drugs help. I'm not a fucking purist, man. I'm not Wiccan.'[273]

In the climax of 'The Dreams in the Witch House', Gilman awakes from a final showdown with Keziah and Brown Jenkin in the world of dreaming. This encounter is described in one of Lovecraft's truly psychedelic passages in which Gilman fails to stop a kidnapped infant from being sacrificed when Brown Jenkin bites its wrist. In an uncanny reflection of Jus's own hearing problems, he is left deafened: 'both ear-drums were ruptured, as if by the impact of some stupendous sound intense beyond all human conception or endurance.'[274]

Inspired in part by the 1970 song 'Killer' by Van der Graaf Generator, 'Torquemada '71', from *Witchcult Today*, brings together two cruel lovers. It imagines the 'necrosadist' Tomás de Torquemada, a real-life Castilian Dominican friar and member of the Spanish Inquisition, transported to the early seventies. He is embroiled in torturous love play with sixteenth-century noblewoman and serial killer Countess Bathory. The song features Liz delivering the spoken-word line '*Oui, la torturatrice*', in a perverse nod to Serge Gainsbourg and Jane Birkin's 'Je t'aime . . . Moi Non Plus'.

'It's kind of a sequel to "I, Witchfinder" in some ways,' Jus told *Decibel* in 2008. 'It's another version of the same character. If I get too wasted, I imagine myself as some reincarnated old geezer living in the time of Caligula. So the Witchfinder is Matthew Hopkins and this is Torquemada reborn in '71.'[275]

Transplanting a centuries-old evil to the early seventies was the thrust of another Hammer film, *Dracula A.D. 1972* (in a similar vein to the modern-day setting of 1970's *The Dunwich Horror*). It was the first film in which Christopher Lee and Peter Cushing were reunited on camera as Count Dracula and his nemesis Van Helsing (albeit in the form of Lorrimer, his descendant) since their original foray in 1958's Hammer classic *Dracula*. Onscreen, both have clearly aged (even the immortal count). They wear shaggier hairstyles and sideburns befitting the era, and Van Helsing smokes like a chimney – otherwise their schtick is the same.

In the film, Dracula's follower Johnny Alucard ('Dracula' spelt backwards) persuades his hip group of twenty-something friends to stage a black mass. One of them is Jessica Van Helsing, Lorrimer's granddaughter, played by Stephanie Beacham. 'Something new but as old as time,' Alucard calls the rite, speaking to how trendy occult matters were in 1972. Unbeknownst to them, he uses the occasion to resurrect Dracula from the grave – in a de-sanctified church in Chelsea, of course. Dracula goes on to pick them off one by one.

It's hard not to see the film as a bit of wish-fulfilment for the conservative forces who were seeking to exact blood-draining punishment on the hippie generation, which in their eyes had outstayed its welcome. Or as Inspector Murray, the detective working with Van Helsing, describes them, 'a bunch of spaced-out teenagers . . . A bunch of kids whose way of life is as foreign to me as . . . ' Van Helsing interrupts him: '. . . as that of a vampire?'

Jus wrote 'Torquemada '71' in the style of Sourvein, leading many to think that it was one of Liz's compositions. It's one of the songs that shows how in sync the band was at this stage.

'*Witchcult Today* is the first real second [incarnation] Electric Wizard album,' Jus said at the time. '*We Live* was the line-up that had been together maybe a few months and Liz had only joined the band that week, so everything was rehearsed and planned. There wasn't a lot of spontaneity going on. But with this line-up it's been going for well over a year now. Liz has been in the band for a long time and we're living together and writing all this stuff together and working out ideas about the band together, which we hadn't done before. It's a real band effort this time, a much more thought-out record . . . it's a fucking *real* Electric Wizard album. If anyone likes *Come My Fanatics* . . . and *Dopethrone* then I personally think that's where it's at for me.'[276]

Jus and Liz collaborated well because they complemented one another. They complemented each other because they approached writing music differently. Liz focused on the riff and rhythm of a song – the big picture. Jus concerned himself with the riff too but also the finer structural points and idiosyncratic details of the song in hand. Liz's approach to writing was rawer; Jus was more refined. Jus often looked at Liz's riffs from another angle, returning them to her in startling new lights. They saw things in each other's writing the other didn't see. It worked.

'Besides the fact that he has a bong surgically attached to his hand, it's pretty much what I consider the perfect life,' Liz reflected in 2012. 'He was one of the first people I ever met that had the same outlook on life and the universe. To finally be able to converse on a daily basis with someone of his intelligence and open-mindedness is like the missing piece to a puzzle. The life we have built together, for a long time, I didn't think was even attainable. We are constantly discussing and creating art and music when we are at home. We've got a voracious appetite for collecting obscurities, travel, books. We obsess on things, explore weird places, converse heavily on the expansion of our mental abilities and watch *a lot* of old movies.'[277]

One of these movies prompted the most experimental piece on the album, which was also a cover version of sorts. 'Black Magic Rituals & Perversions' was inspired by *Le Frisson Des Vampires* (*Shiver of the Vampires*), a 1971 film directed by Jean Rollin.

Le Frisson Des Vampires was one of the films that Jus and Liz bonded over before Liz joined Electric Wizard. The raw fusion of the aesthetics, jumpy editing and outré set pieces in the film gives it a bricolage effect. I watched the film in French without subtitles but don't think there was much of a plot to decipher: a newlywed couple, Isle and Antoine, go to stay in a chateau owned by her cousins, who have been turned into vampires. One of the funnier scenes sees Antoine attacked by a library of books flinging themselves at him off the shelves. Isle is marked to become a vampire. At one point Antoine accidentally shoots a dove with his gun and Isle drinks the blood from its corpse.

The film has a fantastic array of garish costumes and plenty of (female) nudity. It's a French film but has the atmosphere of England. Specifically, the rolling fields and emptiness that had inspired the band while they were in Dorset. This continued after Jus and Liz had moved to the village of Chudleigh in the verdant surroundings of south Devon. Devon opened up new ancient territory to feed into their music.

Jean Rollin had brought together session musicians to form a band called Acanthus, similarly to the way *The Wicker Man* was soundtracked by a group brought together for the film under the name Magnet. The film is part of the canon of lesbian vampire movies, which includes 1971's *Vampyros Lesbos*, directed by Jess Franco, and also *Vampyres*, directed by José Ramón Larraz Gil in 1975. Like *Frisson* . . . the latter has a distinctly English feel as the vampire couple stalks their prey in the winter woods. *Vampyres* was used for an excellent fan-made video for 'Flower of Evil a.k.a. Malfiore' from *We Live*, which brought the themes of that song to life, or at least, undeath.[278] The band have been careful to repost the best fan videos of their music on their own channel, so they weren't lost in automatic copyright takedowns.

With 'Black Magic Rituals & Perversions' they wanted to create a soundtrack that gave some more coherence to a strange, disjointed film. 'It's all graves and coffins and stuff. It's quite a complicated story,' Jus told *Rock Sound*. 'These two chaps at the bottom [of the poster] are vampire hunters, but they eventually get bitten by a vampire. There's lots of lesbian vampire sex and stuff. It doesn't make any sense whatsoever. You have to watch it with the sound off and put some music on. We actually wrote a song based on part of the soundtrack. We do that a lot, horror movie stuff, but we just play it on the guitar.'[279]

The first part of the song is a cover of the film's title theme that plays over the opening credits, originally performed by Acanthus. The original is ominous enough, as Acanthus play it with low gain and twanging guitars. The Wizard just had to apply their customary black-amp power. The second half of 'Black Magic Rituals & Perversions', subtitled 'II: Zora', recreated a black magic ritual in the studio, overdubbed with what sounds like an extended sample from a ceremony in an Italian horror movie. Actually, this was Jus, reading from an Italian horror comic called *The Priestess of Satan*.

The band lit black candles in the studio and created a six-foot-long tape loop, keeping station with pencils in their hands to feed the tape through. Liam employed as many machines as possible to create the song's sound world – feedback, reverb and vocalisations were all sucked into its maw. They were layering on sounds to the point that things were emerging that they didn't know were there. It is Electric Wizard's tribute to electronic pioneer Delia Derbyshire and the BBC Radiophonic Workshop.

The atmosphere in the studio towards the end of 'Black Magic Rituals & Perversions' was mesmerising – the song bouncing off the walls and back in on itself. The band started to spin out as the feedback-drenched organ rang out. They sustained the ambience until the tape ran out: 'I don't think Liam's used to bands recording songs that long,' Jus mused afterwards.[280]

This wasn't the first time the Wizard had created an instrumental derived from a horror movie. One of the outtakes from the *We Live* sessions was called '*Tutti I Colori del Buio*', named after an occult piece of 1972 Giallo directed by Sergio Martino. It was later included on vinyl versions of the *We Live* album. That instrumental derived something of the sinister atmosphere of Bruno Nicolai's score but pared everything right back and filtered it through a megaton dose of distortion. It goes precisely nowhere musically, instead ploughing further into the earth like a cross being hammered into the ground. Fifteen minutes long, it is arguably Electric Wizard's heaviest instrumental track, rivalled only by 'Mind Transferral'.

'*Tutti I Colori del Buio*' was evidence of the anti-evolutionary mindset Jus purported to embrace with Electric Wizard's music. By the time *Witchcult Today* was released, he claimed that *We Live* as a whole had failed because the band tried too hard to evolve for the sake of it. He frequently referred to the band's absorption into the rock world at that time and how he became too much of a 'London' person – a scenester: '[P]eople who don't know me have some pretty wild ideas about what I'm like as a person. They think I'm an arrogant cock, I'm a dickhead, I talk shit about people; I've got a smarmy face, punched-in looking, that kind of shit.'[281]

The *We Live* period had stressed Jus out. He was forced to compete. He felt the pressure and needed to be a band leader, writing all the music and teaching other musicians how to play it. He was relieved to return to being 'the weirdo from Dorset'[282] with his band-as-gang around him, smoking weed and watching movies. He claimed he was happy not to pick up a guitar for six months at a time.

'I don't want to evolve,' he spat. 'Electric Wizard is Electric Wizard. Everything's the same on this album, but hopefully a bit better. I want to get better at what we do, but *We Live* and *Let Us Prey* were the product of trying to evolve and I'm not happy with either of those records, so I don't want to do it anymore. I just want to re-record the same album over and over again! Until I sell a million copies of something, there's no need to change it. There are always going to be new people out there who haven't heard us yet.'[283]

A piece of music which doesn't evolve much is the short instrumental, 'Raptus', which chimes, jangles and seethes with dark energy. The word 'raptus' means a pathological paroxysm of activity to give vent to impulse and tension, often in the form of an act of violence. As a piece of music, it betrayed its name and provided a useful respite or interlude during live performances for the band to recalibrate and indulge in some drone and sustain, drinking in the ambience they had created. The song also harked back to the raw, psychedelic atmosphere of 'Mother of Serpents' from *Let Us Prey*.

Witchcult Today is a cinematic record: from the film-poster adaptation of its cover to its horror-soundtrack sensibility. All it needed was a main character. Where the retro themes of the album – B-movie horror, sex and drugs – meet in most lighthearted fashion is the figure of Drugula, the band's own invention and star of the song 'Satanic Rites Of Drugula'.

'Drugula?' Jus responded to a question from *Metal Maniacs*. 'Well, you know, Dracula's been in his tomb for a few thousand

years and around maybe '69/'70 some Romanian stoners bust
into his tomb, they're smoking some weed, Dracula rises and
sucks the blood of the unfortunate, hot, Euro starlets, which [sic]
are high on LSD at the time and it just leads to a gradual decay
and he turns to drug addiction, basically because he enjoys
sucking the blood of those that are too high. That's how I see
him. He sucks chicks' blood and sucks the drugs from them . . .
whatever. It would make a great movie.'[284]

The song's title is a play on the eighth and final Hammer
Dracula film starring Christopher Lee, *The Satanic Rites Of
Dracula*, released in 1973. For Lee it was business as usual after
his brief sojourn on the side of good in *The Devil Rides Out*.
The silliness of the song's subject matter can't be denied, as it
takes the first-person perspective of Dracula resting in eternal
sleep 'under Saturn's rings' before 'dope smoke violates my tomb'.

At this point in this book, are you wondering whether the
band itself was still violating themselves with dope smoke?

Drugs had taken a backseat to the occult explorations of the
album, but they were still there, feeding the band's deranged
imagination. *We Live* was perhaps the least drug-influenced
album that Electric Wizard had made. Things were back on
track with *Witchcult Today*, where the intoxicants spill out of the
record when it's played, along with everything else.

'No, nothing's changed,' an exasperated Jus told *Metal
Hammer*. 'I smoke pot every day, like I have for twenty years.
It's always been part of the band. We're a drug band. It's not
an issue. When I was nineteen I wanted to drop acid every day.
I'm past that now, but we're not straitlaced. I like to party when
I can. I'll always smoke weed and the band will always smoke
weed. That's what Electric Wizard is all about. You don't ask
people whether they still drink, do you? They're going to drink
until the day they die, and I'm going to smoke weed until the
day I die.'[285]

'Satanic Rites of Drugula' joins 'Dunwich' in having one of the catchiest choruses Electric Wizard had written: 'Bloodlust, druglust, Count Drugula arise'. Nonetheless, it's a bone-heavy composition, with a coffin-wrenching opening and a brutal main riff like an acid-laced stake being driven into the heart of the song. Like Drugula, it is suspended between death, druggy infamy and immortality.

The inclusion of 'bloodlust' in the chorus was a knowing reference to Wes Craven's 1972 film *The Last House on the Left*. In it, Mari Collingwood is celebrating her seventeenth birthday by going to see the band Bloodlust, before she is raped and killed by a group of escaped convicts. Bloodlust are a mixture of early Alice Cooper and Black Sabbath, and otherwise grate against the hippyish tendencies of the soundtrack, depicting how the sixties soured with the advent of the seventies.

'The main protagonists are this weird gang; there's one girl in the gang. A few times I've thought, This is Electric Wizard,' Jus laughed in a 2017 interview with *The Quietus*.[286]

When Electric Wizard played shows with Shaun joining Rob in the rhythm section, they did resemble an 'outlaw biker gang from a seventies' exploitation movie'.[287] The band now treated their fans as their coven, and drew heavily on the material from *Witchcult Today*, playing to an audience that *Kerrang!* felt was 'more secret society than mere fanbase'.[288]

Witchcult Today was a mission statement and a handbook. The band had known exactly what they wanted to do, and they did it. With the album in the world, the band was able to grow again, and bring with them a new 'militia of black-clad, horn-flinging freaks' and drag the 'brain-damaged veterans' along for the ride too.[289] The features and reviews for the album compared it favourably to *Dopethrone* and *Come My Fanatics . . .*, and one or two even felt it exceeded them.

'*Witchcult Today* is more than just a return to form, it's the best Electric Wizard album since 2000's classic *Dopethrone*,' *Kerrang!* said in its review. 'Imagine a horde of evil druids putting Stonehenge on wheels and slamming it through the side of your house. Then imagine the pulverised mess tumbling into a bottomless black hole for a thousand years . . . on acid. In a genre with a veneration for an aspic-entombed past, Electric Wizard have dared to go beyond doom metal's last outpost, and it's an enthralling trip. One-way tickets only.'[290]

On 13 December 2008, Electric Wizard headlined an all-dayer to celebrate Rise Above's twentieth anniversary at the ULU (University of London Union) venue in London. Lee Dorrian took to the stage in a hooded cowl intoning the 'Eko Eko Azarak' chant in high camp style to introduce the band: 'EKO EKO ELECTRIC WIZARD!'

As they opened with 'Witchcult Today', this was obviously a different beast from the band that had toured *We Live*. What was an already febrile atmosphere, at the end of a long midwinter Saturday spent drinking and smoking weed, was elevated by a new collage of B-movie visuals used as a backdrop to Electric Wizard's performance. They played 'The Satanic Rites of Drugula', 'The Chosen Few' and a warped, extended version of 'Raptus', with 'Return Trip' as a nod to their past, and 'Funeralopolis' the nuclear weapon to reduce the audience to dust.

'If the atomisers in each of the guttering smoke machines had been packed with ounces of finest Moroccan hashish, you couldn't imagine a headier atmosphere in which to end the day, and possibly the entire world,' wrote *Metal Hammer* in their review of the gig. 'Electric Wizard are disgustingly, sickeningly heavy, and it's in the interests of sanity – theirs and ours – that they rarely perform live. This is a show that will live in infamy; you were either there or you weren't. Against hallucinogenic back projections of schlock satanism, ritual abuse and Nazi porn, the band deliver a seven-octave mindfuck of brown noise and ball-busting feedback, that leaves hundreds mentally raped. "Songs" subordinate themselves to the calculated cruelty of the sound, and if anyone still insists this band were better way back when, they're obviously already dead.'[291]

Rise Above had pressed up five hundred copies of a new Electric Wizard EP called *The Processean* to sell exclusively at the gig. The cover bore a red skull containing strange imagery within it. The song itself was an instrumental outtake from the *Witchcult Today* sessions, with layers of organ and guitar feedback, driven through in a tribal procession by Shaun's drumming.

When *The Devil Rides Out* poster was adapted for *Witchcult Today*, Electric Wizard left the strange square crucifix dangling from Baphomet's neck. This looks a little like a symbol that was illustrated on the bootleg copies of the band's Radio 1 session – the cross made up of four Ps of the Process Church of the Final Judgement. The Process Church was the group from which the EP took its title.

The Process Church, or simply the Process, was a religious cult which began in the mid-sixties, founded by Robert DeGrimston and Mary Ann Maclean (he was originally Robert Moore, but she convinced him that his middle name, DeGrimston, sounded better). The term derived both from Scientology and also from the name for the movement of a subject who transitions from psychological dependency to 'going clear'. According to *Turn Off Your Mind*, by Gary Lachman (an excellent book about the dark side of the sixties which Electric Wizard read avidly around this time), the mission of the Process was 'to inaugurate the end of the world in the service of satanic destruction, and to arise out of the chaos as leaders of a new age.'[292]

The symbol of the four Ps resembled a Nazi swastika – Hitler was a hero of the Process. Their followers were identifiable by these insignia and by black robes, turtlenecks, silver crosses, Goat of Mendes badges and the German Shepherd dogs which accompanied them. The DeGrimstons – he was charismatic and Christ-like, she was seen as merely aggressive – were accused of exerting mind control and subjecting their members to gruelling sessions to break down their defences.

The Process Church had a slogan equivalent to the Crowleyan axiom of 'Do what thou wilt': 'As it is, so be it'.[293] DeGrimston captured his theology in a book called *As It Is*. The book laid out a complicated theology which embraced both Christ and Satan, where Christ judges and Satan executes the judgement. Their disciples followed one or the other, as well as Jehovah or Lucifer. Christ was a kind of unifying figure of the other three, and symbol of the new age to emerge after the apocalypse. The Process saw bikers like the Hells Angels as the shock troops who would bring about the end of the world.

The Process Church released pamphlets under different themes and preached from a soap box in Hyde Park Corner. They courted pop aristocrats for the pamphlets: interviewing Paul McCartney and girlfriend Jane Asher for the 'Fear' issue. The actors Richard Harris and Stefanie Powers were canvassed. They interviewed Marianne Faithfull for the 'Death' issue, in which Charles Manson was quoted describing death as 'total awareness, closing the circle, bringing the soul to now'.[294]

The skull on the cover of Electric Wizard's *Processean* EP was taken from the 'Death' issue. The band bought it from an old lady on eBay who had found it in a tip and ironed it out. The record itself bore the Process insignia and the cover folded out to an image of Robert DeGrimston with 'Come My Fanatics' inscribed in distinctive Electric Wizard lettering in its lower half, as well as the inverted 'Ankh' symbol (the ancient

Egyptian hieroglyph for life) which became a calling card for the band.

When asked in an interview which period of time she would like to time travel back to, Liz answered: 'The late sixties, early seventies, so I could experience all the films, music and culture I'm into first-hand, like spending the day buying rare occult books that were still to be found in used bookshops, seeing José Larraz's *Deviation* in the cinema, leaving and being handed a Process Church magazine by a black-cloaked Process member, heading to some subterranean, liquid light-filled club and checking out [heavy progressive band] Elias Hulk. Or I'd go back to the turn of the century/*fin de siècle* era so I could hang out at the Café Royal, meet Aleister Crowley, join the Golden Dawn, travel the world and see all the unspoilt exotic and mysterious places as they used to be, when places really were different and not the homogenised shopping mall the world is now.'[295]

After the Manson murders, author and counterculture figure Ed Sanders wrote a book called *The Family* in 1971 (subtitled *The Story of Charles Manson's Dune Buggy Attack Battalion*) which claimed that the Process taught Manson everything he knew. Though they successfully sued Sanders and his publisher, the links to Manson and the death of the sixties was the beginning of the end of the Process. It was an apocalyptic event too far for these self-styled end-timers.

A couple of months before the Rise Above anniversary gig, Electric Wizard released a split EP with Reverend Bizarre. Reverend Bizarre were from Finland but on their 2004 album *II: Crush The Insects* wrote a song about Puritanism during the English Civil War called 'Cromwell'. Their guitarist, Peter Vicar, wanted to 'make a sonic portrait of this man who had the will to change a whole regime'.[296]

The song's galloping riff simulated the Ironsides arriving in London and had a long, evolving second sequence influenced by Pentagram's song 'Burning Saviour'. 'Cromwell' is evidence of the spiritual brotherhood between doom metal bands and shared obsessions of this period in English history, whether the witch-finding craze or the overthrow of God-given power structures in the figure of Charles I. Reverend Bizarre even brought Aleister Crowley's occult injunction into 'Cromwell': 'Love will be my Law, Love under Will/But first there is the Law of Cromwell'.

Reverend Bizarre released their final album in 2007. It was called *III: So Long Suckers* and boasted three songs each over twenty-five minutes in length, and another three over ten minutes. It was a long, knowingly drawn-out goodbye that fitted their long, drawn-out repertoire. The EP with Electric Wizard was another last step in their slowly disappearing existence.

Electric Wizard's contribution to the split was named for a novel that dwelt on the disappearance of life as we know it, *The House on the Borderland* by William Hope Hodgson. Hodgson wrote the book in 1908. It was an influence on Lovecraft and like 'The Dreams in the Witch House' locates the dread of a cosmos in the edifice of a building.

This house is in rural Ireland and the village of Kraighton. Two friends on a fishing trip discover a manuscript which relays the story of a man who is haunted/hunted by supernatural swine-creatures, which seem to rise out of a yawning pit in the earth near the house. The pit is connected by a passageway to a cavernous void directly underneath the house itself. After discovering this along with his intrepid dog, Pepper, the narrator retreats to his home where he barricades himself against the attacks of the creatures. To what extent these are figments of his imagination is uncertain.

Then, the novel changes suddenly, as time elapses at a ferocious rate and the narrator sees all around him reduced to dust, including poor old Pepper. Aeons elapse and he witnesses the sun dying: 'Gradually, even this thread of light died out;

and now, all that was left of our great and glorious sun, was a vast dead disk, rimmed with a thin circle of bronze-red light.' He is whisked by an undefined force to what seems to be the very centre of the universes and the celestial globes themselves, before being reconciled with a long-lost love gazing across the 'Sea of Sleep'.[297]

'The wanderings of the narrator's spirit through limitless light-years of cosmic space and kalpas of eternity, and its witnessing of the solar system's final destruction, constitute something almost unique in standard literature,' H.P. Lovecraft wrote of *The House on the Borderland*. 'And everywhere there is manifest the author's power to suggest vague, ambushed horrors in natural scenery. But for a few touches of commonplace senti-mentality this book would be a classic of the first water.'[298]

Whether the novel is one long allegory of grief or makes a deeper point about the profound hopelessness and dread of our infinitesimal lives, it is difficult to say. But its underground caverns, cosmic dread and that dead sun are reflected too in the work of Electric Wizard. And like the house on the borderland, these symbols are their way of making it clear they sit outside time and space, in a world of their own.

Electric Wizard's 'The House on the Borderland' doesn't tell the story of the book, but calls out to 'Black Amp disciples' and 'covens gathered deep below' to ready their hatred of the world for apocalyptic uprising. The song's confidence is embedded by the fantastic main riff, one of the best of their whole career, which elevates the release to the level of 'Supercoven' for its dark-magic mastery. The presence of black amps in the lyric also ties the song to the immediacy of 'Dopethrone'. Under the denouement of the song, Jus can be heard faintly reading Hope Hodgson's *The House on the Borderland* itself.

They recorded the song at Foel Studio, located in a secluded Welsh valley near the town of Welshpool. The way the studio stood in the valley, it came to be the house on the borderland itself, as purple, misty mountains loomed in the distance – a conduit for forces beyond the band's control. Liz was re-reading Hope Hodgson's book while they recorded, making it natural to use its title and themes. Jus had read it when he was very young and it was one of many formative influences that he used in Electric Wizard's music, which then came to be cultural signifiers of the doom genre as a whole.

Witchcult Today gave definition to Electric Wizard's new form of doom metal – overtly occult with nastier vintage sounds and a seedy underbelly. Once defined, a song like 'The House on the Borderland' drove the imagery home. Electric Wizard's audience was the naked victim on its cover (in an image from occult S&M magazine *Bitchcraft*), having their breast sliced in a remorseless needling – the perverse, 'coveted necromantic' we all secretly crave.

On the weekend of 8–10 May 2009, All Tomorrow's Parties (ATP) held The Fans Strike Back Part II festival at Butlin's, Mine-head, a coastal town in Somerset – a gateway to the deep West Country which begins with Exmoor up and over the hill. The resort consisted of hundreds of identical chalets and a hub of buildings containing pubs, restaurants and venues with stages for 'light entertainment'. There was also a separate swimming pool and water slide centre, populated by tattooed hipsters enjoying the lazy river over the course of the weekend.

ATP established a strange holiday camp vibe, even piping in their own curated schedule to the television sets in the rooms. It was called The Fans Strike Back because the prospective attendees had a free vote to say who they wanted to play. There were high-profile reunion gigs at the festival, including The Jesus Lizard and Sleep – the latter played two sets at 1 a.m. on the Saturday and Sunday nights, the last to feature drummer Chris Hakius and the original line-up.

Electric Wizard were voted on to the bill and played on the Friday night at half past midnight on the Reds stage. ATP created a pack of cards for the event, detailing who was playing and Electric Wizard's card certainly upped the ante: 'Electric Wizard is the heaviest band in the world. The oblivion and ecstasy of crushing doom and high-grade marijuana, a sonic aural trip far, far away from this world, where only cyclopean walls of crackling vintage valve amplifiers set to maximum overdrive and primal ritualistic beats can wash away the filth, drudgery and humiliation of everyday existence. Their music is Doom Metal, the only true definition. A crushing behemoth of funeral march psychedelia. Violent, bleak and ritualistic, they bow to the black altar of the RIFF!!'

Electric Wizard gigs had become an event. ATP pulled together the rally-like assortment of underground culture freaks the Wizard wanted in their coven: punks, metalheads, noise aficionados, and wasters of every stripe. The other side of the ATP playing card showed Liz, Shaun and Jus posing in a bucolic setting, but Rob was absent. He had faded from prominence and eventually left the band altogether.

The weekend itself was chaotic. Sleep called the Wizard straight off their plane from the States to make sure they were well-supplied with weed. The Wizard's chalet became a den of iniquity for the duration of the festival. The band kept losing each other in the ranks of the uniform accommodation.

'I don't really remember the weekend,' Jus told me in 2014. 'We got there late, we got wasted, it was outta control. We had a jam in the chalet at five in the morning on the Sunday. You could hear ". . . the wizard . . ." being shouted out all over the camp. It is kinda weird there, like a concentration camp. I thought we were in *The Great Escape!*'[299]

209

Despite, or probably owing to, the state they were in, the gig was a triumph. It leaned heavily on *Witchcult Today* but brought back 'We Hate You' to showcase how the new line-up tackled the older songs. I was there, and remember the stage seemed to be sunk into the venue – the set had a dark, smoky and oppressive, subterranean feeling. The audience was also unusually rowdy, jostling with each other for elbow room, with a mosh pit simmering away and suddenly boiling over as the band cast its spell.

'It's halfway through the witching hour as Electric Wizard find themselves in front of a packed, expectant room in a holiday camp on the north Somerset coast,' wrote *Kerrang!* 'It's fair to suggest this might be a rather surreal context in which to encounter this motley bunch, these days looking like the cast of [2005 Rob Zombie film] *The Devil's Rejects* had it been made in the West Country in 1973, but the consistently mind-blowing nature of the six albums they've exhaled over the last decade and a half led to their being the second band voted onto the bill by the punters of this half-democratic masterstroke of a festival. The reception they're afforded is duly mental, as the world's slowest mosh gradually erupts in fervent worship, while the band make no concessions whatsoever to curious newcomers, simply getting their heads down and ploughing into a set which mixes the occasional classic with *Witchcult Today* favourites "The Satanic Rites Of Drugula" and "The Chosen Few". Reunion shows from Sleep and The Jesus Lizard might be this ATP's most impressive bookings, but it's Wizard merchandise which appears to be clothing the majority of the festival for the next two days.'[300]

That autumn the band toured the UK and Europe with Blood Ceremony – another band on the Rise Above roster. Far less heavy-going than Electric Wizard, Blood Ceremony's sound was more folk-like and spry. They were Canadian, and singer Alia O'Brien played the flute, so they drew comparisons with a

more fuzzed-out Jethro Tull. Whereas the Wizard reshaped the
soundtracks of seventies' horror movies through their massive
distortion field, Blood Ceremony could easily have provided
the music there and then. It felt good for Electric Wizard to
take them out under their wing, when they hadn't always been
extended the courtesy themselves.

It wasn't always a pleasant experience. As the tour progressed, a bad, persistent smell began wafting through the bus.
On a day off the tour manager insisted they clean it because
something must have died. After searching everywhere for
the source of the stench, they discovered it was coming from
Shaun's duffle bag. They opened it and found a huge block of
blue cheese wrapped in his dirty underwear. As with a lot of
incidents involving Shaun, it defied explanation. And none was
forthcoming from Shaun.

The tour was successful in terms of good shows played to
packed audiences, but Rise Above claimed they didn't make any
money. Yet the Wizard were killing it live. At France's Hellfest
in summer 2009, the band's 'planet-sized doom riffs' flattened
the tent they played in. 'It was a good show, definitely,' Jus
told *Kerrang!*. 'It was heavy as fuck. We were even louder than
[world's loudest band] Manowar!'[301] Electric Wizard found it
hard to believe that they weren't making money. There seemed
to be a culture of 'Don't ask, don't tell' at Rise Above – Electric
Wizard weren't certain what they should be asking and the label
wasn't telling. It soured relations when it came to handling
their touring and seeded greater discontent further down
the line.

Around the time of Hellfest, a booking agent called Mark
Lewis was calling the Rise Above offices on an almost daily
basis. He worked for a booking agency called Elastic Artists in
London, better known for jazz-funk band Incognito than doom
metal. A long-time fan of the Wizard, he asked his boss, Jon

Slade, to let him spend some time pursuing them. Lewis spoke to Will Palmer at the label many, many times but was told that Jus was a nutcase and he wouldn't speak on the phone. But one day, after eighteen months of persistence, Palmer gave Lewis Jus's home number.

Mark Lewis grew up in Northern Ireland during some of the worst atrocities of the 'Troubles', which he described as a living nightmare. Metal was his salvation. Scanning the black metal section in Belfast's Dr Roberts record shop – where he had picked up many black-metal first pressings – he found Electric Wizard's albums. It seemed appropriate that they were shelved there. The band had a long association with black metal as kindred spirits, dating back to Jus's penpal days and the harsh sonic textures of *Come My Fanatics* . . . Lewis was enthralled by the Wizard's music and the stories of the band's chaotic, unreliable behaviour. He went on to work with some of the classic second-wave Norwegian black metal bands, including Mayhem and Ulver. He also had the more poppy Swedish metal act Ghost as a client, who released their debut album, *Opus Eponymous*, through Rise Above in 2010 (they now headline festivals and fill arenas). He was delighted to be professionally involved with many bands whose posters had been up on the walls of his teenage bedroom.

The first few times Lewis rang, Jus didn't even pick up, but after several attempts they eventually spoke. Jus was nothing like Lewis expected; he regarded Wizard with a professionalism that took Lewis aback. Jus said the money simply hadn't been coming in and he was about to go back to carpet-fitting. Lewis explained that he loved the band and thought they had a massive unfulfilled potential as a live force – they were clearly not getting their due in terms of the scale of their shows or compensation. Jus told Lewis he didn't trust anyone, but that he would give him a shot.

Lewis had seen the band live for the first time on 7 September 2008 at London's Scala venue, during the period that he was bombarding Rise Above with phone calls. The show was widely reviewed. As well as the customary extolling of the band's heaviosity, the reviewers were all struck by the shift in the band's shows towards mass ritualistic happenings. 'It feels like everyone in the audience is connected – not in some spiritually uplifting way, however, but like in some sickening H.P. Lovecraft short story,' wrote *Metal Hammer*, noting how Jus and Liz seemed to be 'pulled apart by conflicting sources of energy'.[302] These were of the band's making, and the *Kerrang!* review swore that Jus was 'casting a sinister spell to pull the universe apart at the seams'.[303]

Electric Wizard had succeeded in assembling a line-up that looked and operated like an outlaw biker gang. The memory of *We Live* was dead and buried. Propelled by the success of *Witchcult Today*, the band fulfilled a prophecy of growing a coven of fans around them, drawing in the curious and ingenuous in the process. On record and live, they were in control and conjuring magic. Now they had amassed the audience, the real ceremony could begin.

Chapter Eight
Rituals of Evil

'Make us look like fucking cunts, yeah? I want people to hate us. I want people to fear us. I want the common man to spit at us in the street.' – Jus to John Doran of *The Quietus* in 2009.[304]

On 1 November 2010, All Saints' Day, Electric Wizard released their seventh album, *Black Masses*. For the first time they were on multiple magazine covers – the platform from which they could spread the word was bigger than ever. Now they had lured the audience in through the mirror, the rite could begin.

The album was named for three types of black mass: a particularly good type of squidgy black hash Jus was smoking at the time; the big black of space; and black magic. Long accustomed to an adversarial standpoint against society, it was truly time to let the devil into the music. *Black Masses* was about getting back to the satanic origins of metal, an acknowledgement of the wider metal scene's return to that sound, and then wider society's continued internet-driven depravity.

'This album is more evil, more satanic-sounding,' Jus told *Metal Hammer* on its release. 'We've been obsessing about certain films and very dark shit. We've meditated on the fact that the music we really like has always been inspired by Luciferian thought, by darker movies, books about the devil. I mean, being

214

into metal when I was young was about [Iron Maiden album] *The Number of the Beast* and trying to get a copy of *The Devil's Bible*. It was part of the whole culture and we just obsessed on that and we're trying to solidify those traditions on this record. I think the world's heading into the pits of hell and you're either going to be a Christian or dig it – have your satanic age and just play as loud as possible, do as many drugs as possible, fuck as much as possible, and just do it. We've always talked about the true spirit of satanic heavy metal, what it means to be into heavy metal. Everything's getting a bit wimpy, too clinical or too pussyish.'[305]

The album, once again recorded with Liam Watson at Toe Rag studios, had a nasty, lo-fi sound – more in league with Venom, Sodom, Bathory and early Alice Cooper than doom metal. Jus got to mouth off about the iniquities of modern recording: 'I can't be fucked to sit in front of a screen, moving sliders with a fucking mouse. It gives me migraines. It's misery. Analogue is real shit. I can move, I can twist dials, I can plug things in.'[306]

Black Masses was the most radical departure yet from Electric Wizard's blown-out origins. The band asked Liam for something raw and garage-rock sounding, specifically like The Stooges. Liam decided to produce the album as if it were *Raw Power*, The Stooges' shittiest-sounding album. *Black Masses* ended up like a recovered transmission from the heart of a 'medieval rave-up'.[307] The record was the soundtrack for drug-fuelled hedonism under the guise of a satanic gathering.

Recording is a ritual process. In his book *The Satanic Rituals* (1972), an accompaniment to *The Satanic Bible* (1969), Anton LaVey makes a distinction between rituals and ceremonies. Rituals, he writes, 'are directed towards a specific end that the performer desires', whereas ceremonies 'are pageants paying homage to or commemorating an event, aspect of life, admired personage or declaration of faith.' This distinction is useful:

Electric Wizard studio albums are rituals, where the finished
record is the goal; whereas their live performances are ceremonies: 'a ritual is used to *attain*, while a ceremony serves to
sustain,' writes LaVey.[308]

We can imagine that, in LaVey's eyes, observing Electric
Wizard from a cliff-edge in hell, that the band was walking a
tightrope in terms of their satanist credentials by appropriating
the black mass itself. LaVey thought the black mass was often
mistaken for a type of ceremonial 'pageant of blasphemy',
whereas it was meant to be an over-the-top purging of Christian
dogma. Jus's view of the black mass as an excuse for unleashing
hedonism would probably have met with LaVey's disapproval: 'If
a *Black Mass* is performed by curiosity seekers or "for fun", it
becomes a party,' he writes in *The Satanic Rituals*.[309]

But LaVey took all this a bit too seriously, didn't he?

Black Masses was a priority for Rise Above Records. Electric
Wizard had long been the label's golden calf and *Witchcult
Today* had considerably widened the band's audience. There
was pressure exerted on the band to record *Black Masses* to a
schedule. Rise Above wanted to deliver LPs to high-street shops
like HMV that stipulated a year's lead time for stock orders. No
one involved was used to these kinds of mainstream concerns
and as a result, the alchemy of recording and the release itself
was somewhat hurried.

'They're one of the most unlikely bands you could imagine to
be successful, but I think one of the keys to it is that they've
simply stuck to their guns,' Lee Dorrian said at the time.
'They've never compromised, and they've always kind of known
their direction, even though they've had ups and downs. Justin
very much knows what he wants and where he wants to go in
terms of exploring what Electric Wizard is about and how far he
can push it. Let's not beat around the bush here. Electric Wizard
is not a band that does anything apart from live the lifestyle.

They immerse themselves in occult imagery; they're obsessed with obscure movies . . . it's a lifestyle for them. It's not like some five-minute fad. It's not a fashion or a pose. It's the real thing with them.'[310]

The deluxe, 'Die Hard' edition of the vinyl *Black Masses* contained a small-format comic book called *Crypt Of Drugula* in the style of Italian pulp *Fumetti* comics. Drugula as a character lives on in *Black Masses* in the near-nine-minute comedown at the end of the album, also called 'Crypt Of Drugula'. It is another long, experimental piece in the vein of 'Black Magic Rituals & Perversions', heavy on a crackly atmosphere conjured by the sound of thunder and lightning strikes. Throughout, a lone guitar wails, shrieks and judders through an overdriven wah effect. It sounds like a creature writhing in its pit as low drums seep in from the distance. Another, softer melody line slowly gets louder and adds to the growing unease.

The character of Drugula himself was partly inspired by Bobby Liebling, the singer of Pentagram, who formed in 1971 but only put out their debut album in the mid-eighties. Theirs was a story of what could have been. In 1975, members of KISS had come to see Pentagram perform at home to check out their potential. Two of the members rushed back from their day jobs as janitors for the showcase. KISS were withering in their assessment that their drummer was too fat and they all had bad skin. Liebling blew another one of their chances in the same year when he fell out over his vocal takes with a big-time producer called Murray Krugman, who had offered to record a three-track demo with the band, with a view to getting a major record deal. Krugman had seen the band as a 'street Black Sabbath'.[311] Liebling was certainly a demonic frontman

when he wanted to be, with his wild bug eyes and masses
of hair.

Pentagram gained a reputation at the vanguard of the doom
movement in the eighties with another release in 1987 called
Day of Reckoning. This was partly due to the ungodly guitar
tone of Victor Griffin. Ironic perhaps, because he was a devout
Christian who took traditional doom's idea of judgement before
his saviour very seriously. It wasn't until 2001, when Relapse
Records assembled a collection of Pentagram's seventies' demos
for a retrospective collection called *First Daze Here*, that their
astonishing back catalogue reached a wider audience. But these
demos had been doing the rounds for years in the doom underground and had a tremendous impact on the scene's musicians.
Pentagram was particularly championed by Relapse's Sean 'Pellet'
Pelletier, who also became Bobby Liebling's de facto manager.

Pelletier featured in a 2011 documentary called *Last Days
Here* which depicted Liebling in the throes of drug abuse before
Pentagram reformed for shows in New York and Baltimore in
2009. During filming Liebling turned fifty-four, but he looked
more like seventy-four – older-looking even than his parents,
whose sub-basement he inhabited in Georgetown, Maryland. The
documentary is an eye-opening portrayal of the soul-destroying
reality beneath a band's legend.

At the beginning of the film, Liebling is in the grip of
addiction, claiming he has been a serious drug user for over
forty years. For most of that time he has been hooked on heroin
and crack cocaine. His bandaged arms cover sores, the result
of Liebling's belief that he is infested with parasites, and his
ensuing 'de-breeding' efforts, where he has scratched incessantly
at his dead skin.

I saw the documentary at the London Film Festival and
wondered, like the filmmakers, whether I was witnessing Liebling's final days. He doesn't seem to care about living, or dying.

'If you want me around, I'll stick around,' he says at one point, stoned out of his mind, before searching for a stray crack rock he's dropped.

In his own mind, Liebling is a Peter Pan figure, funded by his parents, refusing to grow up. To others he is a caveman frozen in time with a remarkable musical legacy – his band, Pentagram, the missing link between Led Zeppelin and the Sex Pistols, with a penchant for self-sabotage. With his cadaverous appearance and sunken cheeks, it is easy to see why he inspired Jus to create the immortal drug addict Drugula.

However, the film is a comedy rather than a tragedy. Liebling falls in love with a woman called Hallie, about half his age. He is revitalised and begins dying his grey hair black again. He leaves his parents for an apartment they have rented for him in Philadelphia to be near her. On the day he moves out, the electric hob spontaneously catches fire, at the same time as a crucifix necklace falls off a friend who is helping Liebling pack up. Satan is pleased: Bobby's back.

It's not plain sailing. His relationship with Hallie deteriorates and he falls back into drug addiction, moving back home. She even takes a restraining order out on him. But after his triumphant 2009 Pentagram show in New York, they are reunited, married, and Hallie becomes pregnant. 'There's going to be another me,' Liebling says mischievously at the documentary's conclusion.

Liz met Liebling in the early nineties when she was playing in 13. He was keen to show them his collection of outrageous lamé shirts. He later went through a phase of smoking crack whilst in conversation with an unnerving monkey hand-puppet he always carried with him. Pentagram were Liz's musical heroes and Sourvein recorded a cover of their 'Forever My Queen' in Texas with Clayton Mills of the band Dixie Witch, released on a split with the band Rabies Caste after she left the band.

News of Liebling's baby seeped into 'The Night Child' on *Black Masses*, with its withered, seventies Pentagram-style main riff: 'I am the Nightchild/Shadows gather round me'. It depicts a vampiric creature creeping and crawling at night-time, in search of 'New bodies, new victims/Drug and murder addicted'. The whole of *Black Masses* sounds like one of those recovered Pentagram demo tapes, misplaced amongst one of Liebling's chaotic drawers stuffed with cassettes and CDs.

'In some ways, it was kind of a tribute to Bobby Liebling's new-born son,' Jus said of 'The Night Child' to *Decibel*. 'What Bobby has done in Pentagram, that's what it's all about, I think. That's why I got into rock 'n' roll and heavy metal and punk. It's about being an individual, about creating something that people would remember maybe.'[312]

Hallie wrote to Jus to thank him for the dedication to her son, which was at least half-serious.

The *Crypt Of Drugula* comic book in the deluxe version of the album contained two stories that shared titles with songs from *Black Masses* – the strips themselves were lifted from *Uncanny Tales* magazine which Jus loved as a kid.

The first, 'Black Mass', plays with the notion of dream and reality. 'The tale I am about to unfold is a nightmare . . . ' it begins. The unnamed protagonist is abducted from the street at night by three hooded figures who take him to an underground ritual administered by a white-robed priest who proceeds to have him lashed. Then he is branded on his forehead with a strange bat-like insignia, before a statue of the creature comes to life and tears strips of flesh from him while he is bound to the altar. Aside from its bat wings, it has a beak and what looks like deer antlers. It has more than a little of the Yezidees' satanic peacock about its appearance.

The song itself opens the album with an invocation: 'Lucifer I summon thee to my black mass/I call upon you to complete my evil task'. That evil task is the same it has always been for Electric Wizard – to give oneself to drugs and hate. The difference on *Black Masses* is the band putting that sentiment within a satanic ritual, which is itself what Anton LaVey calls 'a blend of Gnostic, Cabbalistic, Hermetic, and Masonic elements, incorporating nomenclature and vibratory words of power from virtually every mythos.'[313]

If this sounds like a chocolate selection box for naughty children, the black mass had more sinister origins. In the seventeenth century, Catherine Deshayes, otherwise known as LaVoisin, developed her own version (or should I say 'inversion') of the black mass. It purportedly involved the sacrifice of an unbaptised human child. She even roped in willing Catholic priests to engage in heretical acts. She used an aborted foetus in the ritual – Deshayes also performed over two hundred abortions in her lifetime. It is doubly delicious, or horrifying, from our twenty-first century perspective, to think of LaVoisin inverting the Catholic mass by offering up the product of an operation as religiously controversial as abortion.[314]

LaVey's version of the black mass follows a version performed by the Société des Luciferiens in the late nineteenth/early twentieth century. One of LaVey's objectives was to de-shackle Satan from Christian propaganda. He characterised the black mass as a 'psychodrama' that is not about inverting the Catholic mass for purely blasphemous means but to elevate the concept of Satan itself 'to a noble and rational degree'. That said, the chief objective of the black mass was to 'reduce or negate stigma acquired through past indoctrination'. It is a retaliatory act against Christianity, and as such is obsessed with its enemy.[315]

LaVey recorded a black mass in the Church of Satan

headquarters – known as The Black House – at 6114 California Street, San Francisco, on 13 September 1968 for a vinyl release called *The Satanic Mass*. The climax of the black mass involves the celebrant priest inserting a wafer into the vagina of the 'altar' – a naked woman. He then removes it, holds it aloft to a depiction of Baphomet and has some harsh words for Christ:

> Vanish into nothingness, thou fool of fools,
> thou vile and abhorred pretender to the
> majesty of Satan! Vanish into the void of thy
> empty Heaven, for thou wert never, nor
> shalt thou ever be.[316]

The celebrant then takes the wafer and crushes it underfoot. Christ is banished to the void and Satan can rule over the Earth.

'This album *is* our black mass,' Jus told *Decibel*. 'So, we tried to encapsulate everything we feel about this genre of music, heavy doom metal, or whatever we play. For us black masses are towers of amps, rituals, fucking bongs filled with resin, all these things. *Witchcult Today* was sort of a relaxed album, an alluring album, bringing you in, drawing you into the cult. And then *Black Masses* is it. It's ferocious, this one – as ferocious as we get, anyway. That's the intention.'[317]

On 'Patterns Of Evil', the band offer their own vivid description of what their black mass would involve: 'Screaming virgins tortured/Dragged to the Devil's altar'. Their witches' sabbath is an orgy of 'Narcotic chanting', 'Female screams' and 'Naked witches writhing'. The punishment meted out elicits a sexual thrill – the 'obscene kiss'. This song is LaVey's vision of the satanic chamber as 'veritable palace of perversity'.[318]

But 'Patterns Of Evil' is not an ordeal. It moves at a healthy clip: the cymbals sound like they're being tickled by chopsticks (one of the album's failings is its muffled drums). The

atmosphere is oppressive and cloying, but not suffocating compared to previous paeans to suffering like 'I, The Witchfinder'
and 'Master Of Alchemy'.

What's also interesting about the song 'Black Mass' itself is
that with its insistent, cyclical riffing it sounds like a ritual, but
it is also very catchy. It's another instance where Electric Wizard
had come close (ish) to sounding 'pop', something that wasn't
lost on Jus: 'We feel we write pop songs, it's just that they come
via our worldview, our shit-coloured glasses.'[319]

The idea of doing a massive pop single was something Jus
had speculated about ten years previously: 'We'd do a pop single,
I reckon, just for the hell of it. You can have one hit single and
sell a fuckin' load of records. Then you can tell everybody it's
only a fuckin' single, we did it for the money. Wouldn't you?
The albums would still be heavy . . . I don't have a problem
with things like that. If people do it for the wrong reasons, like
they're really honest and they really want to be a pop band,
then fuck 'em. But if you just want to make one pop record,
to stick two fingers up to the music business and the way the
whole system works, and exploit the whole media bullshit, then
fair enough, you should go for it.'[320]

What makes *Black Masses* such a strange, destabilising
album is that it might be a psychedelic pop album disguised as
satanic heavy metal. By 2010, now forty years old, heavy metal
itself had entered a mid-life crisis.[321] Suddenly, it seemed like
everyone was listening to Mercyful Fate again. The nu metal
schism of the nineties had passed, as had the emo takeover of
the mid-2000s. Instead, bands were falling back on tried and
tested formulae and imagery. In 2006, the original line-up of
Slayer had reformed and released *Christ Illusion*, an album
more in tune with their eighties' thrash classics. In 2007, when
Electric Wizard had released *Witchcult Today*, Machine Head
– whose cry 'Let freedom ring with a shotgun blast!' Tim had

pushed Jus to emulate on 'Return Trip' – put out *The Blackening*. Though an instant classic, Machine Head reincorporated some of metal's traditional fantastical themes, allegory and myth on *The Blackening*. They retreated from what had felt like the revolutionary project – which was to bring day-to-day psychological realism into the centre of metal.

In its early years, Electric Wizard had stood outside of this project and had long absorbed other cultural inputs. However, they still had something to say about the forces that control our destiny as human beings. They had been part of metal's modernist drive – severed from the past and reflecting an eternal present.

But by 2010, now that Satan was heavily back in fashion, along with battle jackets, denim and leather, Electric Wizard leaned into the trend. They will always be an acid-and-weed doom band, rather than a speed-freak heavy metal band, which is why their variant of satanic metal on *Black Masses* has a psychedelic, proto-metal texture and spirit.

This dichotomy in Electric Wizard's sound of the period was encapsulated on 'Turn Off Your Mind (azathoth)', with its queasy, thundering, mid-tempo groove and warped vocals. Its title was taken from the instruction by sixties LSD guru Timothy Leary to 'turn off your mind, relax, float downstream', which was famously incorporated into the Beatles song 'Tomorrow Never Knows'. Of course, Azathoth is Lovecraft's demon sultan.

But this is an Electric Wizard song, so inevitably the 'acid burns your mind': 'Colours die and turn to grey/All love has turned to pain'. The comic named after this song in the *Black Masses* deluxe edition (repurposing an old strip drawn by moonlighting Marvel artist Chic Stone) took this to its limit. The protagonist, Joe, is talked into dropping acid, but becomes fixated on a skull in the room: '. . . his eyes rolled about in their sockets until they suddenly fell upon the miniature skull resting on the coffee table . . . he began to meditate upon it . . . an anguished scream rose from his throat as blood gushed from every opening in the skull . . . this he knew was going to be a bad trip . . . ' The trip goes from bad to horrifying. Let's just say at one point Joe witnesses his own dismembered hand nailed to a wall.

'I've seen some pretty terrible things while playing our music,' Jus told *The Quietus* on his return to the bad-acid-trip roots of the band on *Black Masses*. 'It would be impossible to put into words. The music is very visual and is based on things I've seen while taking LSD and listening to psych bands when I'm on acid. The music and those riffs are possibly an attempt to try and convey the experience of LSD better than words can. Psychedelic means mind altering, and we write mind-altering songs. If you've only heard Elvis, I guess something like the cartoon psychedelia of *Sgt. Pepper's Lonely Hearts Club Band* is going to sound pretty fucked-up but to our ears it sounds like playground music. To be truly psychedelic the music has to be able to alter your mind so you lose touch with your body.'[322]

The third tale in the *Crypt Of Drugula* comic book is a photo story called 'Sisters Of Satan'. This features black-and-white photos of a brunette and a blonde woman cavorting together, naked apart from weird leather fetish wear and with a small skull by a bookshelf. The images were extracted from the second issue of volume three of the occult glamour and fetish magazine, *Bitchcraft*. This was also the source of the breast-slicing cover of *The House on the Borderland* EP. There is one caption: '"His Dark Majesty has given us each other," Doreen says to Frederica. "Let us pay homage to our Master through our bodies and our wills."'

The back page of *Crypt Of Drugula* – advertising the next issue, promising more lurid stories including 'The Price Of Passion', with a photo of a bloodied man buried up to his head being tormented by a topless woman – was a replica of a page of

Ed Wood magazine, which never saw a second issue. Similarly, a second issue of *Crypt Of Drugula* is a promise that has yet to be fulfilled . . .

The kind of vintage erotica evident in 'Sisters Of Satan' had found its way into the imagery of Electric Wizard early on. It became much more prominent with *Witchcult Today* and was ramped up further with *Black Masses*. It engulfed the audience at live gigs by way of the videos played on a screen behind the band. Whenever Electric Wizard begins a gig with 'Witchcult Today', the audience is confronted by a long-haired Jess Franco acting in his 1979 film *The Sadist of Notre Dame*. He looks into the camera, aghast at the torture and perversion he sees before him in the catacombs. But when he is staring out of the screen the band used onstage, by extension, the Electric Wizard live audience is also the object of his horror and fascination. In turn, the crowd itself is transfixed by the band and the images of nudity and sadism playing out behind them.

The band had started to use an inverted Ankh symbol around 2000 but it became more prevalent from the *Witchcult Today* era onwards. Jus had long wanted a symbol for the band in the vein of Judas Priest's satanic trident. The Ankh is an ancient Egyptian hieroglyphic symbol which represents everlasting life. Turned upside down, it means eternal death. Before Electric Wizard take to the stage, the inverted Ankh is projected on the backdrop screen and starts to drip blood. Upside down, and in Jus's design, the Ankh also resembles a vagina through which the audience is born, screaming, into the band's domain. Through the cunt of Electric Wizard you enter the world of death. Looking at it another way, the dripping blood is the act of menstruation and concert attendees are earning their 'red wings'.

The Electric Wizard live experience, like the movies they enjoy, goes straight to the hypothalamus. When money isn't in abundance, let sex, blood and death compensate.

Jess Franco's 1973 film *Female Vampire*[323] binds together sex and ritual death. Starring Lina Romay as the mute Countess Irina of Karlstein, there were two cuts of the film – one of seventy minutes and another over a hundred minutes which contained more genuinely pornographic scenes. There is little to no plot but suffice to say that the female vampire likes to drain men's lives through their penises. Being a Jess Franco film, there is also a flogging scene – a staple of *The Erotic Rites of Frankenstein* as well.

Aside from the long, meaningful stares, soft focus and erratic, dreamlike editing, the film has two strong images. The first is the countess emerging from amongst winter trees at its beginning, naked apart from a cloak, boots and a belt – the camera pans up and down her body approvingly. The second is at the film's conclusion, as she writhes in a bath of blood. There are desultory attempts to give her an interior life through the film's voiceover. She complains that a 'malefic influence' forces her to commit what she herself thinks of as 'heinous crimes'. It shows she has a conscience and is a reluctant victim of her corporeal urges: 'Why has my body once again the desire of death? Why can't my senses survive without the last breath of a victim?'

A Romay-type figure appears in the *Black Masses* artwork beneath the black candle that burns on its slipcase, and as the primary image on the LP sleeve. The photograph of the candle was taken by Liz, and the notion was that the candle magically transforms into the woman. It also emulated the idea of having multiple covers, following the trend for bands to use alternate covers in different territories. There was also another naked female vampire as a poster in the album's deluxe vinyl edition.

The overwhelming effect was one of cult exploitation, trash and sex-horror colliding with the contents of *Man, Myth & Magic*, a partwork magazine of pagan mythology and encyclopaedia of the supernatural which began publishing in 1970. The prevalence of the more exploitative photography in Electric Wizard's artwork also spoke to the band's increased control over all aspects of their output. They were behind the camera, and they were pulling the strings – this was their ritual and it was supposed to make you uncomfortable. What are the limits of 'good taste'? What are good morals and who is measuring them? Embrace 'bad taste', perversion and darkness. Do what thou wilt . . .

It was a long way from the confused packaging of *Let Us Prey*, although the bikini-clad model holding a skull aloft inside that album's inlay pointed to this future design pathway. As did the acknowledgement of Lina Romay by name in the 'without whom' list of *Let Us Prey* – Electric Wizard's version of a thank-you list. Similarly, the 'without whom' lists in the inlays of *Witchcult Today* and *Black Masses* are potted guides to Electric Wizard's cultural sphere at the time, and indeed, onwards.

'Justin and Liz do seem to work well together,' Lee Dorrian once observed. 'From the artwork to the photos – the whole imagery, the whole vibe – has become stronger and more focused since Liz has been in the band. And I think that's because you've got two minds working on it as opposed to one. I think they complement each other quite well.'[324]

Electric Wizard's aesthetic evolution was celebrated on the second song on *Black Masses*: 'Venus In Furs'. Another mid-tempo song that has some of Shaun's best hammer-of-the-gods drumming (especially right at the beginning), it has a particularly entrancing bridge section which feels like entering a brightly coloured revel with a seedy underbelly, where the source of addiction this time is a woman: the sorceress and priestess of mars that has haunted multiple Electric Wizard songs. This woman is to be abused ('Queen of the night swathed in saturn black/Your ivory flesh upon my torture rack'), object of fetishist fascination ('To your leather boots I offer prayer') and administrator of toxins ('You rise like a cobra, evil, dressed in furs/But your venom a black drug inside my veins').

This was the nefarious female influence that Black Sabbath and Jimi Hendrix had warned about on 'Evil Woman' and 'Foxy Lady'. 'Venus in Furs' shares a title with a Velvet Underground song, a nineteenth-century novel by Leopold Ritter von Sacher-Masoch (from which we get the term sadomasochism), and a 1969 film, again directed by Jess Franco.

Jus claimed it wasn't really named after any of them: 'It's just meant as an archetypal phrase. To me, it means the sort of archetypal evil woman, a woman that controls men. I mean, every song on the album is about an archetype of evil to a certain extent – as much as I could make it without smoking too much weed and losing sight of the original plan.'[325]

That said, Jess Franco's *Venus In Furs* resonates with the lurid, nightmarish quality of the song. In it a jazz trumpeter called Jimmy Logan becomes obsessed with a blonde-haired woman called Wanda Reed, who is visiting vengeance on a trio of characters who mistreated her in life – we aren't even entirely sure she is still alive, especially since he first encounters her naked body washed up dead on a beach. Each time one of her quarries dies, the film's 'Venus In Furs' theme blares out, played by a band featuring soundtrack composer and keyboardist Manfred Mann. He also appears in the film alongside Logan in Logan's fictional band. Manfred Mann's own band did well out of the horror films of the period: guitarist Mike Vickers wrote the brass-driven funk soundtrack of *Dracula A.D. 1972*.

One of the stand-out sequences in *Venus in Furs* sees a naked Wanda being explored by a middle-aged man in a suit called

Kapp. The contrast between Wanda's flesh and furs, and Kapp's buttoned-up appearance, as well as the camerawork involving multiple perspectives through ornate mirrors, mixes lust, control, dream and reality.

During the film's title sequence the camera pans up Wanda's body, showing her dressed in nothing but underwear, stockings, a brunette bob-style wig and her furs. She is the sixties party girl incarnate, until the solarised, psychedelic effects added to the US print of the film give her an otherworldly quality. This was the effect duplicated on the cover of *Black Masses*. At the end of the film, a title card shows a fragment of a John Donne sonnet: 'I runne to death and death meets me as fast and all my pleasures are like yesterday.' Sex drive and the death drive are one and the same in Franco's film – just as lust is mixed with oblivion in Electric Wizard's song.

The reviews of *Black Masses* acknowledged that this was a different kind of heaviness for Electric Wizard. 'Jus Oborn and Liz Buckingham's guitars are slathered in more reverb, phase and distortion than you imagine possible, creating a maelstrom of fizzing noise that almost sounds synthesised,' wrote *Metal Hammer*.[326]

The review of the album in *Rock Sound* pointed out the strong imagery it evoked, connected to its title, artwork and lyrics: '[I]t's listening to the soundtrack for a demonic ceremony, conjuring up images of underground caves with marks of the Devil carved into the walls, huge pits of fire, psychotic priests sacrificing virgins.' They also swallowed the notion that this was in some sense a 'true heavy metal album' and made it one of their best albums of 2010.[327]

The song 'Scorpio Curse' is marked by the most heavy metal sound on *Black Masses*. It's slower and evinces the pendulum-swinging menace that defines Electric Wizard's earlier work.

Some of the imagery of 'Funeralopolis' returns: the 'dead black asteroid', this time 'crawling with maggots decayed', on a collision course with the sun. It's a song about Lucifer laughing at the damage he has wrought. Cities are full of zombies – Lucifer's children – with their 'deadeyes [sic] and cocaine'. It also might be a fearful song, wary of the very streets the protagonist stalks at night: 'be afraid it's knife or be knifed'.

'It's about our attitude. [That song] is very "fuck the world" in probably the most brutal sense I have ever done,' Jus told *Terrorizer* about 'Scorpio Curse'. 'I was inspired when we were staying in London and I thought about metalheads that lived in the cities; the world isn't a fucking good place right now and anyone that says it is, is full of shit! Electric Wizard is about telling people how it is!'[328]

Electric Wizard's fully fledged embrace of satanic and occult rites meant that the lyrics to *Black Masses* were more inward looking. Only on 'Scorpio's Curse' do we get the broader sweep of cosmic forces and interplanetary derangement that had characterised their songwriting themes from the early days. Jus spent nights staying up until 5 a.m. writing the lyrics to the album, obsessing to the point of madness about every word, and even how they *looked* on the page – whether they were the wrong shape or too long, or had some other esoteric, typographical fault. The evil of the album is inscribed in the words themselves.

The journey into the heart of man's evil that the album charted was countered by the the band's growing popularity in the outside world. In Chudleigh, south Devon, where Jus and Liz were now living, the local youths found out who they were and accosted them with questions about their drug intake and how many groupies they had fucked. One time some fans even staked out their cottage, finding the address because the couple sent merchandise from their home address.

Nearby was the small town of Buckfastleigh and the Holy Trinity church which was burned down in 1992, supposedly by satanists. The church had been the location for a black mass

231

and other satanic shenanigans, including smearing the walls with faeces. No sign of Johnny Alucard from *Dracula A.D. 1972*, sadly. Ne'er-do-wells were attracted to the grave of Richard Cabell, a squire who murdered his wife in the 1600s after making a pact with the devil.

In life, Cabell and his vicious dogs terrorised the village. After he died in 1677, a phantom pack of hounds came to howl at his tomb. This inspired Arthur Conan Doyle to write *The Hound of the Baskervilles*. Cabell's coffin was secured beneath a heavy stone, over which a tomb was built enclosed by iron bars, to prevent his escape.

Electric Wizard lugged their amps and drum kit into the graveyard to pose, playing and headbanging, for a photo in the album sleeve of *Black Masses*. They were jeered by the local hoodies as confused dog walkers looked on. The band still want to play a full gig in the burnt-out ruin of the church.

Black Masses went over well in Europe, especially with the goth crowd, and the lo-fi production pleased black metallers. Electric Wizard started playing bigger gigs and festivals. Mark Lewis came through on his promise from his first phone call with Jus by booking the band a headline appearance at a Portuguese festival called Milhões de Festa in Barcelos, just north of Porto, on 23 July 2010. They had some problems with airport security after Shaun made some comments (for a terse individual he seemed to enjoy opening his mouth at just the wrong moment) but it was smoothed over in time to get to the gig. The show was something of a revelation – there were lots of kids in Electric Wizard T-shirts, some even followed the band down the street, and they started to understand there was a sizable audience in the wider world desperate to see them live. The band got a backline of sufficient power and put on a suitably seismic show.

The booking sealed Lewis's reputation with the band as a master of the dark art of getting great concerts and commanding

better fees for their performances. And for a band that had
grown accustomed to seeing hardly any live income, aside from
a few hundred quid for expenses, his work was very welcome.
Until this point there had been a vacuum where the band's
international touring circuit should have been. Despite the
rumours about the band's reliability, which dated all the way
back to the first reviews of *Come My Fanatics . . .* and one
missed gig in London, Mark Lewis couldn't fault the professionalism of the band. The myth had added to their mystique in the
early days, but it was no substitute for earning a proper living.
Things could get crazy on tour, but they always turned up for
their flights. Soon, high-profile festival bookings fell like dominos
into the band's lap. It wasn't long before Lewis became their
full-blown manager.

At Tuska Rock in Finland in 2011, they played the festival's
second stage on 22 July, before Killing Joke, who were headlining the stage. That was the day of the shootings by Anders
Breivik in Norway, which grounded a lot of flights in the region.
Electric Wizard were supposed to be headlining the second
stage of the High Voltage festival in London the following day.
They didn't think they would make it so they ceded their spot to
newcomers Rival Sons. They did, in fact, make it to the site on
time, but the only taste of heavy metal glory they got was seeing
Judas Priest frontman Rob Halford in a golf cart backstage.

Meanwhile, the legendary Metal Blade label had the rights
to release *Witchcult Today* and *Black Masses* in the US and has
kept them assiduously in print ever since. Yet, their growing
success didn't guarantee stability for Electric Wizard. Rob had
left the band long before the recording of *Black Masses*. In line
with the band's tendency to look at its past not with rose-tinted
glasses but through their shit-stained spectacles, they said that
the band had become lacklustre and deadened after *Witchcult
Today*. Jus sounded strangely like Ricky Gervais's middle

manager character David Brent when he spoke of Rob's departure: 'It's just normal. It happens all the time. It's like being at
the office, I guess. There's always somebody who doesn't work
out.'[329]

Rob's replacement, Tas Danazoglou, was a Greek tattoo artist
who had previously played in a band called Orpheus Child. He
was a positive, enthusiastic presence, very much into the new
satanic leanings of the band. His English was not great and
so, while the rhythm section walked the walk, they couldn't (in
Tas's case), or wouldn't (in Shaun's), talk the talk.

Tas also looked the part – his face covered in tattoos; the band
appeared more out-there than ever. Liz compared it to 'a really
bad motorcycle movie'.[330] (As I've learned from writing this book,
most motorcycle movies are quite bad.) Everyone in the band
was slightly unhinged onstage. At one point, Jus ended gigs by
laying his guitar on the ground and lashing it with a bullwhip.
One night it resulted in breaking his guitar and lacerating
Shaun's forehead. Audiences seemed uncomfortable and confused
during this ritual finale, to the band's disappointment. It was a
short-lived piece of theatre, now confined to history.

'The way they've presented themselves is like a bunch of
outlaws, like some fucked-up biker gang or something from the
late sixties or early seventies that's been fast-forwarded into
the future,' explained Lee Dorrian when he was asked about
the *Black Masses* line-up. 'They're like some outlaw circus and,
because of the way they present themselves, they've become a bit
of an enigma. There's a lot of mystery and aura there that draws
people in and makes them want to know more about the band.
And I think that's something that's really lacking in music these
days. I suppose you could go back to groups like KISS as an
example, bands that had something about them that wasn't just
a straight rock 'n' roll band. If you see photographs of Electric
Wizard now, they look like a collection of individual characters in

this kind of weird cult. It makes you want to be more and more initiated into it. I think you can probably read too much into it, but that's probably quite a good thing from their point of view. The more mystery there is, the better it is for them.'[331]

After *Black Masses*, the demands of playing live only became more intense. Tas had an enthusiasm for the rock 'n' roll lifestyle, but it was countered by the demands of his home life. By this point, Shaun had walked the razor's edge for a long time. Both left the band in 2012.

'Well, Shaun is a bit of a wild creature, and I think being in the real world wasn't really agreeing with him,' Liz told *Decibel* a couple of years later. 'Sometimes when you take something out of the wild, you've gotta put it back. They don't want to be in civilisation. That's pretty much what happened with Shaun. We felt like it was cruel what we did to him. We shouldn't have taken him out of his shed.'[332]

The systematic dismissal of the pair was in line with Anton LaVey's feelings about the need to be careful about any energy that needs to be put into sustaining a relationship within a satanic group that isn't directly focused on the ritual.

'An important point to remember in the practice of any magic ritual or ceremony is: if you depend upon the activities within the chamber to provide or sustain a social climate, the ensuing energy – *conscious or otherwise* – directed towards these ends will *negate* any results you wish to obtain through the ritual!' LaVey writes in *The Satanic Rituals*. 'The line is fine between the desirability for close rapport between participants, and one's need *per se* for close rapport. The ritual will suffer if there is a single person in the chamber who drains the substance from it by his ulterior motives.'[333]

LaVey would have it that the celebrant at a ritual is the sounding board for the emotions of the attendees. Jus and Liz as co-celebrants were responsible for instigating the charge of magical energy that sustained Electric Wizard. Any personalities who would not – or could not – sustain the energy had to be removed, like 'deadwood in any ritual chamber', as LaVey puts it.[334]

Incidentally, in the final chapter of *The Satanic Rituals*, 'The Unknown Known', LaVey states that the 'Satanic Age' would attain maturity in 2002, the year of the first collapse of Electric Wizard. He writes that Satan's reign 'will be filled with wisdom, reason and delight'.[335]

Lacking a bassist and drummer, Jus and Liz also believed they were out of their contractual obligations with Rise Above. They decided to record an EP. Originally pressed on vinyl for a gig at London's Forum venue on 31 March 2012, *Legalise Drugs & Murder* contained two new songs: the title track and 'Murder & Madness'. The EP was released in October 2012 as a cassette with *Terrorizer* magazine. When they later put it out as a digital release in 2016, the song 'Legalise Drugs & Murder' became something of a digital hit, racking up millions of streams.

The song is an anthem for the band in the vein of KISS, recycling lyrics from previous songs ('Black amps tear the sky' from 'Dopethrone' being one), as well as the infamous titular slogan and the refrain 'children of the grave' borrowed from the Black Sabbath song of the same name. It seemed a sly admission to any critics who saw the band as re-treading their lyrical concepts.

The initial vinyl release of the EP had artwork in the style of Sabbath's *Master of Reality* (the album the song 'Children of the Grave' originally appeared on). Already the band was moving away from the *Black Masses* sound, with a pronounced, bowel-scraping bass and a fuller sound, slathered in full-bore distortion and wah pedal. Jus takes a solo and with it a Luciferian flight from the shackles of expectation as to where they might go next. But they carried the *Black Masses* sense of atmospherics with them: an organ joins the ritual and plays the song out in a chilling denouement.

Like 'The House on the Borderland', the song had one of
Electric Wizard's mightiest riffs, here tucked away on an EP.
'Murder & Madness' is more of a jam, propelled by session
player Andrew Prestige's drum groove, layered with whispered
backwards speech and screeching guitar FX.

They debuted the song in front of 2,500 fans at the London
Forum in June 2012 – a collection of people that Electric Wizard
insisted were not the 'cool' crowd, but evidence of the grassroots
support they had amassed. As weed smoke drifted over the
throng, Jus screamed an exultant Ozzy-ish 'Are you high?!' at
his acolytes.

It was getting harder to find the right kind of reclusive people
to slot into the Electric Wizard framework, untainted by the
music business, but they had recruited a new rhythm section by
the time of the performance: Simon Poole on drums and Glenn
Charman on bass. Simon's surname was auspicious, shared with
the name of one of the Dorset coastal smuggling towns nearest
Wimborne. Together, they appeared less outlandish than their
predecessors and gave the band a dependable bedrock from
which to launch their live offenses.

'There used to be a time when the shambolic live performances
of Electric Wizard didn't make sense unless you were on drugs,
so how the Wizard turned into the tight outfit here tonight is
anyone's guess,' wrote *Metal Hammer* in its review of the gig.
'Looking less cartoonish thanks to changes in their rhythm
section, wielding a setlist full of classics – plus a new number,
'Legalise Drugs and Murder' – and accompanied by twisted
lysergic visuals, it's like the quartet channel the horror of Britain's pagan past and expel it in unrelenting waves of doom.'[336]

The 'twisted lysergic visuals' were courtesy of John Moules,
who had just started working with the band. Initially he composed these from hundreds of clips of movies, documentaries and
found footage provided by the band. Moules had been the visual

artist for Hawkwind since 2002. He was the metal guy in their crew who had taken in early shows by Metallica and Slayer in the 1980s, before also taking on, in his words, the 'trippy doom graphics' of Electric Wizard.[337]

'People still find [our success] really hard to believe,' Liz said in an interview in *Terrorizer* when the magazine included the EP as a cassette cover mount. 'We're still perceived as underground but it's getting bigger and bigger. We play gigs where we know it's going to be a good show but there are still promoters out there who don't believe it'll sell, like, "Who is this band? I've not heard of them." It is getting bigger and there are lots more people into the band but it still seems like a secret party.'[338]

When they released the cassette with *Terrorizer* it included four other tracks, including a demo version of 'Satyr IX' from *Black Masses*. The release was credited to Satyr IX productions. In its demo form, the song reeks of evil, burning slowly like the black candle on the album cover. 'I hear the night calling, it knows my name,' Jus sings, and we really believe him – the slow bends and semi-tonal trills of the riff at the halfway mark revel in actual and perceived threat. The song is the energy whirling around the satanic chamber – at first steady, then in frenzy. It is the music of the blood being drawn out of the body by the hungry Countess Irina from *Female Vampire*.

On the six-track EP, there's also a 2012 remix, or 'de-mix', of 'Patterns Of Evil'. Of the two remaining tracks, 'Lucifer (We've Gone Too Far)' sounds almost like the band mocking its own psychedelic, satanic circus. By contrast, 'Our Witchcult Grows . . . ' sounds like an inverted Christmas carol, rather than inverted Catholic mass.

After a ten-year absence, since their tour in 2002, the Electric Wizard party finally returned to the United States to headline the tenth edition of the Maryland Deathfest. Taking place in Baltimore on the weekend of 24–27 May, the 2012 festival was unseasonably hot. But just as Electric Wizard were about to take the stage on the Sunday night, the heavens opened. The deluge was so severe that their set was delayed by twenty minutes.

The audience cooled off and anticipation reached a higher level of frenzy. The band met it by opening with a twelve-minute 'Supercoven'. The orgone energy was flowing strongly at this point as it undulated through the crowd and fans tore down a security fence at the front. The reaction to the following song, 'Satanic Rites Of Drugula', showed how well the Americans had enjoyed the Wizard's output since they last raided the country. The rest of the set was a mixture of classics, new and old, but only 'Black Mass' off the recent album: 'Dopethrone', 'Witchcult Today', 'Black Mass', 'Return Trip', 'The Chosen Few' and crush-the-venue closer 'Funeralopolis'. These songs dominated the band's live ceremonies for the decade that followed.

In 2018, the band put out a soundboard recording of the show on the Lithuanian Creep Purple label. The cover showed a vintage photograph of a naked woman, with a skull in the palm of her hand, not unlike an exploitation-era female Hamlet addressing the skull of Yorick. It was released as a double LP and cassette. The front cover copy promised 'bondage, flagella-tion, torture, domination, satanism': 'Through the ages a myriad of cults have sought to achieve the ultimate sensation in the union of pain and sex'.

Black Masses instantiated an obsession with the depiction of the union of pain and sex that dominated Electric Wizard's aesthetic from that time onwards. The return to America after a decade closed the casket on the painful memories of the disastrous *Let Us Prey* tour in 2002. But maybe they were close enough to Lovecraft's New England for those other gods that had troubled the band before to be roused again.

Because someone from the Wizard's troubled past was about to return.

Chapter Nine
𝔚𝔞𝔨𝔢 𝔲𝔭, 𝔟𝔞𝔟𝔶, 𝔦𝔱'𝔰 𝔱𝔦𝔪𝔢 𝔱𝔬 𝔡𝔦𝔢

icky Kasso came under the influence of Anton LaVey's ideas, with horrific consequences. Kasso bought a copy of *The Satanic Bible* from Village Books on Main Street in the harbour town of Northport, Long Island. It was the early eighties. Kasso was a teenager at the time and what the media would later refer to as a 'self-styled satanist'.

In Northport, Kasso was also known as the 'Acid King' – fond of consuming and selling marijuana, angel dust, LSD and micro-dots of mescaline. In June 1984, aged seventeen, he murdered one of his circle, Gary Lauwers. It was purportedly revenge for Gary stealing some angel dust from him at a party while Kasso slept, and repeatedly failing to pay him back. The nature of the killing made it a global sensation.

Kasso led Gary Lauwers to local spot, Aztakea woods, with two other friends, Jimmy Troiano and Albert Quinones. The location was important. As one boy remembered, 'He was the Acid King and that spot in the woods was his throne room.'[339]

Another boy called Mark Fisher, who had known Kasso since sixth grade, remembered: 'When he was on acid, he'd go back into the dark woods, up in Aztakea, and he would talk to the devil. He said the devil came in the form of a tree, which sprouted out of the ground and glowed.'[340]

240

WAKE UP, BABY, IT'S TIME TO DIE

As Ozzy Osbourne's 'Bark at the Moon' blared from the stereo, Kasso stabbed Lauwers in a frenzy. He taunted him by screaming, 'Say you love Satan!'

When Kasso entered the courtroom to be arraigned for the murder that July, he was wearing an AC/DC T-shirt depicting the devil. In Kasso, the 'satanic panic' of the eighties found its figurehead: a wayward youth out of his mind on drugs, fanatical about heavy metal music, and in thrall to Satan himself.

Blaming juvenile delinquency on the forces of evil wasn't new. It sprung up in the witchcraft trials of the seventeenth century. Horror author Robert Bloch wrote a particularly lurid story in 1958 called 'Spawn of the Dark One', aka 'Sweet Sixteen', in which a civilisation-averse anthropologist lays out his theory that one town's hordes of teenagers on motorcycles with tight jeans and overly made-up faces are the result of their mothers being raped by incubi while their husbands fought in the Second World War. This makes the offspring half-human and half-devil, with an inclination towards lust, rebellion and murderous terror in the long shadow of the war – recycling the horrors of the conflict in their behaviour.

In the eighties, heavy metal became a scapegoat for the shame felt by the beneficiaries of avaricious capitalism. Heavy metal was created in the foundries of the industrial midlands of England, by the children of the traumatised Second World War generation. It was music of the economic recovery, but the social horrors, mental instability and fury of that war were encoded within it as liberal society reckoned with itself during the seventies. Metal musicians' fixation on Satan in the early eighties grew alongside the Great Satan of consumer-oriented living itself. The eighties became a crucible where heavy metal got sucked into a widening gyre created by guilt-ridden evangelicals who were desperate to find ways of diverting attention away from the godlessness of society.

In Northport and far, far beyond, news of the Kasso killing spread like hellfire. What one shop owner dismissed as the action of 'kids high on dope'[341] soon transformed into something more sinister. As Detective Lieutenant Robert Dunn, commander of the Suffolk County Homicide Squad, said, 'This was a sacrificial killing. It's pure satanism.'[342]

The murder became a focus for the community's fears. For Kasso, killing Lauwers had proven both his loyalty to Satan and his manhood. On 7 July, two days after his arrest, Kasso was found dead in his cell, hanging from a bed sheet tied around the bars above his door. He made good on his promise to friends that if he was ever put in jail, he would take his own life.

The media was left with the scant footage and photographs of him just after his arrest. In his sensational and somewhat fictionalised account of the murder (featuring an enormous amount of reconstructed dialogue between the participants throughout), *Say You Love Satan*, David St Clair wrote: '[I]t was his *eyes* – wide, oval, piercing, mocking – that riveted everyone's attention. The reports of satanic rituals and death grabbed readers everywhere, but it was those eyes that put Ricky Kasso on America's front pages and at the top of the six o'clock news.'[343]

Kasso's wild-eyed walk into court, and his strange, drawled yelp, was used at the beginning of the *20/20* news special on satanism – *The Devil Worshippers* – that aired on ABC on 16 May 1985. The sunny, quaint, respectable Main Street can be seen at the opening of Tom Gerald's report: 'Dateline Northport, Long Island – a quiet community rocked by reports a teenager was dragged through these woods toward a late-night ritual of death . . .'

The murder committed by Ricky Kasso, what Kasso came to symbolise, and the media's distortion filter that the whole episode was put through in *The Devil Worshippers*, became the thread running through Electric Wizard's 2014 album, *Time to Die*.

This wasn't the first time Electric Wizard had drawn from *The Devil Worshippers*. The opening of 'Vinum Sabbathi', and *Dopethrone* as a whole, has the infamous sample of Dale Griffis, the police chief of Tiffin, Ohio, from the documentary: 'When you get into one of these groups there's only a couple of ways you can get out: one is death, the other is mental institutions.'

A secret track at the end of *Dopethrone* contains an amusing exchange between *20/20* hosts Hugh Downs and Barbara Walters about the 'serious business' of satanic crimes, downgraded to drug or sex-related felonies because of the pesky absence of evidence. One of the more disturbing elements of the documentary's wider investigation of satanism is the way it gets young children to recount their involvement in the ritual murder of infants. There is a lack of evidence that is concerning, alongside the implication that the nefarious element is not Satan, but rather their parents.

'The problem that exists is that we're getting the stories but we don't have the victims. Once it's proven with one case, it's going to add more credibility to each one of the other cases,' says Sandi Gallant, billed as a 'police intelligence officer'.

'Children are involved in graveyards and crematoria, in funeral parlours, because one of the primary focuses of these people is death,' says Dr Lawrence Pazder in the documentary. Pazder was a psychiatrist and co-author of *Michelle Remembers* with Michelle Smith. The book was published in 1980. It is a discredited account of Michelle Smith's repressed memories of child abuse and possession in a satanic cult, drawn out by hypnosis. Pazder went on to marry Smith.[344]

'Everything is attempted to be destroyed and killed, in that child and in society – everything of goodness. And death is a major preoccupation,' Pazder continues.

Mortality is the major preoccupation of *Time to Die*. 'It's fuckin' heavy man – it mostly concerns death. I think there is

some momentary respite while we meditate on hate and drugs!'
Jus told me at the time. He said he had been pushed back to the
'isolationism and mysticism' of his childhood, as if he had been
sent through 'a time warp'.[345]

The band's teenage obsessions included killers like Richard
Ramirez (the Los Angeles Night Stalker), alongside Ricky
Kasso. These murderers came to be embedded in heavy metal
culture, inspiring numerous songs – creating a feedback loop of
metal, murder and mayhem. Nineteen-eighty-four, the year of
the Kasso killing, when Ramirez's killing spree also began, was
a red-letter year for metal, especially Venom's concept album
where the denizens of hell vanquish their rulers in heaven: *At
War with Satan*. Wimborne was not Northport but the options
for bored kids were the same: drugs, loud music and the occult.
Kasso had first tripped when he was in seventh grade. He drew
a dragon on the classroom board and he saw it start to move. In
their experimentation with LSD, Jus could have been Kasso, but
chose heavy metal over murder.

Liz's aunt lived in Long Island during the Kasso media frenzy.
She had a boyfriend who had been a cop and worked on the Kasso
murder and before that the notorious Amityville murders in 1974
(Kasso himself conducted a ritual outside the Amityville house
one Walpurgis night). The Kasso saga left a strong impression
on law enforcement in the region. In the opinion of the cops,
the kids weren't all right. They were young and inquisitive and
craving experience. They barely understood the consequences of
their actions on others, and themselves. The Kasso murder wasn't
prompted by an inherent, homicidal impulse so much as by an
impressionable boy who nurtured an unhealthy obsession with
death and murder that went too far. The murders were a horrifying expression of wanting to grasp at life by inflicting death.

'I remember reading about it in the newspaper in the back
of my dad's car,' Liz told me in an interview after *Time to Die*

was released. 'That picture of Ricky in his AC/DC shirt, the whole satanic panic. I was totally obsessed and continued to be for many years. Turns out, Justin pretty much was the English Ricky when he was a teenager, he just didn't actually kill anyone. But eerily similar situations happened. We like to think that Ricky would have been into Electric Wizard and would have identified with the lyrics: the outsider, the alienation.'[346]

But what prompted this sudden reversion to these childhood concerns for both Jus and Liz? It was most probably the unexpected return of Mark on drums.

Walter Hoeijmakers, the artistic director of the Roadburn festival in Holland, had repeatedly asked the band to play. That evolved into an offer to curate the Saturday of the festival – to make it like a druggy 'happening' from the glory days of the late sixties, just as the festival was acquiring more artistic leanings. On 19 April 2013, Electric Wizard put on the Electric Acid Orgy. They had some interesting ideas of how to achieve it. Their ambition was a 'multimedia headfuck' and 'total sensory annihilation'.[347]

Electric Wizard wanted it to feel like there was no escape for the audience – disorientation should be baked into the experience. Their idea to fill the corridors of Tilburg's 013 venue full of billowing smoke was rejected on safety grounds. As was giving acid out as the audience arrived. But they had their revenge elsewhere. One was unleashing Genesis P-Orridge on the audience who, within a few seconds of starting, 'had pissed off everyone'.

As a teenager, Genesis P-Orridge – born Neil Megson – heard the words 'COUM Transmissions' in the summer of 1969, when P-Orridge was in the car on a family trip to Wales and started to get disembodied visions and aural hallucinations. P-Orridge went on to set up the COUM art collective in Hull, which in one of their pamphlets stated: 'COUM is the folk music of tomorrow because there is no tomorrow.'[348] After the collapse of industrial pioneers Throbbing Gristle, P-Orridge founded Thee Temple ov Psychick Youth in 1981, another art collective and chaos magic practitioners. They were falsely accused of child abuse in a Channel 4 documentary in the early nineties. P-Orridge went to the United States and became part of a new project called The Process which in part resurrected the symbology of The Process Church of the Final Judgement. P-Orridge embodied a lot of the subversive practices that enthralled Electric Wizard, if not exactly everyone else.

Jus invited one of his favourite original doom acts, Dream Death, to appear, as well as Uncle Acid & the Deadbeats, and seventies psych rockers The Pretty Things. As a band that originated dual guitars in the 1960s and had a claim to write the first rock opera with 1968's *S.F. Sorrow* (Jus struggled to see why anyone would want to make that claim), The Pretty Things were a tough sell to Walter. They tended to play the more general audience Dutch festivals. But he eventually agreed, and The Pretty Things let Jus choose their setlist – heavy numbers only, please. Newer blood, like Satan's Satyrs, also appeared. Their teenage bassist, Clayton Burgess, had previously written to Electric Wizard enclosing the Satan's Satyrs demo and they in turn encouraged Walter to let the band play on the bill.

The Wizard also created a cinema room billed as 'The Electric Grindhouse Cinema' featuring 'the darkest side of seventies' exploitation cinema'. It was a twelve-hour bad-taste marathon from 'when cinema was still considered art and art meant tits and ass to the grindhouse cinemas of the seventies,' said Jus.

'Dirty sleazepit theatres in 42nd street NY, Soho, Copenhagen, Paris, SF, etc. and across the world started out by showing "arthouse" films with an emphasis on sex and/or violence but by the seventies this had devolved into pure sex and violence epics,' he said in advance of the festival. 'Any film with the right ingredients could make money on the thriving underground circuit and some directors used this breeding ground to explore their own cinematic obsessions . . . Jess Franco, Jean Rollin etc. . . . and some just sunk to the bottom for money, money, money . . . Harry Novak, 42nd street S&M etc. . . . either way they got darker, sicker, more depraved, shocking and sleazy. They have a primal roar that is unique compared to modern cinema. They are harsh, violent and evil, like early Sabbath, Stooges, Pentagram, etc. We have handpicked from our personal collection an eclectic selection of obscure oddities.'[349]

The films included *Janie* – about a girl who spontaneously starts killing people to a red-hot, fuzz guitar soundtrack which had been recorded live to the film – and *The Sinful Dwarf* – itself an 'acid test' movie for prospective Electric Wizard band members.

The Sinful Dwarf is a 1973 'dwarfsploitation' film starring Torben Bille, a former Danish children's television presenter, as Olaf Lash. He walks with a cane and wears a red plaid shirt like a lumberjack or grunge musician. He lives with his drink-sodden mother, Lila – an old-time cabaret performer. In their attic they keep naked sex slaves, lured and kidnapped by Olaf. The slaves are kept strung out on heroin supplied by the toy shop's owner (code name 'Santa Claus'). The film was made by Danish porn barons in the UK and features a host of Danish actors putting on terrible cod-English accents.

A couple come to rent a room in the house – the implausible writer Peter and his wife, Mary. As Peter walks the streets in the daytime attempting to meet with 'editors', Mary creeps about the house attempting to discover the source of the strange noises she can hear at night and explain why she sees so many men coming and going. We get to see the couple have sex with each other, as well as the enslaved heroin addicts with their 'clients'. The latter sex scenes, with their frenetic action and backing music, are where the film is at its most distasteful. Jus has described the soundtrack as 'demented proto-Squarepusher-meets-Hendrix', with an intensity that 'blows your mind into space'.[350] As with other films discussed in this book, there is the obligatory flogging scene.

After taking one too many risks creeping about, Mary is captured by Olaf and Lila – they fake a note to Peter saying she's left him. Olaf injects Mary with heroin while bearing his sweaty, toothy grin, from which the film derives its manic intensity. Once you've seen that face, you don't forget it. But the worst is yet to come – Olaf later rapes Mary with the handle of his cane. The 'little bastard', as the police call him, eventually jumps from a window to his death.

The Electric Grindhouse Cinema even featured a hardcore porn section taken from Jus's Super 8mm collection of ten-minute porn 'loops'. He showed Italian pornographer Lasse Braun's seventies loops *Hooked* and *The Vikings* – the latter depicts a Viking raid in full costume with real sex. But Jus felt that might have crossed a line: 'A lot of people didn't seem to think it was acceptable to have twenty-foot spurting cocks,' he later reflected.[351]

Another unhappy customer was the musician who had unwittingly agreed to provide accompaniment whilst the porn loops were playing. He was a good friend of Walter's and complained bitterly. Walter was not happy about it at all. Electric Wizard wanted to create a 'no escape' vibe at the Electric Acid Orgy. It was as if they were paying tribute to the spirit of *Last House on Dead End Street*, a movie notorious for supposedly being 'snuff' – films in which those featured were said to be killed for real – back when the idea of the snuff movie was popularised following the rumours that the Manson Family filmed their murders in the late sixties.

'If *Last House on the Left* is the cinematic equivalent of
Black Sabbath then this squalid, claustrophobic and evil film
is Electric Wizard,' Jus told *Terrorizer* in 2012 of *Last House on
Dead End Street*. 'Its quasi Manson-esque tale of Terry – the
leather-jacketed, speed dealer, Sabbath fan and pornloop
maker – is so nihilistic and grim that the very film seems dirty
and acid-burned. The music and editing borders on genius and
madness and creates the genuine ambience of drugged, satanic
hippies that will rape and kill. That's what we are all about;
from super-groovy, hunchbacked S&M to forcing squares to
fellate severed goat hooves – a truly depraved work of art.'[352]
Electric Wizard running amok with Walter's festival gave the
impression that Liz and Jus were curating their own version of
the movie, with an audience and promoter unable to stop them.

Last House on Dead End Street was made in 1972 but wasn't
released until 1977. Like many films of its ilk, it existed in
multiple forms: one was called *The Cuckoo Clocks from Hell* and
teetered near to three hours long. The film's crew all took pseud-
onyms, leading to rumours it was financed by the Mexican mob.

Director Roger Watkins, originally credited as Victor Janos
(Watkins himself didn't come forward as its director until the
2000s), plays Terry Hawkins, himself a film director. Hawkins
has spent a period in jail for drug abuse. (Watkins purportedly
blew most of the film's three-thousand-dollar budget from his
parents on amphetamines.) When Hawkins leaves prison,
he vows to make a film that will shock everyone to the core.
He recruits a cast of indigent street people, forces a no-hoper
cameraman – a man he's stolen from before – to film it, and
persuades some porn distributors to put it out. The final third
of *Last House on Dead End Street*, where people are brought
to an abandoned warehouse to be killed off, is as grimy as it's
vicious. The soundtrack, though all stock music, is terrifying in
its intensity, particularly during the dismemberment of a young

woman underneath a white cloth. The concealment makes it more horrific, as the blood gushes beneath and stains the bright white fabric.

The film is a comment on the nature of pornography and the human urge for depravity. In its marketing it dared viewers to believe it was real. Once again, the nature of truth and reality itself was in question.

During Electric Wizard's headline set, fans got their first look at the band with Mark back in the line-up. Older, with longer hair, he himself looked more Manson-ish than before. He played the later material steadily – songs like 'Witchcult Today' and 'The Night Child' were fine, even if Mark did seem uncertain where to pause in the former. Being Mark, he added smatterings of fills whenever the opportunity arose. This was a much bigger stage than he had played on before, in front of the giant video backdrop of horror movies. They even started the set with 'Return Trip' in his honour, and 'Son Of Nothing' made it into the setlist for the first time since 2002.

By the time they ended with 'Funeralopolis', the excitement was clearly overflowing. Mark mistimed the drum break into the final speeding barrage, then compensated by going haywire around the kit. It managed to throw Jus and Liz completely off their axis, putting the guitarists at opposite ends of the riff sequence. The beauty in the simplicity of some of their music is that even when this happened, the band were able to convey some cohesion. The song is supposed to end in meltdown, and was extended, like the jams of old, to over thirteen minutes in length. Maybe this was the effect of Nyarlathotep, the Crawling Chaos, dressed in black in the front row – back again to admire his protégés, who had made so much effort to reassert control over their music.

'It was really weird,' Mark said of rejoining the band. 'I did hear something was going on with Shaun, so I wondered about that. And I really wanted to be back in Electric Wizard because it was a big part of my life. I wanted to be jamming with Justin again because that's where my career started, really. So then I bumped into Justin and Liz at the Camden Underworld. I was a bit worried because I thought Justin might be nasty to me. But he was really nice. Shortly after that was when Liz got in contact with me about having a jam with Justin.'[353]

It wasn't as spontaneous as that. Mark had been hovering around the band on social media long before he received that invitation. At first, it wasn't clear he was rejoining at all. He jammed with Jus, then Jus and Glenn (still playing bass with the band). And then finally with Liz. Jus and Mark had spent a decade playing together and fell back into their jamming style of playing.

'Before, Justin had to write everything the way it had to be,' Liz later explained. 'There wasn't a jam component with Shaun, really. With Mark it was a lot easier to just let things go and form naturally and organically.'[354]

'I think we can expect total fuckin' destruction,' Jus told me in January 2014, trumpeting the new material the band was working on. 'We have needed Mark back, he's definitely the best drummer for the Wizard. The whole feud had gone on so fuckin' long that we forgot what it was. As soon as we jammed it was over. Liz was like, "This is meant to be." We have this connection, I guess, from those early jams: my riffs and Mark's style is perfect. Liz is my mirror image so it all makes sense; everything is more volatile and destructive now but I feel happier. Everyone is [playing] a lead instrument again, that's the old way. We kept getting these bloody "followers". We need "leaders" in the band: lead drums, lead bass, lead guitars, lead vocals!'[355]

Initially, Electric Wizard were galvanised by the return of Mark. Jus, in particular, was happy to have his old friend back in the band and to be able to play with him now that the Wizard had grown so significantly. But perhaps like a hit of Ricky Kasso's angel dust it was an intense high that couldn't last. Outside of the creative business of writing new songs, the business of the band itself was darkening. The band saw themselves as out of contract with Rise Above, something which they had signalled with the independent recording of the *Legalise Drugs & Murder* EP. For what became *Time to Die*, the band had established their own imprint, Witchfinder Records, and sub-licensed the recording to Spinefarm Records, part of the Universal Group.

When they travelled to London to meet Mark Lewis and sign the Spinefarm deal, Jus decided to take a piss against Universal's headquarters. This might have been a quasi-tribute to Ozzy Osbourne, who famously bit the head off a dove when meeting executives in the boardroom of CBS records in 1981 and got arrested on another occasion for urinating on the Alamo. Jus simply combined the two, demarcating his own mythic rock territory. He also elected to smoke some homegrown opium in the car when they picked up one of the label's publicists.

The Wizard saw the relationship with a major label as an opportunity to become 'the biggest metal band in the world'.[356] They had never hidden their ambition to be as big as possible. *Black Masses* had given them a taste, and they wanted more. This didn't mean watering their sound down. Quite the opposite, they promised a 'super-heavy' record as if to compensate for making a deal with the man. Nevertheless, Rise Above was furious and soon legal wrangling began, which brought to the surface years of tensions around whether Electric Wizard was getting fairly compensated for their sales.

Back in 2001, *Dopethrone* had clearly been successful and the band got the first inkling they weren't seeing the rewards from what was clearly selling. On their first US tour (itself proof of the album's success), Jus was asked by the *Midwest Metal* fanzine about what most people don't see about the business of being in a band: 'Ah, the fact that we don't get fucking paid! Fucking everyone else gets paid before you, the cunt at the record shop gets paid before you. The bastard answering the phone at the record label gets paid before you, that sucks. Loads of people, myself included, will tell you it's not about the money, but you do this for ten years and if it's not about the money maybe it's time to give up and get a job, you've got to pay the rent! [I]f records are in the shops, someone's making money, there's something getting passed around and it's fucking passing me [laughing]! But I think it sucks because that's why so many bands get down, a lot of bands split up over this shit. If it's not the money, it's that you're putting in a lot of hard work and nothing comes of it. Labels take a lot of money, man, it's like a sick institution, where do record contracts come from? It's like one was invented early on and now all people do is add more pages, our last one was like one hundred pages!'[357]

In 2013 and 2014 there was a sense of brinkmanship about the band in the middle of their legal problems. They were teetering on the edge of existence. They ploughed that negative energy into the rehearsal room. The recording of the album was a purging of those frustrations, but it was also the dark stain left behind after a horrible year – like that left on the ground of Aztakea woods by the decomposing body of Gary Lauwers. Death became an overwhelming concern of the band.

'It was just our state of mind during the creation of the album', Liz reflected. 'First we just wanted to *die* from all the legal torture and abuse that was being flung on us for a year straight. I mean literally a year of constant psychological torture and torment. We just wanted to lay down and die. Then some "good Samaritans" offered us some help with our plight, and subsequently things/people were exposed for what they were really doing and that then made us want to *kill*. I mean, [we were] really, really fucking angry, and so we just put all that hatred and passion into the album. So death is the overriding theme – it was unavoidable. Many things needed to die. Many things did die. And really we just felt like we were gonna die, just trying to finish and put this album out. The thing is cursed. There are double meanings all over it. Is it cursed? Or did we curse it? It continues to be cursed. We've created a monster.'[358]

Nineteen-eighty-four had been a year in the history of heavy metal in which fans felt they could die for their allegiances. Electric Wizard sought to recreate that emotional intensity, as ridiculous as it might be: the belief that metal can end the world and also save your life. But the album is almost about the slow death of that same long-held belief. The tumult of the period marked the end of Electric Wizard's protracted innocence, an innocence that widely defines heavy metal fans. Under the armour of their battle jackets, the perennial metalhead struggle is to protect and maintain that innocence and enthusiasm against non-believers.

Most of the songs on *Time to Die* were written before Mark joined, composed in isolation by Jus and Liz, as they had for the previous decade. They had begun writing the material around the recording of *Legalise Drugs & Murder* without a full-time rhythm section in place. The songs were liberated from the compromises of writing with consideration for other musicians' abilities. The material felt particularly free and something precious that Jus and Liz sought to carry forward and protect. But Mark 'brought a lot of attitude and baggage with him', in Jus's words, which meant he wasn't just taking instruction.[359] Mark left his own imprint on the album.

Glenn left abruptly before the recording of the album, so when it came to recording 'lead bass', Jus drafted in his far-out associate, the eastern European Count Orlof. He was credited with 'session necrobass' in the liner notes. Orlof's style throughout recalls Tim's way of playing, drenched in fuzz and high in the mix, vying for parity with the guitars. Difficult to work with, the secretive bassist disappeared into the shadows after tracking his parts.

The album's production was troubled. The rough tracks laid down at Toe Rag studios (again with Liam Watson) were powerful and pointed to the album being 'the one'. It sounded like everything they had ever wanted to record. But somewhere along the line it got emasculated in the mixing. The band took the mixes to Skyhammer Studios where they worked with producer and Conan bassist Chris Fielding to restore some of its muscle. It was the start of the disintegration of the album project and the atmosphere in and around the band, bit by bit.

The song 'Time To Die' collided the old with the new. It has the pitch-black atmosphere of *Black Masses* but is slower than most of that album. The Hammond organ that breaches through was played by Mark and infuses the song with the horrifying feeling of 'Night of the Shape' on *Let Us Prey*. The song, like the album, sometimes feels like a re-animated *Let Us Prey*, but with the swirling eddies of electricity that have given it life now whirling out of control. It is suffused with a no-fucks-given attitude. Lyrically it doesn't even seem that concerned with its own unease: 'This barren earth defiled by man/Raped and tortured, yeah whatever man'.

The purest expression of the album's nihilism is on 'I Am Nothing'. It's an unusual song for Electric Wizard, with a relentless head-down chug – acting as a steamroller driven by Saturn's Children, the Supercoven and the Old Ones, all recalled in the lyrics to exact remorseless death on 'Mindless slaves to their lust and technology'. The song crashes into itself at the halfway point with explosive chord reverberations and Mark's battery accentuates the uncovering of old horrors. It then yawns into the void of space like 'Weird Tales' before it, succumbing to chaos. The song 'Sadiowitch' does a similar thing by quoting the wailing drum 'n' bass vocal sample of 'Ivixor B' from *Come My Fanatics* . . .

It's like Electric Wizard were forcing themselves, and their audience, back to the scene of their previous crimes to look at what they had done. Ricky Kasso did the same. For weeks after Gary Lauwers' murder, he bragged about what he had done and took disbelieving children to look at the corpse. 'The really gross part was smelling it like four blocks away,' recalled seventeen-year-old Mark Florimonte. 'It smelled like a swamp that was after a thousand years, something just decaying for a thousand years and there's maggots.'[360]

Before Gary Lauwers was murdered, he had accompanied Kasso to attempt to dig up a skull in an American Indian grave-yard to use in a black magic ritual. Kasso was arrested for grave desecration, but Lauwers escaped. 'I creep amongst the graves and crypts/I love the dead, the living make me sick,' Jus sings on 'We Love The Dead'.

Electric Wizard weren't just disinterring their past on *Time to Die*. The attitude and intent of Detroit garage rock was plain in 'Funeral Of Your Mind' – a driving ode to the way Kasso's mind burned out long before his body. It could also be aimed at Mark and Lee Dorrian.

> You never fucking listened anyway
> Now you realise it's too late
> We had all the answers you can't find
> It's the funeral of your mind

'It's pretty much a tribute to all the bands we were digging at the time,' Liz said of the song. 'The whole pace and vibe is very different from all of our other songs. I like playing it a lot, it's a classic dual guitar song. It's the type of song where every instrument is totally doing its own thing, and it all comes together and you really feel what it's all about to be in a band.'[361]

The band seemed to absorb some of the reactionary fervour of
the Baader–Meinhof era again. The spirit of krautrock – Amon
Düül II, Message, Necronomicon, German Oak – is abroad on
the album, if not directly in the sound. What krautrock and the
Detroit sound of the sixties shared was an attacking mode, a front-
foot confrontational style against . . . well, what have you got?

'It's something I've always liked,' Jus told *Guitar World*. 'To
me, a lot of that is early American hard rock. I know punk
appropriated some of the bands along the way. But Grand Funk,
Amboy Dukes and MC5 – they're rock and metal bands. I particularly like that it's very aggressive music that's also politically
and revolutionary based. And especially because of how we were
feeling at the time, I picked up on how that music is just punching you in the face. That was our attitude for our record too, like
"Yeah, you want some? Come on then!" So influences like The
Stooges definitely bubbled to the surface.'[362]

All of this got wrapped into the song 'Lucifer's Slaves'. With
it, the notion of the undead biker gang from *Psychomania* was
back: 'We are Lucifer's Slaves/Born dead we'll never be saved'.
The engine-revving main riff gives Mark the space to hit all his
signature fills. Jus handled the Hammond organ on this one. A
cataclysmic collision midway through simulates the bike careening off the road, killing all the civilians in its path. It's also
the doomiest moment on the whole album, straight out of the
playbook of older songs like 'Chrono.Naut'. Instead of launching
the song out into the void, it seems to open a black hole in the
centre of the song. It is the ultimate act of destruction and one
also of creation: 'We are the Antichrists/We are the New Reich/
Fuck your world, fuck everything . . .'

The invocation of the 'New Reich' signals its representation of
biker gangs who used the iconography of the Second World War
with abandon, even down to wearing German military helmets of
the period. The proliferation of swastikas and iron eagles used by

COME MY FANATICS

The Skulls gang in the Roger Corman-produced 1967 biker film *Devil's Angels* (directed by Daniel Haller, who also made *The Dunwich Horror*) makes this uncomfortably clear. What makes *Devil's Angels* more jarring is the casting of John Cassavetes as the gang's clean-shaven and oddly conscientious leader, Cody. The film was released the same year he starred as an imprisoned member of the Chicago Outfit crime syndicate, with an intense problem with authority, in *The Dirty Dozen*. Cody ends up deserting his own gang at the end of *Devil's Angels* as they go on the rampage against his wishes.

When I spoke to Jus about the film he sneered at Cody's dewy-eyed departure in its finale – is that tears in his eyes, or just the headwind? But I wonder whether Jus has identified with Cody in the moments he has been the reluctant leader of a bunch of reprobates, and when he's been compelled to be the 'reasonable one'. There have been several times he could have ridden off towards the horizon.

In Alex R. Stuart's 1972 New English Library novel *The Devil's Rider*, biker gang the Sons Of Baal are led by Sam. Sam looks like Rasputin. He has eyes 'which beam out ancient energies'.[363] He is a conduit for the 'Diamond Nine', the manifestation of a cosmic 'vampire energy' with an 'enslaving hatred for the human race'.[364] Not unlike the beat prose-poetry of *Freewheelin Frank*, the book – set in England – is written in odd, highly stylised transatlantic prose, where phrases like 'the necrobike wailed the banshee blues' are admissible.[365]

Anton LaVey had designated 'nine' as Satan's number. There is a myth of Nine Unknown Men carried down the years and reported in sixties' bestseller *The Morning of the Magicians* (more of which later): they are guardians of science practised in a moral way, a notion which *The Devil's Rider* subverts.

The novel also plumbs ancient Assyrian mythology – Ishtar and Marduk, rather than Christ and Satan. The rape of women

258

is another recurrent feature of biker lore – even if the bikers are being falsely accused, or framed, as in *The Northville Cemetery Massacre*. The confrontation with authority in *Devil's Angels* pivots on the bikers being accused of raping one of the town of Brookville's beauty queens. In *The Devil's Rider*, this happens at a rock concert of a band called the Dear Departed, after which the victim – a plant used by the police – becomes the 'old lady' of one of Sam's lieutenants.

The main female protagonist of the novel is Ish, who is quiet and seems disapproving. She represents a counter-energy to Sam and The Nine: 'an alternate essence with different wishes for mankind.'[366] The story reaches its climax at the dawn of midsummer at Stonehenge, with hundreds in attendance. The bikers are slaves to Sam's grander scheme – a sublimating energy meltdown where Sam and Ish vanish.

As they prepare to convene at Stonehenge, at one point the gang are being watched by a hidden couple on the B3048, northeast of Andover. With his supernatural senses, Sam points in their direction forty yards away, even though they are invisible. Apprehended, Sam's piercing eyes drain their energy. Sam's eyes still glow when the moon disappears behind a cloud.

The scene is reminiscent of one in *Say You Love Satan*. Ricky Kasso's friend Jimmy Troiano looks out of the window of the psychiatric hospital he's in and sees the back of Kasso's head in another wing. Troiano had no idea Kasso had also been admitted to the hospital. He pledges his love to Satan (in the rather needy way they do throughout the book). He calls on Satan to get Kasso to turn his head. It works. The doctors refuse to let them meet until Kasso – who is in there for psychiatric examinations into his suicidal tendencies – attempts to hang himself in protest. When Troiano is reunited with Kasso, St Clair writes, he saw that 'the glitter in his eyes was even stronger'.[367]

Like Sam in *The Devil's Rider*, Ricky Kasso pledged himself
to explore death. He daubed satanic graffiti on the gazebo in
the park by Northport's harbour, although in the substances he
used, he seemed to resist the really hard stuff – the black drug
which takes the soul away, and replaces blood with 'her venom',
as heroin is personified as an evil mistress on *Time to Die*'s
'Sadiowitch'. The other reason was that it was easier to sell the
softer drugs to the younger kids – cocaine and heroin meant
dealing to adults.

Time to Die isn't only directly about Kasso, or just about the
state Electric Wizard found themselves in around this time. It is
about how those situations were distorted and manipulated by
other entities, particularly the media. 'Destroy Those Who Love
God' is named for something spoken by one of the children made
to recreate a satanic ritual in *The Devil Worshippers 20/20*
special. The instrumental makes the documentary the 'ritual of
death' itself, with its fixation on child abuse, tortured animals
and human corpses. 'Police have found no proof and made no
arrests, but that's no surprise,' the reporter says, blissfully free
of irony.

The documentary soon moves to put the blame at cinema
and heavy metal's door. At one point, they play Led Zeppelin's
'Stairway to Heaven' in reverse so we can discern the message,
'My sweet Satan'. But what was the song the kids in Northport
played while they scrubbed the gazebo clean of its graffiti?
'Stairway to Heaven', played forwards, as God intended.

Saturn has played its role at the conclusion of two previous
Electric Wizard albums: 'Saturn's Children' on *We Live* and
'Saturnine' on *Witchcult Today*. As the character Pam puts it
near the beginning of 1974's *The Texas Chainsaw Massacre*,
from an astrological perspective Saturn is a 'bad influence'.
The planet is retrograde during the terrible events of that film,
enhancing what she calls its 'malefic' character.

'They have a primal roar that is unique compared to modern cinema.' Jus on the films handpicked by the band as part of the Electric Acid Orgy at the Roadburn Festival in 2013.

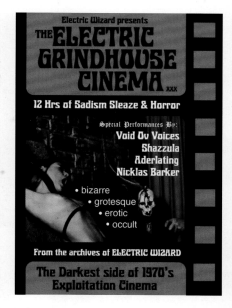

Poster for a 2013 secret gig as Legalise Drugs & Murder in Stockholm.

The horrific *Last House on Dead End Street* (1977).

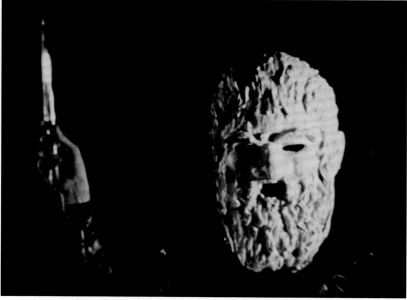

Back from the dead: Mark returns to the Electric Wizard lineup for *Time to Die*.

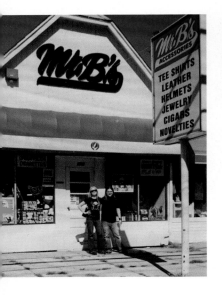

Jus and Liz outside Mr. B's Accessories in Northport, Long Island, in 2003. This was where Ricky Kasso acquired the knife with which he went on to commit murder in 1984.

Mark, now with longer hair and bigger cymbals, rehearsing with Jus during the *Time to Die* period.

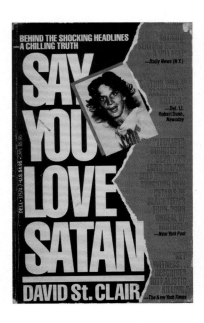

The Devil himself: Ricky Kasso's unnerves on the cover of this infamous true-crime version of events.

The *Time to Die* lineup:
(L-R) Clayton, Liz, Mark
and Jus.

Poster for the 'Sadiowitch'
video directed by Shazzula.

Poster for the band's first
performance at the Camden
Roundhouse in 2015.

More than a shade of
Freewheelin Frank in this
2015 US tour poster.

Jus and Clayton going to
it at New York's Webster
Hall in 2015.

The Chosen Few
roar through the
Ritz, Manchester
in 2014.

Pushing the boundaries of
human decency in tour posters
from 2017-2019.

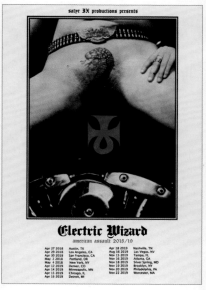

Necromaniacs Unite! Promo for *Wizard Bloody Wizard*.

Subtitled *Secret Societies, Conspiracies and Vanished Civilisations*, the cult classic of 'fantastic realism'.

The *Wizard Bloody Wizard* lineup with Simon (left) and Clayton (right).

Wizard Bloody Wizard is unleashed.

Up on the moor, no one
fucks with Electric Wizard.

Liz and Simon onstage
during the 2019 US tour.

The lineup for Psycho
Las Vegas in 2019 with
the Wizard one of the
headliners.

Liz onstage at Psycho Las
Vegas with her customised
1967 Gibson SG.

The cover of 'L.S.D.', released in 2021.

Electric Wizard at Desertfest London 2022 with Haz on bass.

On a triumphant return trip to the Camden Roundhouse at Desertfest London in 2022.

WAKE UP, BABY, IT'S TIME TO DIE

Here, the devourer of his children is supplanted on the instrumental 'Saturn Dethroned' as crows caw in the background, and the bass, Hammond and drums jam the album out. A crow cawed after Kasso had finished stabbing Gary Lauwers, which he took as a sign from Satan that his work was done. But perhaps the message here is that, similarly to *Dopethrone*, the work of authority and systems of oppression is never over – society will keep devouring its children.

The album ends as it begins, with the sound of a stream of water – back to the false rural idylls of Northport, and Wimborne. The album's front cover was drawn by Jus in a late-night frenzy, the band's name draped around an inverted cross as multiple eyes stared back at him – at points it felt like he had overdone it and it was mocking him. The inner sleeve has photos of the satanic graffiti on the gazebo in Northport. The gatefold of the album was a photograph (taken by Liz) of a body posed face down next to a stream, wearing an Electric Wizard, inverted-Ankh patch on the back of a denim vest. One of the chosen few – snuffed out.

The lyrics to 'Funeralopolis' are reproduced and laid over the photograph – a timeless message that binds the two eras of the band together.

Funeral planet
Dead black asteroid
Mausoleum
This world is a tomb
Human zombies
Staring blank faces
No reason to live, dead in the womb
Death shroud existence
Slave for a pittance
Condemned to die

261

Before I could breathe
Millions are screaming
The dead are still living
This world has died
Yet no-one has seen . . .

The last word on *Time to Die* also harks back to *Dopethrone*.
It is left to Chief Dale Griffis, from the start of 'Vinum Sabbathi', who adds one final warning about getting into a satanic
group – or a rock group of Electric Wizard's nature – with an
extended version of that original sample: 'When you get into one
of these groups there's only a couple of ways you can get out:
one is death, the other is mental institutions. Or a third: you
can't get out.'

Electric Wizard had always treated the last track on their
albums as if it pointed to the next record: a taste of things to
come. This wasn't the case with *Time to Die*. 'Saturn Dethroned'
could easily be their epitaph. The future looked bleak. 'We've
been through it all, and shit doesn't change,' Jus said after its
release. 'Nothing gets better. It isn't like you're going to live a
happy life and everything will be great. That's all bullshit. It
still fucking sucks.'[368]

When Electric Wizard invited Clayton Burgess, bassist with
Satan's Satyrs, to audition over a weekend in late November
2013, he didn't think twice. A stranger in a strange land,
they picked Clayton up at Taunton bus station and drove him
'thumping and bumping' down country roads in a jeep back to
their lair. It was his first time in England and, in his words,
'utterly surreal'. Burgess, who then joined on bass, was only
twenty-one but his creativity and fluidity in Satan's Satyrs

had impressed Jus and Liz. The Wizard's invitation to play the Roadburn Festival in 2013 had blown his mind. Playing on a bill with his heroes spurred on Satan's Satyrs to take their band to the next level.

'They fuckin' rip . . . I honestly don't hear that much music that has any real energy and aggression these days,' Jus told *Vice*. 'You need people screaming, "What the fuck is this racket? Turn it off . . ." and that's exactly what I thought when I heard Satan's Satyrs.'[369]

Clayton's first gig was February 2014. He said he learned enough from Jus and Liz to fill a library, but he also watched the tail-end of the drama of *Time to Die* unfold as a fan. He could see Electric Wizard from the inside and outside.

'What I love about the band still is their connection to young people,' Clayton said in an interview years later. 'It's not about the thirty-five-year-old, tattooed-up, bearded, trucker-cap guy. Sure, they'll be at the concert too, but it's really about the young people. Just as in the same way it was when all our favourite groups in the seventies were playing to the youth. They were playing to the kids. Electric Wizard has that attraction and is grabbing that section of the audience, that demographic. And I love that about it. That youthful energy is such an important element of rock 'n' roll. Rock music, heavy rock, whatever you want to call it – it's integral.'[370]

Any despondency in the band now centred on Mark. He played about ten gigs with Electric Wizard after he rejoined, travelling to rehearsals every weekend on his motorbike. Mark was prominent in the marketing of *Time to Die*. He appeared in a coffin for publicity photographs and was depicted in the T-shirt sent out as part of a bundle with the album. But the wheels came off at the Temples Festival on 2 May 2014 in Bristol. The band headlined the Friday night, atop a bill of friends in Brutal Truth, Blood Ceremony, Moss, Witchsorrow and others. They started the set with a new song, 'Incense For The Damned', the song that opens *Time to Die*. The album wouldn't be released for another five months.

'Incense For The Damned' had been around in one form or another since Shaun's time in the band. The song opens with funeral-march drum hits, akin to the huge, stabbing chords of Gustav Holst's 'Mars, the Bringer of War' from *The Planets*. It's a dictatorial statement of intent where a life condemned to monotony is liberated and lifted by marijuana. 'Like Caligula is how I would treat this world if it were mine . . .' Jus sings.

But Mark was all over the place. It wasn't a complicated drum pattern – he simply couldn't nail it down at the gig. For a band now accustomed to their gigs being large ceremonial affairs, this was a ritual humiliation.

'It was a disaster,' Jus later told *Decibel* magazine. 'Mark was drunk – and more. And he had other problems weighing on him that didn't put him in the right frame of mind. We'd been super-fucking-tolerant for a long time, but there's only so long you can drag your name through the dirt.'[371]

'I had a few too many drinks,' Mark conceded in the same interview. 'That's just rock 'n' roll. The thing is, I've never had any problems with drinking and drumming, but that night something hit me for six. It was just not a very good gig, really, but I feel like it wasn't all down to me.'[372]

After the disastrous performance, Mark Lewis put it to the band that they ask Mark to sit out the summer's remaining gigs (including a headline slot at Hellfest in France). Lewis suggested he ask Simon Poole to temporarily come back in on the drum stool. No one wanted to fire Mark, not least because of how excited they had been to get him back in the group, but Liz and Jus had grown increasingly frustrated with Mark's 'performance impotence' on bigger stages, as well as his excessive drinking. He was even struggling with the *Dopethrone* material. Something was bothering him, preventing him from excelling in this line-up. He seemed to be getting off on pressing the self-destruct button. It turned out Electric Wizard couldn't reanimate part of the corpse of the former line-up and expect it to function properly.

'When you break up with someone, you should stay broken up,' Liz told *Decibel*.[373]

Lewis rang Mark and suggested he take a break, just two or three shows, to sort himself out and get off the drink. He was even ready for Mark to say, 'No,' and carry on in the band regardless. But Mark began crying down the phone. 'I can't believe you're sacking me!' he sobbed. Lewis tried to placate him, repeatedly saying that he wasn't sacked. But Mark hung up. The whole affair felt like both a cry for help from Mark and a dagger to the heart of the band. Mark later sued for what he saw as his fair share of publishing royalties from the album, which was temporarily withdrawn while that was settled.

More immediately, Simon was successfully drafted back to complete the summer's festival run and he learnt the new songs at speed. It put him in the odd position of replacing both a replacement drummer and a founding member in one. It was the kind of loyalty to the cause that meant he remained in the band.

The legal disputes with Rise Above and Mark soured *Time to Die* for the band. It was hard to dissociate it as a work of art from the circumstances of its creation. The *Decibel* interview was a forum for a war of words between Jus and Lee Dorrian over their dispute. 'I owe somebody a smack in the mouth,' Jus said bitterly.[374]

It was a question of whose version of events was closest to the objective truth. In the aftermath of the killing of Gary Lauwers, Kasso's friend Jimmy Troiano was put on trial for second-degree murder. The arguments revolved around whether Troiano held Lauwers down while Kasso stabbed him, and the two differing

confessions Troiano had signed. All of this was complicated by
the state of mind of the participants. The other witness, Albert
Quinones, was so bombed out of his skull on LSD and angel dust
that he was transfixed by a tree seeming to intermittently bend
to touch the ground and then be overrun with cats.

In his summing up, Troiano's defence attorney had this to say
about the 'truth' of the matter: 'I will argue that there remains
a reasonable doubt, in fact, much more than reasonable doubt,
as to what is real and what is not . . . and to what is truth and
what is not, as to what is believable and what is not.'[375]

What was left after Mark's second departure from Electric
Wizard was the attitude of *Time to Die*. As a partial return to
Electric Wizard's roots, it had been a creative success. After the
psychedelic pop malevolence of *Black Masses*, it was a confrontational mind-mangler of an album. Simply, it was a much heavier
proposition: the sound of a band with everything to lose and
embracing the fact.

'A lot of outside influences were making us a bit paranoid,
feeling everyone was against us, so it was quite an aggressive
album,' said Jus looking back. 'But we thought we'd stay on it,
because the last few albums have been quite cinematic, based
on movie stuff, the occult, black magic. We thought we'd do one
that's a lot more realistic, a lot more serious, at least on one
level.'[376]

'It's just gotten to that point where if you give a fuck, you're
contrived,' Liz said. 'That's not creating real, honest music any
more. You have to create what's in your soul and heart. If you
give a fuck too much, that's impossible to do. But after the year
we've had, it was easy to say, "I don't care. I just want to write
the heaviest music possible. Fuck it, here it is."'[377]

'I don't think we do give a fuck about anyone,' Jus said,
sounding like he had in the old days. 'Not like, "Fuck everyone,"
but I don't give a fuck what people think about our band or our

music. I've had enough of the government and being pushed around by any motherfucker. I've had it. That's what this album is about. That's why I've moved miles away. I don't give a fuck about anyone. This is our statement. If people don't like it, I don't care. I've had it with "liking" and "sharing" and all this bullshit. Bands used to be *badass*, you know? Now they're just trying to please everyone and sell fucking records. I don't know what they're trying to do. It's not rock 'n' roll, anyway. Not to me.'[378]

He might not have cared if anyone liked it, but the critics did receive the album well. By this point, Electric Wizard was getting mainstream music press coverage in places like *NME* and much of it pointed to how full of life this morbid album found the band.

'The latest effort from England's reigning doom entities Electric Wizard deserves every accolade thrown its way,' trumpeted *Pitchfork*. 'Following their last disappointing effort, *Time to Die* holds its listeners close, inviting us into a warped echo chamber of horrors filled with eldritch evil . . . It's rare to see a band as established as Electric Wizard come back from a slump with renewed vigour and a fresh shot of hellfire coursing through their veins, but with *Time to Die*, they've both surpassed expectations and proved that they're still as vital as they ever were.'[379]

'Greening puts in a remarkable performance, complete with seemingly endless tom rolls that Bill Ward could be proud of,' wrote *Drowned in Sound*. 'It's great that Electric Wizard are still around and are still pushing the limits of heavy music – not just for metal itself, but for British metal in particular.'[380]

'Immersed in macabre kitsch and THC'd into hellish oblivion, the Wizard's trademark sound eschews experimentation in favour of the fervent pursuit of inconceivable, remorseless heaviness, replete with mesmerising repetition and enough reverb to make the whole harrowing enterprise feel like a slow-motion nose-dive into the abyss,' wrote the *Guardian* in a review which favoured long sentences. 'The bleak, lumbering likes of "I Am Nothing" "and Lucifer's Slaves" are the mutant children of Black Sabbath's revered blueprint, driven by anti-cosmic desolation and wielding immense hypnotic power.'[381]

Electric Wizard refused to die. When I interviewed Liz after the release of the album, I asked her what comes after death – where does Electric Wizard go next?

'It goes to hell,' she replied.[382]

Chapter Ten
As Saturn's children dream

As suicidal as *Time to Die* sounded, it was very successful. It charted in the US, UK and mainland Europe. If, when they had formed, you'd told Electric Wizard – or Sunn O))), or Sleep, for that matter – that in 2015 they would be selling out theatres, playing big stages at festivals and growing their audiences, they would have had little reason to believe you.

Doom metal had crossed a threshold and received broader artistic appreciation. Even the *Guardian*'s review of *Time to Die* noted the phenomenon: 'Electric Wizard will probably regard their recent assimilation into the world of hipster approval as an accidental bonus wrung from their own slithering persistence.' Signing to a major label brought its fair share of 'Shoreditch berks',[383] it sneered.

The band were not complaining. Riding high on the popularity of *Time to Die*, they headlined the London Roundhouse in May 2015, with Simon back on drums and Clayton still on bass. It was a triumphant moment to sell out a venue which had hosted Led Zeppelin, Hawkwind and the MC5. That hipster embrace saw them invited to play much more diverse festivals, like Primavera Sound in Barcelona – where Tyler, the Creator's thudding headline set drowned out the echo from Sunn O)))'s appearance.

'We always had a fantasy that we'd end up in the tabloids, getting busted for having satanic sex orgies,' Jus told the

Guardian that year. 'We're always having them but no one cares! We were always the greatest band that you've never heard of, but it's starting to turn around. The world's our oyster now. We're aiming for the Royal Albert Hall next . . . for an English rock band, that's the crowning glory, isn't it? We'll all crash our Lamborghinis afterwards and that'll be the end of it. There's a sense of inevitability sometimes. I get scared that the grim reaper's there behind me, cackling.'[384]

The previous October, the band played at the Ritz venue in Manchester, a gig promoted by Kamran Haq at Live Nation. Haq went on to book bands for the Download Festival at Donington Park (including Electric Wizard). The band had done a signing session earlier in the day for which Jus wore a pair of black leather gloves.

Their live performances had reached a level where they felt they were wrangling huge forces – they sounded enormous, largely thanks to Konstantinos 'Costa' Kostopoulos, who had handled their front-of-house sound for many years at that point. But the more powerful they became, the more draining the exertion of playing live. When the band came offstage it was like they had been at war. Electric Wizard often needed a week to reacclimatise to the pace of 'normal' life after a tour. War has physical and mental consequences.

The Wizard also felt a sense of shock in the wake of *Time to Die*. Somehow, they had pulled it off. They had made a success of the most turbulent period in the band's troubled history – by choosing to sink to the bottom. They took it on the chin, like a true heavy band should. There was something operatic about *Time to Die* – over an hour of depressed and mean-spirited doom metal: it was the whole Electric Wizard experience. But it had left its scars – financial and personal. The changing world around them was not helping. More and more it was starting to resemble Amon Düül II's song 'Apocalyptic Bore', a world with neither hate, nor love – a chastened place where everything is grey and boring.

Jus had been feeling nostalgic for a while. Nostalgia can make you vulnerable, and he probably wouldn't have gone through the process of recruiting Mark if he hadn't been pining for the past. After his second tenure in the Wizard, Mark himself went on to form a new band with Tim and Lee Dorrian, called With The Dead, who released their self-titled album in October 2015. It was hard not to see Mark's seeming self-sabotage at the Temples Festival the previous year as a ploy to get sacked and use the ensuing drama to launch With The Dead. Their album might be the only example of a metal diss record. Jus was certain the 'fuck-you' Dorrian shouts on their song 'The Cross' is his ex-associates taking aim at him.

Certain musical influences continued to hound Jus and Liz. The garage rock elements of *Time to Die* had worked well. Jus had often fantasised that in 1971 a tunnel had been constructed between Detroit and Wimborne – connecting the two working-class population centres and smuggling the Detroit sound into the underground tunnel network of the Dorset town.

Living in a secluded farmhouse in Devon was also working for the couple. In their new location they rehearsed in the darkness of the barn and came into the light to record in the studio which they had been diligently assembling in a room off the house's entranceway. The walls of the house were two to three-feet thick, as had been the walls of Lodge Farm, the fourteenth-century hunting lodge where King Crimson rehearsed in 1981. As Robert Fripp explained in the *Robert Fripp: New York – Wimborne* documentary he made in the mid-eighties: when Crimson played in the front room they couldn't even be heard in the kitchen.

Jus and Liz had long harboured a desire to self-produce their albums, and the production challenges of *Time to Die* forced them to act on it. The Wizard's farmhouse was partly Victorian

and gave them the feeling of recording in a place that was a
cross between the eighteenth-century ex-workhouse Headley
Grange and the Welsh cottage Bron-Yr-Aur – two locations
where Led Zeppelin recorded and wrote music. Not that Led
Zeppelin had to spend a year struggling with vintage equipment
bought from eBay.

Jus acquired a Tascam sixteen-track tape machine, Mackie
desk, Neve preamp, Copicat tape delay, Roland space echo, and a
couple of other reverbs and compressors. It was a simple set-up
designed to keep a short, uncluttered path for the sound signal
to follow from band to tape. Jus and Liz had observed Liam
at Toe Rag Studios enough to know that this was the secret to
keeping the sound live and raw.[385]

That vintage sixteen-track recorder broke and caused a
six-month delay in recording. Conan's Chris Fielding (who had
worked on the later mixes of *Time to Die*) was on hand for
technical assistance. The doom alliance also extended to Virginian band Windhand and their guitarist Garrett Morris, who
engineered some of this next album, including the basic tracks,
so Jus could concentrate on playing. They had worked together
on the 2016 album *Still They Pray* by the Virginian band Cough.
Jus produced Cough's album and its first track in particular,
'Haunter of the Dark', with its nod to the Lovecraft story, has
the magnificent roar of 'Return Trip' and 'Supercoven'.

The Cough project provided some vicarious thrills at a time
when Electric Wizard were resetting their sound. Cough drew
the line at titling their album *Still They Prey* in case it was
perceived as a homage to *Let Us Prey*. What did it matter?
Electric Wizard had lifted their fourth album title from the
Judas Priest song 'Let Us Pray/Call for the Priest' from 1977's
Sin After Sin album.

With a little help from their friends – and the operational
inconveniences of true independence aside – Electric Wizard was

in control of the destiny of its sound. In building and perfecting the home set-up, which became known as the Satyr IX recording studio, Jus worked over his vocal takes twenty or thirty times a song. Liz had pushed Jus in the studio ever since she joined the band. As the ultimate fan-turned-member she held Electric Wizard to a gold standard of heaviness. Most importantly, up on the moor in Devon, no-one fucked with them.

'When I was younger, television was the thing that always dragged you in, like social media is today,' Jus told *Metal Hammer*. 'But when I stopped watching TV, it was a really freeing thing, to not be on the same wavelength as everybody else, with the same news, the same thoughts, the same reference points. Things have only got worse now, so being completely out of the loop will either be distressing or entertaining, depending on your point of view. I must admit, we are really digging it.'[386]

Primitivism became an aesthetic choice. The band was rebounding hard against what had come before. They went back to old blues and rock 'n' roll records, to get the original blood rush that made that music so vital and provocative at the time it emerged: leather-bound Gene Vincent was a role model. Electric Wizard's sound had morphed down the years, from its early doom origins of Trouble, Saint Vitus and Pentagram, it had quickly incorporated more leftfield influences: Loop, My Bloody Valentine and dance culture. Electric Wizard's music was changing again, in a band where change is a continuum of sorts.

Heavy music culture had become more stratified as the second decade of the twenty-first century evolved. The proliferation of choice and the flattening of the landscape on digital platforms meant that bands clung to genre labels to define what they were doing. But truly great bands exist beyond genre bounds – their name is enough.

On the one hand, Electric Wizard was always developing. Each release had marked sonic differences. This was largely down to textures, tones and production. But live, songs that were written twenty years apart shared the same shapes and intensity, bound together by the lyrical motifs. This led to a feeling of deliberate arrested development, or evolution in a bubble. Already physically displaced, as they started to shape their next album, it wasn't the first time Electric Wizard had felt left outside of the times they were living through.

'I feel like doom grew away from us,' Jus told *Iron Fist* magazine. 'We haven't changed, but the world keeps moving around and changing and developing, and I guess we've been left behind somewhere. I mean a heavy band should be about the music – I remember a few times in the past in this band where we played, we rented the rehearsal room, we got the fifty-watt combos, we were rehearsing, and then someone's coming in telling us to turn down – and we're playing pure shit fifty-watt combos! Why the fuck do we have to turn down? Then I realise it's the music – there's something about creating resonation, creating good music and heavy music that's beyond amplification and beyond sound. You can play it clean, you can play it on an acoustic guitar, it would still have that effect on people.'[387]

Jus and Liz felt they didn't have anywhere left to go with the downtuned sound, droning on the low E and lashing the audience with distortion. This time the apostasy was against what was expected of them – the new album was to be a palate cleanser after the bitter pill of *Time to Die*. They resolved to do something different and, to them, terrifying: take the foot off the pedal.

Electric Wizard's ninth album, *Wizard Bloody Wizard*, was released on 17 November 2017. It was billed as 'six hymns to death, drugs, sex and violence'. Its title immediately recalled Black Sabbath's fifth album, *Sabbath Bloody Sabbath*, released in 1973. Liz handled the photography for its cover (as she had for *Black Masses* and *Time to Die*): a female torso with the

album title stencilled in blood across the stomach. There was
a more extreme version with the title carved into the stomach,
but the band chose the more schlocky option, in keeping with
their aesthetic. This could have been *House Of Whipcord* star
Penny Irving's torso – it wasn't a disturbing image by any
means, instead cheaply titillating in a seventies way, with horror
overtones.

Liz tackled the issue of the cover's nudity directly: 'It's heading towards not being allowed to do anything anymore, and not
being allowed to think for yourself, when you should be able to.
It's Victorian, some stuff. What's wrong with breasts? Why have
they become obscene, according to Facebook? It's bizarre.'[388]

'I like the art of the record sleeve,' Jus concurred. 'I wanted to
design one where you go into a record shop and think: I've got
to hear this. That's how I approach music – with wonder. The
cover's also tongue-in-cheek. The title, even though it's a Sabbath reference, was meant to be a withering English comment
said by Alan Partridge or in *On the Buses*. "You've got a naked
body, you've got blood on it. Wizard bloody wizard . . . "'[389]

In an episode of *I'm Alan Partridge* called 'To Kill a Mocking
Alan', from 1997, the outmoded and cringeworthy former television presenter (played by Steve Coogan) assails two Northern
Irishmen with his opinion of U2's song about the Bloody Sunday
shooting of unarmed protesters in Northern Ireland, 'Sunday
Bloody Sunday': 'It really encapsulates the frustration of a
Sunday, doesn't it? You wake up in the morning, you've got to
read all the Sunday papers, the kids are running round, you've
got to mow the lawn, wash the car, and you think, Sunday,
bloody Sunday!' The Partridge reference flew over people's
heads when *Wizard Bloody Wizard* was released. Despite long
having given consciously and unconsciously hilarious interviews,
that kind of humour was not something Electric Wizard was
known for.

One of the album's prerogatives is the submergence in, and submission to, the feminine. The serpentine blues riff descent of 'Wicked Caresses' sees it coil its way back towards the sentiment of 'Priestess Of Mars' from *Let Us Prey*. Whereas that song was about someone lost and desperately searching the terrain of inner and outer space for 'enchanted flesh beneath the moon', in 'Wicked Caresses' she is already part of the black mass: 'Inside her coffin/She spreads her wings'. Instead, Jus sings from the perspective of a man who wants to be enslaved by an ice maiden's touch: 'I need her evil but she's so cold'.

Like its cover, the lyrics of the songs are full of wry mischief. Jus and Liz spoke about having a new, positive mindset. It was the positivity that came with self-righteous rebellion. The band had always pulled its audience away from day-to-day reality, but this album crafted a more communal atmosphere after the solipsism of *Time to Die*.

'I think that is the real message of the band,' said Jus. 'I mean the negativity and everything else is just accepting the world for what it is and going for it, but the MC5, White Panther kind of rock 'n' roll fucking-in-the-streets, that is our real goal. I just like singing about it – the world's like that, I don't want to paper over it or pretend it's something different and start singing love songs or whatever, but I think with music, however hate-filled the music is, the people who're listening to the music are enjoying it, and you can't escape it – it's a positive thing!'[390]

The White Panther Party was founded as an act of anti-racist, counterculture solidarity with the Black Panther movement in 1968. For a long time, Electric Wizard has used the White Panther manifesto on their Facebook page: 'We demand total freedom for everybody! And we will not be stopped until we get it. We are bad. There's only two kinds of people on the planet: those who make up the problem and those who make up the

276

solution. WE ARE THE SOLUTION. We have no problems. Everything is free for everybody. Money sucks. Leaders suck. School sucks . . . We don't want it! Our program of rock 'n' roll, dope and fucking in the streets is a program of total freedom for everyone. We are totally committed to carrying out our program. We breathe revolution. We are LSD-driven total maniacs of the universe. We will do anything we can to drive people crazy out of their heads and into their bodies.'

I don't think the White Panthers envisaged their followers looking to get high on virgin blood and screams, but the song 'Necromania' shares the White Panther's convictions. Here the undead creep in the shadows, be it with 'black whips of leather' or 'death her pleasure'. It all amounted to what Jus called 'more of a satanic party album than a miserable riffs album. I don't know . . . it's a bit more sexy, maybe?'[391]

This was slightly uncomfortable, unusual terrain for Electric Wizard. 'Necromania' is spry-sounding by the band's standards, dancing on Simon's chopped-up backbeat and Clayton's swooping bass. The rhythm section was busier on this album than ever, leaving Jus and Liz to groove on two or three principal riffs and layer in fuzz, phaser and wah textures. They imagined they were taking on the fourth Stooges album, when James Williamson was still on guitar. Clayton was already a fan of The Stooges' Ron Asheton's bass playing. The Wizard wanted to capture a free and pure rock 'n' roll sound.

'I wanted to do that style quite purely, without being retro or trying to home in on one particular band, like "We want to sound like Sabbath", "We sound like [Alice] Cooper",' Jus said of *Wizard Bloody Wizard*. 'I just wanted to sound like a band from that era, that cusp moment when everyone's a little bit rock 'n' roll but really heavy, [when] acid rock turned into heavy metal . . . When I was recording, all I was listening to really was *Master of Reality* and *Led Zeppelin II* – that was like my trying to keep the reference points really tight, not trying to go off in too many directions, production-wise.'[392]

Opening song 'See You In Hell' does something Electric Wizard had never done before: it swaggers. It sounds like a slowed-down Status Quo. The grinding meat-and-two-potatoes riff earned it a performance video and lead single status: 'I like the idea of attacking blues again, to reinterpret it,' Jus said.[393]

The lyrics take vindictive glee at a dying world populated by turned-off minds. Here the emotionless denizen with 'feelings petrified' has resolved himself to a life of doing Satan's evil bidding:

I need something to fix the pain
Baby, baby, please stick the needle in
Then I'll be dead and blue
Just like you

The song, and its message, was blunt. Despite its claims to the contrary, it came from caring about the apathy of the modern world. It bludgeoned and stabbed to see if there was any life out there. Electric Wizard's gigs have never been a sea of phones – ironically their own use of a big-screen backdrop ensured that the easily bored at least had some sex and violence to occupy them. It was like the reverse of the 'Ludovico' technique used on Alex in *A Clockwork Orange*. Rather than clamp their audience's eyes open and force them to feel horrified, Electric Wizard let the film images roll for them to feel . . . anything.

'When I was growing up, it was part and parcel of rock 'n' roll that you'd be provocative in any way possible, to fuck with the system and the status quo,' Jus lamented. 'But it doesn't seem to be like that very much anymore. We'd like people to become immersed in the music and to not be thinking about taking a fucking selfie. People need to *feel* music again.'[394]

There were other sonic tricks and techniques to get the adrenaline flowing. The stuttering, then full-throttled drive of 'Hear The Sirens Scream' evokes bikers roaring down the street, with the police in hot pursuit, like 'Knights of fuzz riding/On blackened steeds'.

Vehicular-driven deviance inspired the song. In 1976, Kenneth Rowles directed *Take an Easy Ride*, a grubby, thirty-eight-minute-long sexploitation short disguised as a public information film about the dangers of hitchhiking. It blends seemingly authentic vox pops with several dramatic sequences, each showing the dangers of hitching a ride.

'At times you may wish the wife and kids were out of the way as you pass that mini-skirt thumbing a lift,' says the voiceover at the beginning. 'The producers of this film wish to give you the opportunity to judge for yourselves whether hitchhiking should be . . . *banned*. Is it a form of Russian roulette?'

Of course it is. We follow the fates of two teenagers on their way to a pop festival, a single woman travelling to see her boyfriend at the barracks in Bovington, Dorset (home of the tank museum Jus frequented as a kid), and two other female friends who request a lift 'anywhere' on the coast. The teenagers are raped and murdered, the single woman is coerced into a threesome with a married couple against her will and the two friends stab a driver to death after they mug him.

The short film is shot in the summer heat. Towards its conclusion, an ambulance and police car tear down country lanes with alternating sirens wailing. The red-hot-fuzz guitars of the soundtrack merge into the siren of another police car as the music festival is shut down.

On 'Hear The Sirens Scream', Electric Wizard also emulate the two-tone wail of the police siren, with a hair-raising effect that is the opposite of that to the Kiiry off the shoulder of Ivixor B, lulling spacecraft to their doom on *Come My Fanatics* . . .

279

We are the night
We hate the light
We have no future
We are the doomed
Drugs our religion
Violence our hymn
Killing for freedom
Then the sirens scream again

The biker life is grim. You look like a vagrant; your jeans are
threadbare, and you stink of petrol. But at least you have your
patch, your chopper, and the night. In a 1985 BBC documentary
about The Outcasts biker gang, the only thing that saves one of
their members from being burnt alive at home is the screams of
the woman he's sleeping with, after his house in Great Yarmouth
is firebombed. Whether a biker riding the night air, or Jus crashing his fantasy Lamborghini, on *Wizard Bloody Wizard* death
merely lurked in the background; it was no longer imminent.

'The Reaper' simulates this disquiet: 'Hopeless and drugged/
Slip into the void,' Jus sings. Droning Hammond and the slow
burn, layered palette of the guitar parts makes it the album's
most psychedelic track, recalling 'Raptus' from *Witchcult Today*
and the final stages of 'The House on the Borderland'. At just
over three minutes it is the shortest song on Electric Wizard's
shortest album – the band's only creative restriction on themselves was that *Wizard Bloody Wizard* fit on one vinyl record.

By contrast, the album's closing song, 'Mourning Of The
Magicians', was its longest at over eleven minutes. Throughout
its steady procession, dissonance encroaches like a lurking fear.
The guitars provide an enshrouding cloak of mystery while
the bass traces the song's unusually catchy hooks, eventually
unleashing the full band before they crawl back within the song
again. Clayton's dextrous playing is even reminiscent of Paul

McCartney. At one point he plays a bassline which sounds very similar to The Beatles song that is referenced in the chorus of sorts: 'Come together/And feel it now'.

The song's title is a mutation of *The Morning of the Magicians*, a book written by Louis Pauwels and Jacques Bergier and published in 1960. The book examined the esoteric powers seeking to influence world events. With the subtitle 'Secret Societies, Conspiracies and Vanished Civilisations', the book explored 'fantastic realism', as its authors called it: 'It has nothing to do with the bizarre, the exotic, the merely picturesque,' they write. 'There was no attempt on our part to escape the times in which we live. We were not interested in the "outer suburbs" of reality: on the contrary we have tried to take up a position at its very hub.'[395]

The book is optimistic of the birth of a new age – one of 'ultra-consciousness' and the 'awakened state'. The book was a totem for the sixties and of the dawning Age of Aquarius. It explores then-new (ish) ideas of heightened awareness and the seed of superintelligence in children of the time – they cite an English study of five thousand children which detected a sudden rise in the level of intelligence and of IQs of a sample of 140 children between seven and nine years of age which could be credited to strontium-90, a radioactive substance that penetrates the body and which didn't exist before the first atomic explosion.[396] The book's hopes for awakened supernatural potential in human beings is tied inextricably to the awesome and terrifying start of the nuclear age.

Likewise, it grapples with the fall-out from the Second World War and some of the dangerous theories of cosmogony that might have fed it: 'The rise of Nazism was one of those rare moments in the history of our civilization, when a door was noisily and ostentatiously opened on to something "Other",' they write.[397]

Pauwels and Bergier write about how the Germans sent scientists to the Baltic island of Rügen to prove that they were

living inside a hollow Earth. Once there, radar was aimed at
the sky at a 45-degree angle so that the concave curvature
of the inner Earth (they supposedly believed we lived inside a
hollow planet) would enable them to locate the British fleet by
using dead straight infrared rays to reflect an image
of it.[398]

The budding astronomer Swithin in Hardy's *Two on a Tower*
argues that the idea of a hollow Earth is really one of denying
the threatening reality of the immensity of the universe: "'The
imaginary picture of the sky as the concavity of a dome whose
base extends from horizon to horizon of our Earth is grand,
simply grand, and I wish I had never got beyond looking at it in
that way. But the actual sky is a horror.'"[399]

Even more aberrant was the doctrine of eternal ice (in
German, '*Welteislehre*'), originally propounded by Austrian
engineer Hanns Hörbiger. One of the tenets of this theory was
that the Earth had gone through four geological epochs under
four different moons. Each successive moon had fallen and, as it
fell, there were periods of hundreds of thousands of years where
it revolved around the Earth at a distance of four to six times
the circumference of the Earth, hugely closer than the moon's
orbit in reality. According to the theory, the marked changes in
gravity that resulted caused the development of larger animals
and vegetation – gigantism was prevalent.[400]

This created a succession of epochs of giant kings who gov-
erned and educated the smaller, more savage human race. Also
– according to this theory – twelve thousand years ago the Earth
acquired its fourth satellite, our present moon. The resulting
gravitational effect caused the flooding of a second Atlantis in
the North Atlantic (the other was in the Andes). This was the
Great Flood of the Bible.

During this fourth moon phase, the giants still living became
degenerate – reflected in the mythology of giants fighting

amongst themselves and with men. Giants had become monsters; one of them, Saturn, devoured his children.[401]

In this case, Saturn's children were the humans left in
ignorance. Perhaps this explains why the magicians of Electric
Wizard's song were in mourning. The children of Saturn appear
yet again in one of their album closers: 'Distorted shadows
scream/As Saturn's children dream'.

The Morning of the Magicians points out that the old books on
alchemy said that the secrets of matter itself were to be found
on the planet Saturn. Back in 1960, nuclear physicists spoke of
the 'Saturnian' atom as a central mass around which rings of
electrons revolved.[402] Incidentally, scientists recently discovered
that trinitite – a glassy material made when sand was fused
during the world's first nuclear blast – contained icosahedrite,
a quasicrystal with fivefold symmetry. In other words, nuclear
explosions create pentagrams.[403]

Saturn's children dream of enlightenment, to be awakened
into a higher consciousness like the astral children in Arthur C.
Clarke's *Childhood's End*, the book with an influence on *Come
My Fanatics* . . . As gods are dragged to hell and crucified, the
order of the world is inverted.

On 'The Mourning of the Magicians', Electric Wizard are led
by Saturn's children into the light, to higher consciousness,
and the tears flow as they venture back into the burning sun of
'Return Trip':

> The children call to me
> We have the answers that you seek
> I know it's been too long
> But at last, the light has come
> As you die

Electric Wizard wanted to make a rock 'n' roll album, and with
Wizard Bloody Wizard they achieved that aim. Their souls were

long ago sold at the crossroads, but they were bartering with their own reputation this time. The album channelled the notion that had been growing inside Jus that hard rock and metal music had attained its own status as a form of folk music. Electric Wizard were as entitled as anyone else to share in its traditions.

They paid the price for this to some extent in the album's reviews. *Metal Hammer* seemed particularly slighted. They gave it six out of ten and sniffed that it was 'amongst the blandest of their canon': 'Jus Oborn has spoken of his desire to create a record that harks back to the stripped-down, heavy blues of the likes of the likes of Zeppelin and Blue Cheer, and the results are as alarming as that sounds.'[404]

This didn't damage the band's live reputation in any way. They toured the album extensively as a dependable and thrilling entity. They followed manager Peter Grant's advice to his charges Led Zeppelin to play the same core set of songs when they performed live – to not be fooled by a hardcore contingent who wanted them to foray deeper into their back catalogue.

Electric Wizard were invited to headline the Dark Mofo festival in Hobart, Tasmania, in June 2018 – the depths of the Australian winter. The organisers had flown the band out first-class and the city seemed to be taking the festival's 'dark and dangerous' theme seriously. It was a large and well-funded arts event which greeted the band with inverted crosses down the city's main drag. To the band it felt like a brainwashing campaign making use of government grants. They loved it. It was the band's first gig in Australia since the tour supporting *We Live* in 2005. The intervening years had seen them arrive at a new pinnacle.

The set was partially captured by a young Australian film-maker, who had his own vision for using Electric Wizard's music in a sick and twisted way. To soundtrack a film was an ambition long nurtured by the band and one they soon realised.

Chapter Eleven
𝔕𝔢𝔱𝔲𝔯𝔫 𝔗𝔯𝔦𝔭

In October 2021, Electric Wizard released a new song called 'L.S.D.' – which, of course, stands for 'Lucifer's Satanic Daughter'. The vinyl version was put out by Creep Purple, run out of Lithuania by Paulius Plytnikas, who the band met via the *It's Psychedelic Baby* magazine website. Creep Purple is a high quality, DIY operation which acts as a kind of back-up for Witchfinder Records releases – the digital versions can be found on the Witchfinder Records Bandcamp page. The single was part of the soundtrack of the film *Lucifer's Satanic Daughter* made by a deranged young Australian director called Chandler Thistle.

Thistle's relationship with Electric Wizard began when he started to make his own, unofficial, videos for the band's songs. He directed a particularly accomplished clip for 'Satanic Rites Of Drugula' in 2015, clearly with zero budget for the Halloween party-shop Drugula costume. But the drone shots, psychedelic effects and innovative camera work showed promise. In one sequence Drugula took a hit from a bong filled with water mixed with a victim's blood. Thistle then took the viewer on a cosmic journey through one of Drugula's stoned red eyes into outer space. The band fed the video out through its media contacts and made sure it scored over a hundred thousand YouTube views.

The band's support of Thistle is an expression of passing forward the mutual support that is embedded in the metal fanbase.

'There is a community there,' Jus told *Psychology Today* in 2018. 'There are people making T-shirts, making patches, doing interviews. And that helps everyone – it is important. It isn't just a little fantasy for yourself. In the metal world, a kid can design a T-shirt and send it to his favourite band, and the band would say that's fucking cool – we're going to do it. The bands love that shit. That's what helps – everyone wants word of mouth – not big adverts in *Rolling Stone*. The word of mouth is way better. And everyone is involved with it on some level. A whole community is there to be involved in.'[405]

The B-side of 'L.S.D.' is a superb recording of 'Satanic Rites Of Drugula' from the 2017 edition of the Brutal Assault metal festival, an event which takes place in the eighteenth-century Josefov fortress in the Czech Republic, built by Emperor Joseph II. The festival is set against the fortress walls, which is a bigger, badder version of Littledean jail, where *House Of Whipcord* was filmed. Bands reach the stage through a long, submerged tunnel, like gladiators emerging into the colosseum. The live version of the song worked even better in this setting now that Jus had come to introduce it with an exaggerated eastern European accent: 'I vant to drink your blood . . .'

When Electric Wizard played the Dark Mofo festival in Hobart, Tasmania, in 2018, Chandler Thistle came along with his camera. He captured some footage of Jus testifying to the satanic nature of rock 'n' roll outside the venue and filmed the band's set inside. The footage found its way into *Lucifer's Satanic Daughter*, which Thistle crowd-funded and billed as a 'psychedelic slasher' film. Electric Wizard liked the kid and put a decent chunk of their own money into the production, with Jus becoming an associate producer.

The film plays as a kind of long-form tribute to Electric Wizard, and heavy music more broadly. In the opening, one of the kids screams, 'Legalise drugs and murder!' at a group of protesting evangelical Christians. Electric Wizard's songs are used throughout, at times giving it the feel of a giant music video collage. While sitting around the fire listening to 'Funeralopolis', one of the kids comments that dropping acid is 'like a heavy riff – starts off slow then really comes and gets ya'. The kid in question is Ricky, a reinterpretation of Ricky Kasso, who once again murders a kid called Gary around a campfire.

The film uses the Electric Wizard myth of Ricky Kasso as presented on *Time to Die*, recycling liberal amounts of audio from the *20/20 Devil Worshippers* documentary to thread the real-life killings through the film. It retrospectively confirms *Time to Die* as Electric Wizard's unintentional concept album in the vein of The Who's *Quadrophenia*. Otherwise, *Lucifer's Satanic Daughter* is a chaotic collision of a marauding witch, kids lost in the woods and undead Knights Templar – a lift from Amando de Ossorio's 1972 film *Tombs of the Blind Dead*, which spawned three sequels and was a huge inspiration to Cathedral.

Lucifer's Satanic Daughter doesn't have a plot. Instead, it's a tableau of various extreme and drug-crazed sequences: a ventriloquist's dummy comes to life and brandishes a switchblade; bikers stomp heads and cover their victims with their own menstrual blood; and the witch bites off a kid's dick during fellatio. The cast look like they had a lot of fun making it and, judging by some of the performances, I think many of them were high as kites in the process – method acting still has its place in twenty-first-century filmmaking.

What the film (deliberately) lacks in coherent narrative it makes up for in exuberant camerawork and visual effects. There's a fantastic, 360-degree fisheye lens used on the interior roof of the camper van during the film's opening, which kicks off a succession of lysergic visuals credited to Owsley Stanley and Liquid Light Lab. There's also a never-ending well of sick ideas as each character reaches their demise. Judging by Electric Wizard's favourite films, the key to successful exploitation cinema has always been a similar recipe: gross-out ideas, some interesting camerawork, dodgy performances and easy on the storyline.

Electric Wizard's 'L.S.D.' gets an airing in its entirety towards the end of the film in one of the climactic orgies of psychedelic mayhem and violence. Electric Wizard have been a filter for an array of horror and exploitation cinema images, archetypes and aesthetics, and now they have fully stepped through the mirror and reversed that process: they are the influence on a new wave of trash filmmaking and its ritualisation of blood, bongs and boobs. Also, finally, the Wizard have soundtracked a film in the way they had promised a soundtrack recording to follow up *We Live*.

As for the song itself, it has the swing and bite of *Wizard Bloody Wizard* but returns to the more fuzzed-out tones of the band's past. The shape of the main riff's body and stinging tail recalls Electric Wizard's earliest work – it wouldn't sound out of place on their debut. But the atmosphere and composition as a whole could only have been written by the current line-up. On the record's sleeve, drummer Simon has been redubbed Simon Lust – the name of a member of the band Mystic from the 1973 film *Horror Hospital*. In the opening of the film, Mystic play the song 'Hand of Death' in a club with walls adorned with prints by nineteenth-century illustrator Aubrey Beardsley. *Horror Hospital* stars Robin Askwith and Michael Gough (it also features two biker heavies who don't take off their helmets and a more sympathetic dwarf character than Olaf in *The Sinful Dwarf*, called Frederick). Electric Wizard's new bassist Haz Wheaton played on 'L.S.D.' He used to be in the latter-day Hawkwind, closing the circle with one of the original influences on the band.

Jus sounds like he's having as much fun with his vocals as the actors tripping balls in the film. He sits confidently out front of the mix: 'Only seventeen/On the cover of a magazine'. This harks back to the lyrics of 'Demon Lung' on the first Electric Wizard split with Orange Goblin, then called Our Haunted Kingdom, released in 1996. The cover featured Kip Trevor of the occult seventies' folk-rock band Black Widow, poised with a knife to sacrifice a naked woman on stage. The image appeared on the cover of the Japanese edition of their 1970 single 'Come to the Sabbat'.

This nightly ritual, which Black Widow performed on a woman called Katie at the climax of the set with the song 'Sacrifice', attracted the attention of publicity-hungry Wiccan Alex Sanders. He warned the band they might accidentally conjure a she-devil. According to Maxine Sanders, Alex's widow, Katie then grew hysterical about the mock sacrifice, believing, too, that it was verging on black magic. The band asked Sanders if he knew a witch who would be up for playing the part of the demon goddess instead. After a volunteer from the Sanders coven dropped out, Maxine Sanders stepped in at the last moment to play the demon Astaroth.[406]

On Electric Wizard's wah-heavy and light-footed 'Demon Lung' Jus sings, 'She'd been to places her mother's never seen/When she was fifteen/Now she's squirming across the floor/Begging me to do it again. Yeah! Yeah! Yeah!' Only the breakdown in the song's final third resembles the band that went on to record Come My Fanatics . . . , with a wrung-out, slow-mo blues section, layered soloing and a repeated wailed request for someone to 'load' the demon lung.

Looking up the lyrics for 'L.S.D.', I came across an even more sinister song called 'Satan's Daughter' by none other than Shaun's favourite, Gary Glitter:

She is Satan's daughter
Can't you see?
She's just a vicious child
She is Satan's Daughter
And she only wants to use you
For a little while

It's clear that demonic women have obsessed rock musicians over the last fifty years. It's a tale as old as time.

On Sunday 1 May 2022, Electric Wizard headlined Desertfest at London's Roundhouse. It was the first time the band had returned to the venue since 2015, and the world had changed completely.

'Back from the grave . . . ' they proclaimed in the run-up to the gig, their first performance since 2019 and the ensuing suspension of live music during the Covid-19 pandemic. Re-entering the auditorium through its large doors was like walking into the hall of kings, with a sold-out crowd seeking oblivion and ecstasy, in thrall to the Wizard once again. Isolation, a condition so necessary to the creative health of the band, had become common over the two previous years – and so we craved ceremony and blasphemous communion at the feet of the band.

As 'Procreation (Of the Wicked)' by Celtic Frost thundered over the PA, to be replaced with the thunder, lightning and procession-ary drumming of the studio version of 'Crypt Of Drugula' from *Black Masses*, the inverted Ankh that glowed red above the stage began to drip blood. By this point I had come to know the band personally while writing this book, but my anticipation of the performance was undimmed. Like the best rock bands, Electric Wizard take on another guise onstage – they become gigantic and otherworldly, intermediaries between our world and theirs.

This was hammered home when they opened with 'Return Trip'. The last time I saw them in 2019 the first song, as was customary, had been 'Witchcult Today'. It lures the initiates into the ceremony. The visceral shock of the opening chord of 'Return Trip' was making another point: the pessimism and paranoia of the Wizard's worldview had been vindicated. We were doused in the fiery abandon of the song right at the start of the gig because we weren't simply entering their world anymore – it had already merged with our own.

It's hard to convey how overwhelming to the senses an Electric Wizard concert was after the extended hiatus. The roar, screech and fuzz of the Marshall stacks flooded the venue with a white-hot intensity. During 'Return Trip', Jus kept walking back to his amp, adjusting the dials as if he was searching for the perfect, tinnitus-inducing frequency. Costa Kostopoulos still handles sound and he is too organised not to also become their tour manager in recent years. Maybe it is working with such high volumes that means he can shout loud enough to peel paint when confronted with decibel restrictions in mainland Europe. While Kostopoulos orchestrates the mix from the front, Rainer Lauer runs the monitors and stage sound. That is, when he's not assisting the band in his capacity as its 'official' joint roller.

If the sonic assault of Electric Wizard's shows is not enough, the visual concoction mixed for each song will get you. John Moules still provides the psychedelic backdrop of movie clips and trippy video sequences for the band. He works alongside Anne Weckstrom, a Finnish lighting designer with experience in creating potent ambience – for museum exhibitions and the opera, as well as for bands like Sunn O))) and Mayhem. The feeling of stepping into a live horror film when witnessing the Wizard, or at least a seedy cinema projecting all manner of exploitative filth, can also be credited to their efforts.

At the Roundhouse, this was particularly potent during 'The Chosen Few', with the huge, widescreen chopper sequences from 1968 biker movie *Hells Chosen Few* playing in the background. The brightness on screen affirms that sense of a song that reaches for the light. The prolonged diminuendo of the song is the dying whisper of the chosen few who 'look up in the sky'. On the night it felt like a reflection on the fallen members of the band who had stopped believing in Electric Wizard.

No song encapsulates the new era of global uncertainty we have entered as powerfully as 'Funeralopolis'. Already an anthem and the template for a generation of doom metal, as the finale it felt like an invitation to dance around the fires of its promised nuclear devastation. And as the world deteriorates in conflict, environmental collapse and dying societal systems for which replacements seem impossible, the song is a monstrous testament to how desperate things feel. 'This world is so fucked, let's end it tonight' sounded gloriously over-the-top in 2000, but twenty years and counting later, it is grimly aspirational.

Electric Wizard have achieved their aims. The fact that their disgust and addictive fascination with the depravity of humanity is now widespread is our problem.

Epilogue
The Shout

For the sake of argument, let's say there are three forms of truth: the truth, the whole truth, and nothing but the truth. This book speaks the truth — maybe only *a* truth — about Electric Wizard. I can't argue it is the whole truth, and certainly not that it is nothing but the truth.

Who am I, to purport to speak any truth about the band? Well, I am one of the band's long-time fans; one of their fanatics. One who risked crossing through the mirror to tell the band's story.

There are things that I haven't been able to say in this book and some details that have been suppressed for the sake of the individuals involved. There were hints of other things, especially concerning Wimborne, which soon fell silent.

I sensed there was a conflict in the band between wanting to be unburdened of certain things and the pain involved in doing so. Other elements of the band's story were to be locked away for ever, only glimpsed.

When I found out where they were living in Devon, I immediately thought about Jerzy Skolimowski's 1978 film *The Shout*. Its opening scenes involve a cricket match at an asylum. These were filmed at Hartland Abbey, a grand eighteenth-century house set back from the coast a few miles west of the town of Bideford on the River Torridge. The film's most dramatic sequences take place in the sand dunes of Braunton Burrows, north of Bideford, across the estuary of the River Torridge where it meets the River Taw. The dunes border Saunton Sands beach.

As a child, I spent a few family holidays at the Saunton Sands hotel, which stands on a cliff overlooking the beach at its northernmost point. It's an extraordinary beach, which stretches for miles southwards and is popular with surfers. When the tide is out, there are extensive rock pools abutting the cliffs and a wide expanse of white sand.

In the summer of 1987, when I was five years old, my family encountered a strange sight viewed from the hotel lawn: hundreds of metal-framed hospital beds stretching, in a snake-like formation, down the middle of the beach at low tide. The beds were being photographed for the cover of the new Pink Floyd album, *A Momentary Lapse of Reason*. Members of the band were sitting in the lounge of the hotel bar watching it all unfold. The speed of the incoming tide surprised the crew, and cover designer Storm Thorgerson's team had to rush to bring the beds in before they were claimed by the sea.

Pink Floyd had filmed some of the war sequences in their film of *The Wall* in the dunes of Braunton Burrows. In *The Shout*, it is here that the dark and inscrutable Crossley (played by Alan Bates) unleashes a 'terror shout' taught to him by the aboriginal people of the Northern Territory of Australia, which can kill any living thing within earshot.

My brothers and I used to play in the burrows as kids. We called one particularly impressive dune, set well back from the beach, the 'Big Dipper'. It never felt like an intimidating place, but the burrows seemed to be endless. Looking back, I can imagine us stumbling upon a Crossley stalking the area in his long black coat, before he draws in his breath, throws back his head and unleashes his death-scream.

THE SHOUT

In the film of *The Shout*, Crossley inserts himself into the lives of Rachel and Anthony Fielding, played by Susannah York and John Hurt, who live in an isolated cottage. Seeing the film made Liz want to follow suit and move to a remote part of north Devon. By contrast, Jus was repulsed by Alan Bates's portrayal of Crossley and grimaced as he told me that he could practically smell the character's thick polyester jumper when he watched it.

The film is adapted from a short story of the same name by Robert Graves, published in 1965. Its narrator encounters Crossley at the cricket game in the asylum grounds, where Crossley is a patient. A doctor says that Crossley has 'delusions' that he is a murderer: that he claims he killed two men and a woman in Sydney, and that his soul has been split into pieces. The narrator sits in the scoring box with Crossley as a thunderstorm approaches: 'I had no fear of physical violence, only the sense of being in the presence of a man of unusual force, even perhaps, it somehow came to me, of occult powers.'[407]

Crossley begins to tell the story of his arrival in the Fieldings' lives: '"My story is true," he said, "every word of it. Or, when I say that my story is 'true', I mean at least that I am telling it in a new way. It is always the same story, but I sometimes vary the climax and even recast the characters."'[408]

On being told of the terror shout, which Crossley claims he took eighteen years to perfect and was taught by 'the chief devil of the Northern Territory',[409] the narrator of the story tells him of other shouts from mythology: the shout of Irish warriors that drove armies back; the terrible shout of Hector of Troy; and the sudden shouts in the woods of Greece attributed to the god Pan, infecting men with madness and fear – from which the English word 'panic' is derived.

When I read the story of the terror shout, I thought of the roar of Electric Wizard's amplifiers. They are capable of evoking delight, hysteria and fear, and of inducing sickness, euphoria

and a trancelike state. The power the band wields is as hard to
define as it is to deny. Like Crossley's, it is awe-inspiring, and it
is terrible.

As I drove back from my first meeting with Jus and Liz in the
week of the summer solstice, back east down the A303 where
Stonehenge haunted the evening twilight, I wondered if I was
Crossley – a malign presence inveigling myself into their lives
and making them explain themselves. But as time went on,
it became clearer that I was more like Graves's narrator and
they were Crossley, keepers of hidden knowledge telling me the
version of the truth they wanted to tell.

After all, they are the Electric Wizard: possessors of unusual
force and occult powers.

I returned to Wimborne on the winter solstice, 2021. It was cold
and grey. Masked shoppers made their way through the streets.
With resurgent Covid cases, it was the most paranoid Christmas
ever.

I went first to Square Records, which we had missed on my
visit with Jus and Liz. The shop had moved down the road from
its former position next to the Minster and we assumed it had
closed down. I asked the grey-haired man behind the counter
whether he remembered the band: 'Ah, the Wizard. Fantastic!'
he said.

We didn't get much of a chance to speak as the phone rang
and he served customers. But he managed to point out that the
shop's counter was the same as the one at which Robert Fripp
signed records in the BBC's *New York – Wimborne* documentary,
which meant it was thirty years old and going strong.

I had a look around the Museum of East Dorset on the high
street, then tried to go into the Minster but couldn't because

there was a funeral in progress. The Quarter Jack rang out and I passed two hearses on my way back to the King Street car park.

I wanted to visit two of the other sites in the Robert Fripp documentary. The first was Witchampton, about four miles north of Wimborne. As I drove up, I passed the west entrance to Gaunt's House near Holt. There is a squat, thatched building here called Alice Lodge which was built in 1809 in a style known as 'cottage ornée' – 'ornate cottage'.

Witchampton was always going to struggle to live up to its name, though it is a pretty village with a fine church. They used to make moulded papier-mache flowerpots (which allowed seeds to germinate quickly) at the Witchampton Paper Mill, opened in 1780. The mill also produced wallpaper, writing paper and card for boxes – all known as *witchware*. It closed in 1991.

I made my way into the churchyard of St Mary's and wondered about this book project. From my pitching the book to Mark Lewis, through the slow process of negotiating our creative relationship, engaging a publisher and signing a contract, I had always felt the book was tentative – like it might never happen and could be killed at any moment.

Even if I crashed and burned and the book was suppressed for ever, perhaps I should feel privileged to count myself amongst the serried ranks of collaborators who have been sacrificed at Electric Wizard's altar. I thought of Gore Vidal, who had written the original screenplay for 1979's *Caligula*, one of Electric Wizard's favourite films. *Penthouse* magazine financed the film and its founder, Bob Guccione, brought in Tinto Brass to direct it. Brass rewrote Vidal's script and Vidal distanced himself from the project. It was later credited as only being adapted from his screenplay. I'm no Gore Vidal, but this kind of thing can happen to any writer in a big collaboration. I was more than a little paranoid that it might happen to me.

I drove on to my final destination a couple of miles up the road: Knowlton church. On the site are the remains of a small Norman church built in the 1100s and remodelled in the fourteenth century. What makes it fascinating is that it stands inside a late Neolithic henge monument dating from between 4000 and 2500 BC. The henge consists of a ring bank with two entrances and an internal ditch. The site is presumed to have been used for ceremonial purposes before the Normans built their own site of worship.

The landscape whirled around the site with desolate winter views. It felt like a centrifuge for immense primal power – the same forces Electric Wizard harnessed. Robert Fripp had spoken of Wimborne as being the centre of the universe. Thomas Hardy was compelled to write a book about a couple's lives set against the immensity of space when he lived in the town. It was being in a region this open to the heavens that drove Electric Wizard to grapple with that void. The Wizard had flown down from the clouds on the back of a dragon, which whisked them off on an astral journey. They made devotions to the ancient ones 'under starless sky'.

In the Fripp documentary he speaks in the ruins of Knowlton church, on what looks like a similarly cold day, about his decision to leave King Crimson in 1974 and join Sherbourne House. Sherbourne House was the home of the International Academy for Continuous Education, a spiritual institution founded by the philosopher J.G. Bennett. There, Bennett expounded on the teachings of the Russian philosopher and mystic George Gurdjieff, perhaps most famous for his methods for achieving higher consciousness, known as 'The Work'. Pauwels and Bergier wrote of him in *The Morning of the Magicians*. Bennett was keen to help the Aquarian generation, who found 'freedom' in the late sixties, to negotiate the spiritual and existential complexities of the much bleaker seventies.

'The difficulty about talking about spirituality is that
we make it something *other*, something apart or outside of
ourselves,' Fripp says in the documentary. 'The so-called "inner
life". There's really no inside and no outside. Unless we wish it
to be there. Quite a while [it seemed] that all the contradictions
of being a rock musician . . . It was simply not giving me the
answers I needed. The questions which took me away from
Wimborne weren't being answered even by Crimson.'

Knowlton is a similar site to that of the deconsecrated church
in Buckfastleigh, Devon, the place of inspiration for *The Hound
of the Baskervilles*. These are places to ask difficult, devilish
questions of ourselves which are not easily answered – by God,
Satan, or rock music.

In the 1970 film *The Blood on Satan's Claw*, the uncovering
of a deformed skull on farmland known as Tarrant's field by
an eighteenth-century ploughman called Ralph Gower (the
film's representative of our modern-day conscience) unleashes a
demonic power which possesses the local children, led by Angel
Blake. The children sacrifice one of their friends, Cathy, to the
demon Behemoth in a black mass. Dark of fur and terrifying,
Behemoth lurks during the ritual in the real-life ruins of St
James's, the Norman church in the Vale of Bix Bottom, in the
Chiltern Hills of Oxfordshire, where the scene was filmed.

The Blood on Satan's Claw is a folk-horror film about the fear
of burgeoning female sexuality. But, like *Mark of The Devil*, it is
ultimately about the inviolability of male power. In the strangest
and most consequential scene in the film, the district judge
elects to leave the village as the satanic panic is unfolding, only
to return after things have escalated beyond control, pledging to
use 'undreamed-of measures' to tame the disturbance.

If there is any doubt that he leaves only in order to return
with the utmost violence, he says this to the village squire on
his departure: 'I shall not forget you. I shall return, when the

time is ripe. But you must have patience. Even while people die. Only thus can the whole evil be destroyed. You must let it *grow*.'

As a viewer, the film asks: whose side are you on? Behemoth's youthful coven which indulges in a spot of murder along the way, or the torch-wielding mob of justice who want to preserve the status quo?

Electric Wizard were allowed to grow in Wimborne but, once their influence spread, they were driven out of town before they tainted it with the devil's mark any further. Ultimately, they had their revenge on their oppressors, in the form of witchcraft, lust and unholy sonic terrors, taken to a global audience.

As I finished my perambulation of the earthwork, patting over-friendly dogs and dodging zig-zagging children, I spotted a man with long black hair comforting a child by the ruins. As I got closer and he looked up, I could have sworn it was Tim from the first Electric Wizard line-up. I pretended to need a better look at the church to get nearer. The man raised his head again – it wasn't Tim. I drove home.

I first read the name Electric Wizard when I came across the review of *Come My Fanatics . . .* in the issue of *Kerrang!* published on 11 January 1997. Hunting the magazine down for this book, I instantly recognised its cover – it features Jonathan Davis of Korn wearing his then trademark Adidas tracksuit with the banner, 'Korn, 3 Colours Red & the future sound of music', previewing 'the noise of '97'.

Context is everything, and the context of 1997 was one of upheaval in heavy music. Korn were at the vanguard of nu metal, emergent but not yet fully defined. Metallica had cut their hair and released the contentious album *Load* in 1996 – there's a smaller photo of drummer Lars Ulrich from their then recent winter tour of the UK, where I saw them play at Earl's Court. Also on the cover is L.G. Petrov of Entombed, Swedish death metal originators who had switched to a death 'n' roll sound with *DCLXVI: To Ride, Shoot Straight and Speak the Truth*. Petrov sadly died of cancer in 2021. Also in the roll call were Chino Moreno of Deftones and Gwen Stefani of No Doubt, both of which were to blow up in the years to come – No Doubt spectacularly so.

I was fourteen at the time I bought that issue of *Kerrang!* and ripe for this sea change in metal. I saw Korn at Brixton Academy the following month and lost a shoe during the first song. I hopped on one foot for the rest of the gig. I've never seen a crowd jump in unison like it until I went to see hip-hop collective Odd Future (featuring Tyler, the Creator who played Primavera Sound in 2015 alongside Electric Wizard) at the same venue when I was thirty. That time, I watched the seething mass of teenagers from the back.

In 1997, Electric Wizard would have spat at the idea they were part of this new movement. But since the new forms of metal emerging were diffuse, fragmented and shattered heavy metal's orthodoxy, they were part of it by default. When I bought *Come My Fanatics . . .* it was the two-CD set that Rise Above reissued in 1999 which also included the debut album, both with marijuana plant images on the CDs, printed in different shades of green. Why there was a two-year gap between reading about the band and buying the album I don't remember. But by then I was well into my weed-smoking journey. I bought *Dopethrone* when it came out the following year and sat in my student halls in Edinburgh at the foot of Arthur's Seat. We liked to smoke on the rocky outcrops of the ancient volcano. I blasted the album continuously in my room, looking out at my very own dopethrone.

I look back at the mid-to-late nineties with a lot of affection, but like many I think this period of relative stability and prosperity had me fooled. *Come My Fanatics . . .* was a transmission from a dismal future, a vision of the 'world-without-us'[410] that presaged the growing climate crisis, millenarian paranoia and the hidden workings of power, while many in the western world were revelling in their freedoms.

'It was a similar period in history. I think it always is,' Jus told me about the nineties, in our 2017 interview looking back at *Come My Fanatics . . .* 'I don't think that anything changes from that point of view. It's just different baddies involved every time. It didn't feel like it was a simpler time. There were still things to be scared about then: the threat of nuclear war had only just gone past. Our country wasn't in a great state. And metal was totally fucked at that point. We were really making a musical statement. When you're younger everything is a reaction against the world.'[411]

Electric Wizard opened a black hole within themselves where the hidden chaos of the universe seemed to rush in. *Come My Fanatics . . .* was rife with cosmic pessimism. The special, anointed Earth – blessed by civilisation – was just another planet, on the verge of collapsing in on itself. In the grand scheme of things, our lives are meaningless. The other problem is that 'the grand scheme of things' is also unfathomable.

The same qualities that H.P. Lovecraft attributed to the weird tale in his essay 'Supernatural Horror in Literature' (first published in 1927) could be applied to early Electric Wizard: 'A certain atmosphere of breathless and unexplainable dread of outer, unknown forces must be present; and there must be a hint, expressed with a seriousness and portentousness becoming its subject, of that most terrible conception of the human brain – a malign and particular suspension or defeat of those fixed laws of Nature which are our only safeguard against the assaults of chaos and the daemons of unplumbed space.'[412] In Electric Wizard's case a 'hint' became a sonic deluge.

Lovecraft was not the first writer to explore cosmic fear, though he was perhaps its exponent *par excellence*. Thomas Hardy, in *Two on a Tower*, dwelt on the terror of empty space and how it reveals itself in increments. As his astronomer Swithin declares: 'Until a person has thought out the stars and their interfaces, he has hardly learnt that there are things much more terrible than monsters of shape, namely, monsters of magnitude without known shape. Such monsters are the voids and waste spaces of the sky.'[413]

I think it's a mistake to see this as purely nihilistic. It is nihilistic but it is also liberating. The experience of listening to the first era of Electric Wizard is one of becoming one with a cosmic force beyond explanation – the heaviness that first found expression in Black Sabbath is one of the great mysteries of the universe. It compels you to live in the present moment.

However, harnessing that energy is fraught with difficulties. It is almost too *real*, and that crawling chaos can only be subjugated to musical order for so long unless you demarcate your own magical space to operate within. The first line-up of Electric Wizard refused to do that. They were young, working-class men, who, if they made it past the year 2000 at all, couldn't see themselves living much beyond it.

'I think I can listen to them quite objectively now,' Jus told *Iron First* magazine of the early albums in 2016. 'I think I'm listening to some kids in their early twenties who are really venting their fucking frustrations with the world on the shittiest, cheapest equipment imaginable.'[414]

There is a long-running tension in the band's view of their music as being outside of time and space, yet also a product of its environment. The countryside around Wimborne nurtured a music which reflected its surroundings, which were (in Jus's words) 'bleak and silent and huge'.[415] In that environment one of two things happened with the band. Either they didn't see many other people, and they became paranoid; or they did encounter too many of them for their liking, and it fed their misanthropy. One day, as a child riding his bike with a friend, two farmers' kids held Jus up at shotgun point, took them to their farm's courtyard and let a flock of geese attack them. They screamed for mercy for hours. Experiences like that are formative.

It's a risk to dwell on clichés about the hidden brutality of the countryside. But these things happened. The young people of Wimborne hated authority, especially the police. They lived in a conservative part of the south of England full of wealthy retirees, an area which was also going through a heroin epidemic. *Dopethrone* is a difficult album for Jus to love because it conveys a miserable struggle against power and their own victim status, against what Wimborne was, and what it represented: *I am full of hatred for this place I call my home.*

Their environment bred two (sometimes conflicting, sometimes complementary) impulses: to start a revolution, and to fuck it all off. The biker and Baader–Meinhof mindset came out of the former impulse, but anger is an expensive fuel. The mayor advised Jus to leave Wimborne after too many run-ins and only a few years later, the band collapsed in on itself. They had been crushed by reality.

Isolation followed. When Liz joined the band, they drew a magic circle around themselves. They turned their attention to the hidden forces within. They made it very clear with *Witch-cult Today* that this is *our world now* – enter if you dare. Jus and Liz speak about writing songs as a form of method acting – putting themselves in situations in order to nurture an emotional foundation for a song, even if it makes them miserable. In their own words, they are introverted, contemplative and obsessive.

The music they produced as a result has been widely credited for reinvigorating occult metal music. But I've always felt the

music of this phase of the band was less about occult practice
than the way occultism is represented in wider culture. The
films, books and characters who gripped their imaginations
became necessary tropes for the inevitable crop of bands that
imitated what mark II Electric Wizard were doing. Their idiosyncratic interests became working templates.

When Jus lived in London for a short period in his early
twenties, he stayed in a tower block. He found the experience
unnerving and bewildering. For the first time, there were thousands of people sleeping around him every night. He wondered
what they were doing and what they were thinking. He worried
that they were corrupting his dreams. He almost went crazy.
As he lay in bed, Jus might have been thinking of the warning
words about cities spoken by the patriarch Judge Taylor from
Leigh Brackett's novel *The Long Tomorrow*: "'The cities were
sucking all the life of the country into themselves and destroying
it. Men were no longer individuals, but units in a vast machine,
all cut to one pattern, with the same tastes and ideas, the same
mass-produced education that did not educate but only pasted a
veneer of catchwords over ignorance.'"[416]

In the capital, Jus also did some flat-sitting for Tracey Emin,
a friend of some art-school pals, got wasted and puked on her
newly polished wooden floor. It was all part of the effects of the
ill-starred city on him. He was grateful to return to Dorset and
thenceforward regarded the capital city, and Londoners, with
suspicion.

Electric Wizard stand outside of the spaces many bands
operate in – in the form of the cities, even if they haven't exactly
stood outside of time. But thirty years into the band's existence,
it's also true that they have created timeless music. They believe
that metal has aged enough – with its own hallmarks and
traditions and history – to be called folk music. They see themselves as part of that tradition. Electric Wizard have superseded

their genre – their music is not stoner or doom or punk or heavy
rock any longer: it's Electric Wizard.

'I like to hope we've made a big difference,' Jus said in 2007.
'I'm not sure if anyone would admit it, but we were the first
band in England that really pushed it without copying anyone.
The problem with British bands is that they always copy American bands. We [the English] *invented* heavy shit in this country.
English bands always push it too far. We've got heaviness in
our blood here. How could Sabbath exist otherwise? They're a
product of British society. They didn't have anything to aspire to
and they didn't copy anyone.'[417]

Electric Wizard are a folk band with an unusual vision of
England. As a sprawling pile-up of the horror films and mythol-
ogies, exploitation cinema, pulp novels and heavy music of the
tail end of the twentieth century, it is more authentic than some
false memory of a bucolic countryside. Decent weed and bad
acid opened a gate in Dorset to somewhere else that couldn't be
closed. Instead of mind transferral, it is as if the band has been
paying out this cultural ephemera for a constant supply of the
raw, unknowable material of heaviness itself.

They told me that after they played the Graspop Metal
Meeting festival in Dessel, Belgium, in 2011, they were informed
by the merch team that they hadn't sold any T-shirts, except for
one. It was sold to David Coverdale, the frontman of Whitesnake
and former lead singer of Rainbow. They had pleased a classic
rock musician, the singer on Deep Purple's 1974 album *Storm-*
bringer, and counted him as a fan. It symbolised the transition
of power from the founding generation of heavy metal to their
successors. For a band that was perceived as shambolic in its
infancy, they had (largely) tamed chaos to their own ends.

We need new myths – new rock 'n' roll stories. Once you
know theirs, Electric Wizard reconfigures the English musical
landscape – Liverpool, Manchester, London, Wimborne and the

West Country. In the time it takes to watch *Get Back*, Peter
Jackson's exhaustive documentary about The Beatles recording
one album, you can listen to almost the whole of the Wizard's
back catalogue. And once you've listened to it, you know that
these children of Saturn are inheritors of the legend of English
heavy rock. The hammer of the gods has been passed on.

Electric Wizard never feared death, but they worried about
mortality. Or rather, whether they would be remembered. From
childhood it bothered Jus that the snuffing out of consciousness
meant everything someone achieved in their life 'doesn't mean
shit any more'.[418] Electric Wizard, like any rock 'n' roll band, is
an attempt at immortality. No tombstone required.

For many, Electric Wizard is still a hidden English band.
Maybe one day Jus and Liz will have the *Dopethrone* swimming
pool they joked about a few years ago. Like the metal genre
itself, they don't need the average person who will never get it
to understand how powerful their music is, and they don't really
want your respect either.

The weirdest thing that Jus ever said to me was that he sees
the foundational elements of music as drums and vocals. For
a guitar player, in a band that changed how that instrument's
potential for power was perceived, I thought it was a selfless
and self-effacing thing to say. Liz told me she believed heavy
music long preceded heavy rock and metal – it was a mindset
and feeling that composers and artists have tried to express over
time. She said that heavy metal is as relevant as ever and her
passion for it is undiminished, even if it does 'feel like a sinking
ship' at times. But, she added, isn't that what it's all about?

The Wizard convey something about the unknowability of life
that is very rare, if not unique. The witchcult, the supercoven,
the thirteen gathered on a moonless night, symbolises a community. When they play live it still feels like they are on the brink
of revolution and that they can change people's lives.

COME MY FANATICS

Throughout writing this book I have needed to separate myself as one of the fanatics of the band from my position as their documentarian. This journey has been an attempt to reach into their world and extract some truth. This book itself is a magical portal to their hidden powers. But Electric Wizard are the keepers of their story. Ultimately, I am under their control. I have been since I was a teenager. Because when you get into this group, you can't get out.

Endnotes

1   *Heroes in the Wind: From Kull to Conan*, Robert E. Howard
     with introduction by John Clute, Penguin Books, 2009, p.x.
2   'The Mirrors of Tuzun Thune', Howard, op. cit., p.45.
3   Howard, op. cit., p.47.
4   Howard, op. cit., p.49.
5   The historical information about the town and surrounding
     area in this chapter was found in several books and in the
     Museum of East Dorset on Wimborne high street. The books
     are: *Wimborne Minster: The History of a Country Town* by Jude
     James (The Dovecote Press, 1982); *Wimborne: A Miscellany:
     Book 1* by M. V. Angel (Wild Geese Publishing, 2017) and *A
     History of Wimborne Minster: The Collegiate Church of Saint
     Cuthberga and King's Free Chapel at Wimborne* by Charles
     Herbert Mayo (Bell and Daldy, 1860).
6   'A Cult Above', Dayal Patterson, *Metal Hammer*, December
     2010.
7   *Freewheelin Frank*, Frank Reynolds, New English Library,
     1969, p.20.
8   https://www.youtube.com/watch?v=ng8Ll7x08Vk
9   Reynolds, op. cit., p.52.
10   Reynolds, op. cit., p.70.
11   Reynolds, op. cit., p.35.
12   Reynolds, op cit., p.53.

13 From Hardy's 1895 preface to the book.

14 This information is from Claire Tomalin's biography of Hardy, *Thomas Hardy: The Time-Torn Man* (Viking, 2006) and Angel's *Wimborne: A Miscellany: Book 1*.

15 *Two on a Tower*, Thomas Hardy, Penguin English Library, 2012, p.34.

16 Hardy, op. cit., p.35.

17 'Spitting at Mortality with Jus Oborn', Michael Friedman Ph.D., *Psychology Today*, 23 July 2018: https://www.psychology-today.com/gb/blog/brick-brick/201807/spitting-mortality-jus-oborn

18 'In The Crypt of the Wizard', Nick Ruskell, *Kerrang!*, 18 November 2017.

19 https://www.gauntshouse.com/what-we-do/

20 'Aristocrat transforms his ancestral seat into training centre preparing new age disciples for the coming apocalypse', *Daily Mail*, 18 March 2016: https://www.dailymail.co.uk/news/article-3498402/Aristocrat-transforms-ancestral-seat-training-centre-preparing-New-Age-disciples-coming-apocalypse.html

21 Hardy, op. cit., p.3.

22 *Turn Off Your Mind: The Dedalus Book of the 1960s*, Gary Lachman, Dedalus, 2021, p.179.

23 'Let Us Press Pley: Jus Oborn Of Electric Wizard's Favourite Horror Films', Harry Sword, *The Quietus*, 31 October 2017: https://thequietus.com/articles/23490-electric-wizard-interview-favourite-horror-films

24 Lachman, op. cit., pp.243–4.

25 Reynolds, op. cit., p.88.

26 Reynolds, op. cit., p.88.

27 'Want your marriage to last? Live in Dorset! East of the county has highest number of married couples', *Daily Mail*, 14 February 2013: https://www.dailymail.co.uk/news/article-2278304/

Want-marriage-Live-Dorset-East-county-highest-number-married-couples.html

28   'The Doom That Came to Dorset: The Making of Electric Wizard's Dopethrone', Anthony Bartkewicz, *Decibel*, September 2007.

29   'Just Like Witches', J. Bennett, *Decibel*, February 2011.

30   'The Whisperer in Darkness', *The Call of Cthulhu and Other Weird Stories*, H. P. Lovecraft, Penguin Classics, 2002, p.251.

31   'Mean Streets', Catherine Yates, *Kerrang!*, 30 March 2002.

32   *Bad Acid*, Tab 1.

33   An early pressing of the album's sleeve misprinted the lyric as 'Just one beer before he dies', somewhat undermining its emotional tenor.

34   *Bad Acid*, Tab 2.

35   'Treasure Chest: An Intimate Portrait Of A Life In Rock: Jus Oborn', Nick Ruskell, *Kerrang!*, 11 July 2009.

36   Hardy, op. cit., p.68.

37   'Electric Wizard: Un-Lords of the Dopethrone', *Midwest Metal*, spring/summer 2001.

38   *Bad Acid*, Tab 1.

39   'Electric Wizard: Dorset for E's and Wiz', Chris Chantler, *Terrorizer*, September 2000.

40   'The Dark Knight of the Soul', Tomas Rocha, *The Atlantic*, 25 June 2014: https://www.theatlantic.com/health/archive/2014/06/the-dark-knight-of-the-souls/372766/

41   *The Alien World: The Complete Illustrated Guide*, Steven Eisler, Octopus Books, 1980.

42   Eisler, op. cit., p.15.

43   Eisler, op. cit., p.22.

44   Eisler, op. cit., p.22.

45   Eisler, op. cit., p.22.

46   *Childhood's End*, Arthur C. Clarke, Pan, 2010, p.240.

47   Clarke, op. cit., p.164.

48 '21st Century Birth Pains: Electric Wizard's Come My Fanatics Revisited', Dan Franklin, *The Quietus*, 31 January 2017: https://thequietus.com/articles/21643-electric-wizard-interview-come-my-fanatics-anniversary

49 *The Long Tomorrow*, Leigh Brackett, Gollancz, 2014, epigraph.

50 Brackett, op. cit., p.194.

51 'Rise Above Records Turns 25: From Electric Wizard To Iron Man', Dan Franklin, *The Quietus*, 27 December 2013: https://thequietus.com/articles/14115-rise-above-records-lee-dorrian-interview-cathedral

52 *The Quietus*, January 2017.

53 Review of *Come My Fanatics . . .*, Andrew Carter, *Terrorizer*, January 1997.

54 'Doped To Infinity', Dom Lawson, *Kerrang!*, 21st October 2000.

55 'A Long Strange Trip', Jim Martin, *Terrorizer's Secret History of Doom Metal*, April 2012. This is a reprint of an interview originally from 2006.

56 'A Long Strange Trip', Jim Martin, *Terrorizer's Secret History of Doom Metal*, April 2012.

57 'Electric Wizard: Doom Across America', J. Bennett, *Boston's Weekly Dig*, April 2001.

58 *Decibel*, February 2011.

59 'In the Crypt of the Wizard', Nick Ruskell, *Kerrang!*, 18 November 2017.

60 *Bad Acid*, Tab 2.

61 'Electric Wizard: Dorset for E's and Wiz', Chris Chantler, *Terrorizer*, September 2000.

62 *Serpent Eve*, vol. 1, autumn/winter 1998/1999.

63 'Black God's Shadow', *Jirel of Joiry*, C. L. Moore, Gollancz, 2019, p.34.

64 Moore, op. cit., p.47.

65 *Bad Acid*, Tab 2.

66 *Bad Acid*, Tab 1.

67   'Electric Wizard: Fanatics' Return', J. J. Koczan, *Metal Maniacs*, November/December 2007.

68   'Bad Acid (Label Profile)', *Aural Innovations* #6, April 1999: http://www.aural-innovations.com/issues/issue6/badacid.html

69   Review of *Supercoven*, Gregory Whalen, *Terrorizer*, May 1998.

70   *Bad Acid*, Tab 2.

71   *Bad Acid*, Tab 1.

72   *Bad Acid*, Tab 2.

73   *Serpent Eve*, vol. 1, autumn/winter 1998/1999.

74   Live review of London LA2 show, Marion Garden, *Terrorizer*, June 1999.

75   *Bad Acid*, Tab 2.

76   *Hitler's Children: The Story of the Baader–Meinhof Terrorist Gang*, Jillian Becker, J. B. Lippincott Company, 1977, p.57

77   Becker, op. cit., p.47.

78   Becker, op. cit., p.151.

79   Becker, op. cit., p.73.

80   Becker, op. cit., p.74.

81   *Bad Acid*, Tab 2.

82   *Kerrang!,* 11 July 2009.

83   Live review of the Camden Barfly on 25 May 1999, Ray Zell, *Kerrang!*, 12 June 1999.

84   *Vincebus Eruptum* magazine, 2000.

85   *Terrorizer's Secret History of Doom Metal*, April 2012.

86   *Terrorizer*, September 2000.

87   'The Dunwich Horror', *The Essential Tales of H.P. Lovecraft*, H. P. Lovecraft, Quarto Publishing Group, 2016, p.184.

88   Lovecraft, op. cit., p.185.

89   'Electric Wizard: Total Horrorshow', Darren Sadler, *Rock Sound*, May 2002.

90   Lachman, op. cit., p.42.

91   *Vincebus Eruptum*, 2000.

92   *H.P. Lovecraft: Against the World, Against Life*, Michel Houel-

lebecq, Weidenfeld & Nicolson, 2006, p.57.

93   Houellebecq, op. cit., p.53.

94   Houellebecq, op. cit., p.57.

95   'The Story Behind Electric Wizard: Dopethrone', Malcolm Dome, *Metal Hammer*, February 2007.

96   'The Bong Remains The Same', Dom Lawson, *Metal Hammer*, December 2007.

97   *Bad Acid*, Tab 2.

98   *Serpent Eve* fanzine, November/December 1998/1999.

99   *Serpent Eve* fanzine, November/December 1998/1999.

100 *Decibel*, September 2007.

101 *Bad Acid*, Tab 1.

102 *Bad Acid*, Tab 1.

103 'The Whisperer in Darkness', *The Call of Cthulhu and Other Weird Stories*, H.P. Lovecraft, Penguin Classics, 2002, p.234.

104 Lovecraft, op. cit., p.234.

105 Lovecraft, op. cit., pp.234–5.

106 'The Dream-Quest of Unknown Kadath', *The Dreams in the Witch House and Other Weird Stories*, H.P. Lovecraft, Penguin Books, 2005, p.167.

107 Lovecraft, op. cit., p.433.

108 Lovecraft, op. cit., p.240.

109 Lovecraft, op. cit., p.243–4.

110 Lovecraft, op. cit., p.245.

111 Lovecraft, op. cit., p.248.

112 Lovecraft, op. cit., p.249.

113 Lovecraft, op. cit., p.248.

114 'Nyarlathotep', *The Call of Cthulhu and Other Weird Stories*, H.P. Lovecraft, Penguin Classics, 2002, p.32.

115 'The Dream-Quest of Unknown Kadath', *The Dreams in the Witch House and Other Weird Stories*, H.P. Lovecraft, Penguin Books, 2005, p.249.

116 Lovecraft, op. cit., p.250.

117 'The Altar of Melek Taos', G.G. Pendarves, *Weird Tales*, September 1932, pp.305–6.

118 Pendarves, op. cit., p.300.

119 Pendarves, op. cit., p.299.

120 Pendarves, op. cit., p.308.

121 Pendarves, op. cit., p.315.

122 *Decibel*, September 2007.

123 'A Witch Shall Be Born', *Heroes in the Wind: From Kull to Conan*, Robert E. Howard, introduction by John Clute, Penguin Books, 2009, p.412.

124 Howard, op. cit., pp.412–3.

125 Howard, 'Queen of the Black Coast', op. cit., p.366.

126 *Terrorizer*, September 2000.

127 *Terrorizer*, September 2000.

128 *Metal Hammer*, February 2007.

129 *Kerrang!*, 11 July 2009.

130 *Metal Hammer*, February 2007.

131 *Terrorizer*, September 2000.

132 *Metal Hammer*, February 2007.

133 *Vincebus Eruptum*, 2000.

134 *Decibel*, September 2007.

135 *Decibel*, September 2007.

136 *Kerrang!,* 11 July 2009.

137 *Decibel*, September 2007.

138 All of these videos can be found here: www.youtube.com/user/Rolphonse

139 'Introducing Electric Wizard', Malcolm Dome, *Metal Hammer*, October 2000.

140 *Decibel*, September 2007.

141 'The Shadow Out of Time', *The Dreams in the Witch House and Other Weird Stories*, H.P. Lovecraft, Penguin Books, 2005, p.357.

142 Lovecraft, op. cit., p.351.

143 Lovecraft, op. cit., p.351.

144 Lovecraft, op. cit., p.343.

145 Lovecraft, op. cit., p.358.

146 Lovecraft, op. cit., p.359.

147 Lovecraft, op. cit., p.360.

148 Lovecraft, op. cit., p.380.

149 *Terrorizer*, September 2000.

150 '10 Favourite Horror Films of Electric Wizard's Jus Oborn!', Brad Miska, *Bloody Disgusting*, 23 November 2017: bloody-disgusting.com/editorials/3470577/10-fav-horror-films-electric-wizards-jus-oborn/

151 'INTERVIEW: Electric Wizard Talk New LP', Dan Franklin, *The Quietus*, 20 January 2014: thequietus.com/articles/14305-electric-wizard-new-album-interview

152 *Metal Hammer*, February 2007.

153 *The Quietus,* January 2014.

154 'Spitting at Mortality with Jus Oborn', Michael Friedman Ph.D., *Psychology Today*, 23 July 2018: www.psychologytoday.com/gb/blog/brick-brick/201807/spitting-mortality-jus-oborn

155 *Terrorizer*, September 2000.

156 *Metal Hammer*, February 2007.

157 'Novel of the White Powder', *The Great God Pan*, Arthur Machen, Penguin English Library, 2018, p.82.

158 Machen, op. cit., p.80.

159 *Kerrang!*, 30 March 2002.

160 *Terrorizer*, September 2000.

161 *Kerrang!*, 21 October 2000.

162 *Vincebus Eruptum*, 2000.

163 *Vincebus Eruptum*, 2000.

164 *Metal Hammer*, February 2007.

165 *Decibel*, September 2007.

166 He did this on one video-recorded occasion, at Jaxx nightclub, Springfield, Virginia on 10 March 2001.

167 'The Haunter of the Dark', *The Call of Cthulhu and Other Weird Stories*, H.P. Lovecraft, Penguin Classics, 2002, p.348.

168 *Kerrang!*, 21 October 2000.

169 Review by Graham Bent in the October 2000 issue of *Metal Hammer*.

170 'The top 20 best metal albums of 2000', *Metal Hammer*, 29 September 2020: https://www.loudersound.com/features/the-top-20-best-metal-albums-of-2000

171 'Critical Mass: *Terrorizer* critics' albums of the decade', *Terrorizer*, December 2009.

172 'Warhorse: Apocalypse Now!!', Darren Sadler, *Rock Sound*, June 2001.

173 *Boston's Weekly Dig*, April 2001.

174 *Midwest Metal*, spring/summer 2001.

175 *Boston's Weekly Dig*, April 2001.

176 'Electric Wizard: Thrilling, Chilling and Bellyaching', Darren Sadler, *Rock Sound*, June 2001.

177 *Boston's Weekly Dig*, April 2001.

178 There is loads of footage from the 2001 and 2002 tours on YouTube. When I make reference to songs and incidents in particular gigs, I'm not linking directly to videos in case they disappear, but they are worth seeking out.

179 *Midwest Metal*, spring/summer 2001.

180 *Midwest Metal*, spring/summer 2001.

181 Backstage, Mark interrupted Jus having a conversation with Homme, camcorder in hand. Homme greeted him saying, 'I'll bend over and you can film the inside of my ass.'

182 'Oral History: Liz Buckingham', *Terrorizer,* September 2009.

183 *Decibel*, February 2011.

184 'Enter the Supercoven', J. Bennett, *Decibel*, January 2008.

185 'Masters of Reality', Ronnie Kerswell-O'Hara, *Terrorizer*, October 2012.

186 *Rock Sound*, June 2001.

187 *Rock Sound*, June 2001.

188 *Rock Sound*, June 2001.

189 *Decibel*, September 2007.

190 *Terrorizer's Secret History of Doom Metal*, April 2012.

191 *Kerrang!*, 11 July 2009.

192 'The Outsider', *The Call of Cthulhu and Other Weird Stories*, H.P. Lovecraft, Penguin Classics, 2002, p.43.

193 Lovecraft, op. cit., p.43.

194 Lovecraft, op. cit., p.45.

195 Lovecraft, op. cit., p.46.

196 Lovecraft, op. cit., p.47.

197 Lovecraft, op. cit., p.47.

198 Lovecraft, op. cit., p.47.

199 Lovecraft, op. cit., p.48.

200 Lovecraft, op. cit., p.49.

201 Lovecraft, op. cit., p.49.

202 *Kerrang!*, 30 March 2002.

203 *Kerrang!*, 30 March 2002.

204 *Kerrang!*, 30 March 2002.

205 *Kerrang!*, 30 March 2002.

206 *Kerrang!*, 30 March 2002.

207 *Midwest Metal*, spring/summer 2001.

208 *Kerrang!*, 23rd March 2002.

209 *Terrorizer*, April 2002.

210 Lovecraft, op. cit., p.49.

211 'The Day of Doom: Electric Wizard and Warhorse Hit Town', Ronnie Kerswell, *Rock Sound*, August 2002.

212 *Rock Sound*, August 2002.

213 *Rock Sound*, May 2002.

214 Lepers TV interview 2002: www.youtube.com/watch?v=wi1OwLkHrd4

215 forum.theobelisk.net/viewtopic.php?f=1&t=3914

216 'Shambleau', *Northwest of Earth*, C.L. Moore, Gollancz, p.20.

217 Moore, 'The Tree of Life', op. cit., p.276.

218 Moore, 'The Tree of Life', op. cit., p.276-7.

219 http://forum.theobelisk.net/viewtopic.php?f=1&t=3914

220 *Kerrang!*, 11 July 2009.

221 'Doom Pioneers: Liz Buckingham', Darren Sadler, *Terrorizer's Secret History of Doom Metal*, April 2012.

222 'Electric Wizard's Liz Buckingham: On Heavy Music and Taking the Hard Road', Kim Kelly, NPR, 24 October 2011: www.npr.org/sections/therecord/2011/10/24/141563482/electric-wizards-liz-buckingham-on-heavy-music-and-taking-the-hard-road?t=1635242905165

223 'The Last Thirteen Questions: Electric Wizard: Liz Buckingham', *Metal Hammer*, December 2009.

224 *Terrorizer's Secret History of Doom Metal*, April 2012.

225 *Terrorizer's Secret History of Doom Metal*, April 2012.

226 This quote and some of the following detail about 13 is from an interview with Alicia Morgan in issue 9 of the *Salt* zine, the date of which I haven't been able to uncover.

227 *Terrorizer's Secret History of Doom Metal*, April 2012.

228 *Terrorizer*, September 2009.

229 *Vincebus Eruptum*, 2000.

230 *Decibel*, January 2008.

231 *Decibel*, February 2011.

232 *Metal Hammer*, December 2007.

233 *Terrorizer's Secret History of Doom Metal*, April 2012.

234 *The Quietus*, 31 October 2017: https://thequietus.com/articles/23490-electric-wizard-interview-favourite-horror-films?page=3

235 *Decibel*, February 2011.

236 *Decibel*, January 2008.

237 *Decibel*, January 2008.

238 *Decibel*, February 2011.

239 *Decibel*, January 2008.

240 'Phoenix Knights' by Chris Chantler, *Terrorizer*, June 2004.

241 *Terrorizer*, June 2004.

242 Live review of their Fiddlers, Bristol, performance on 1 May 2005, *Kerrang!*, 21 May 2005.

243 Live review of their Concorde 2, Brighton, performance on 25 February 2006, *Kerrang!*, 25 March 2006.

244 'Thee Plague of Gentlemen Frontman Imprisoned for "Unimaginable" Criminal Acts', Blabbermouth, 17 July 2006: https://blabbermouth.net/news/thee-plague-of-gentlemen-frontman-imprisoned-for-unimaginable-criminal-acts

245 The following quotations about the film are taken from the booklet of the *Eureka! Masters of Cinema* series DVD and Blu-ray edition of the film.

246 'J.F.C. Fuller and the Black Arts' by weekiwitch, *Ecstatick Magick*, 24 June 2013: ecstatickmagick.wordpress. com/2013/06/24/j-f-c-fuller-and-the-black-arts/

247 *The Great Beast: The Life of Aleister Crowley*, John Symonds, Panther Books, 1963, pp.79–80.

248 Lachman, op. cit., pp.237–8.

249 'You Terrible Cult: Electric Wizard Interviewed', John Doran, *The Quietus*, 19 November 2009: thequietus.com/ articles/03261-electric-wizard-interview

250 *Terrorizer's Secret History of Doom Metal*, April 2012.

251 *The Quietus*, 31 October 2017.

252 *Metal Hammer*, December 2009.

253 'High Voltage' by Dara Conn, *Terrorizer*, December 2007.

254 *Metal Maniacs*, November/December 2007.

255 *Metal Hammer*, December 2007.

256 J. Bennett in *Decibel*, January 2008.

257 *Metal Hammer*, December 2007.

258 *Terrorizer*, December 2007.

259 *Decibel*, January 2008.

260 'Studio Reports: Electric Wizard', *Rock Sound*, October 2007.

261 Lachman, op. cit., pp.249–50.

262 *Decibel*, February 2011.

263 *Metal Hammer*, December 2007.

264 *Metal Maniacs,* November/December 2007.

265 'Introducing W.G. Sebald: Thoughts from the late Roger Deakin', *Five Dials*: fivedials.com/fiction/w-g-sebald/

266 *Metal Maniacs*, November/December 2007.

267 'The Dreams in the Witch House', *The Dreams in the Witch House and Other Weird Stories*, H.P. Lovecraft, Penguin Books, 2005, p.303.

268 Lovecraft, op. cit., p.322.

269 Lovecraft, op. cit., p.310.

270 Lovecraft, op. cit., p.327.

271 Lovecraft, op. cit., p.329.

272 Lovecraft, op. cit., p.329.

273 *Metal Maniacs*, November/December 2007.

274 Lovecraft, op. cit., p.330.

275 *Decibel*, January 2008.

276 *Metal Maniacs*, November/December 2007.

277 *Terrorizer's Secret History of Doom Metal*, April 2012.

278 Electric Wizard - Flower of Evil a.k.a. Malfiore, published on YouTube by Electric Wizard on 12 May 2015: www.youtube.com/watch?v=1FUAAFpqdkI

279 'Electric Wizard: Come My Fanatics', Ronnie Kerswell, *Rock Sound*, December 2007.

280 'Smoke & Mirrors', Alex Deller, *Zero Tolerance*, January/February 2008.

281 *Decibel*, January 2008.

282 *Rock Sound*, October 2007.

283 *Metal Hammer*, December 2007.

284 *Metal Maniacs*, November/December 2007.

285 *Metal Hammer*, December 2007.

286 *The Quietus*, 31 October 2017.

287 Live review of Electric Wizard at the London Scala on 7 September 2009, Jim Martin, *Terrorizer*, October 2009.

288 Live review of Electric Wizard at the London Scala on 7 September 2009, Nick Ruskell, *Kerrang!*, 19 September 2009.

289 From the *Terrorizer* review of the gig at the Scala.

290 *Witchcult Today* album review by 'Damien', *Kerrang!*, 10 November 2007.

291 Live review of Electric Wizard's headline performance at the Rise Above twentieth anniversary show at ULU, Greg Moffitt, *Metal Hammer*, February 2009.

292 Lachman, op. cit., p.262.

293 Lachman, op. cit., p.271.

294 Lachman, op. cit., p.275.

295 *Metal Hammer*, December 2009.

296 Writing under his real name Kimi Kärki in an essay called 'Confessions of metal and folk: Remembering and Contextualizing the Creative Process', in the collection *Music, Memory, Memoir* (ed. Robert Edgar, Fraser Mann and Helen Pleasance), Bloomsbury Academic, 2019.

297 I read the Project Gutenberg version of the novel hosted on its own webpage: https://www.gutenberg.org/files/10002/10002-h/10002-h.htm

298 From Lovecraft's essay *Supernatural Horror in Literature*: www.hplovecraft.com/writings/texts/essays/shil.aspx

299 *The Quietus*, 20 January 2014.

300 Live review of the Wizard's ATP set on 8 May 2008, Olly Thomas, *Kerrang!*, 30 May 2009.

301 Live review round-up of Hellfest in Clisson, France, 19–21 June 2009, Nick Ruskell, *Kerrang!*, 4 July 2009.

302 Review of the Scala gig on 7 September 2009, John Doran, *Metal Hammer*, November 2009.

303 Scala gig review, Nick Ruskell, *Kerrang!*, 19 September 2009.

304 *The Quietus*, 19 November 2009.

305 *Metal Hammer*, December 2010.

306 *Decibel*, February 2011.

307 *Metal Hammer*, December 2010.

308 *The Satanic Rituals: Companion to The Satanic Bible*, Anton Szandor LaVey, Avon, 1972, p.17.

309 LaVey, op. cit., p.17.

310 *Decibel*, February 2011.

311 As quoted in the 2011 documentary *Last Days Here*.

312 *Decibel*, February 2011.

313 LaVey, op. cit., p.21.

314 LaVey, op. cit., pp.33–4.

315 LaVey, op. cit., p.34.

316 LaVey, op. cit., p.51.

317 Decibel, February 2011.

318 LaVey, op. cit., p.16.

319 *Metal Hammer*, December 2010.

320 *Vincebus Eruptum*, 2000.

321 If we designate heavy metal's date of birth as 13 February 1970, when the first Black Sabbath album was released (which I think we should).

322 *The Quietus*, 19 November 2009.

323 Also well known as *The Bare-Breasted Countess*, though I watched a version from the Wizard Video Collection with the eighties' VHS title of *Erotikill*.

324 'Doomsdays of our Lives', J. Bennett, *Decibel*, October 2014.

325 *Decibel*, February 2011.

326 *Black Masses* album review, John Doran in the *Sübterranea* section of *Metal Hammer*, December 2010.

327 *Black Masses* album review, Darren Sadler in *Rock Sound*, December 2010.

328 'The Cult Is Alive', James Minton, *Terrorizer*, December 2010.

329 *Decibel*, February 2011.

330 *Decibel*, February 2011.

331 *Decibel*, February 2011.

332 *Decibel*, October 2014.

333 LaVey, op. cit., p.19.

334 LaVey, op. cit., p.25.

335 LaVey, op. cit., p.220.

336 Live review of the London Forum gig, Toby Cook, *Metal Hammer*, June 2012.

337 John Moules interview, *It's Psychedelic Baby* magazine, 1 May 2015: www.psychedelicbabymag.com/2015/05/john-moules-interview.html

338 *Terrorizer*, October 2012.

339 *Say You Love Satan*, David St Clair, Corgi Books, 1990, p.138.

340 'Kids in the Dark', David Breskin, *Rolling Stone*, 22 November 1984: davidbreskin.com/magazines/3-features/kids-in-the-dark-2/

341 St Clair, op. cit., p.12.

342 St Clair, op. cit., p.14.

343 St Clair, op. cit., p.318.

344 'The Satanic Panic in the Missouri General Assembly': www.senate.mo.gov/LegislativeLibrary/Panic.html

345 *The Quietus*, 20 January 2014.

346 'Going To Hell: Electric Wizard's Liz Buckingham Interviewed', *The Quietus*, 7 October 2014: thequietus.com/articles/16409-liz-buckingham-interview-electric-wizard

347 *The Quietus*, 31 October 2017.

348 Information gleaned from the 2021 documentary *Other, Like Me: The Oral History of COUM Transmissions and Throbbing Gristle*.

349 'Electric Wizard Proudly Presents the Electric Grindhouse Cinema at Roadburn 2013', Lee Edwards, *The Sleeping Shaman*, 9 April 2013: www.thesleepingshaman.com/news/electric-wizard-proudly-presents-the-electric-grindhouse-cinema-at-roadburn-2013/

350 'Screen Bloody Murder!', *Terrorizer's Secret History of Doom Metal*, April 2012.

351 *The Quietus*, 31 October 2017.

352 *Terrorizer's Secret History of Doom Metal*, April 2012.

353 *Decibel*, October 2014.

354 *Decibel*, October 2014.

355 *The Quietus*, 20 January 2014.

356 *Decibel*, October 2014.

357 *Midwest Metal*, spring/summer 2001.

358 *The Quietus*, 7 October 2014.

359 'Hex, Drugs and Rock & Roll', Brad Angle, *Guitar World*, December 2014.

360 Breskin, *Rolling Stone*, 22 November 1984.

361 *The Quietus*, 7 October 2014.

362 *Guitar World*, December 2014.

363 *The Devil's Rider*, Alex R. Stuart, New English Library, 1975, p.45.

364 Stuart, op. cit., p.136.

365 Stuart, op. cit., p.24.

366 Stuart, op. cit., p.91.

367 St Clair, op. cit., p.97.

368 *Decibel*, October 2014.

369 'Electric Wizard A to Z', Harry Sword, *Vice*, 14 June 2014: www.vice.com/en/article/6w3896/electric-wizard-a-to-z-jus-oborn-interview

370 Shooting the Shit 666 podcast, 20 October 2020.

371 *Decibel*, October 2014.

372 *Decibel*, October 2014.

373 *Decibel*, October 2014.

374 *Decibel*, October 2014.

375 St Clair, op. cit., p.389.

376 'Electric Wizard interview', Jim Martin, *Iron Fist*, 4 November 2016: www.ironfistzine.com/2016/11/04/electric-wizard-

interview-ive-not-got-a-lot-of-admiration-for-people-that-weaken-and-dilute-metal/

377 *Decibel*, October 2014.

378 *Decibel*, October 2014.

379 *Time to Die* album review, Kim Kelly, *Pitchfork*, 1 October 2014: pitchfork.com/reviews/albums/19622-electric-wizard-time-to-die/

380 *Time to Die* album review, Joseph Rowan, *Drowned in Sound*, 30 September 2014: web.archive.org/web/20141003074412/ http://drownedinsound.com/releases/18446/reviews/4148291

381 'Electric Wizard: *Time to Die* review – immense hypnotic power', Dom Lawson, *Guardian*, 25 September 2014: www.theguardian.com/music/2014/sep/25/electric-wizard-time-to-die-review

382 *The Quietus*, 7 October 2014.

383 'Electric Wizard: *Time to Die* review – immense hypnotic power', Dom Lawson, *Guardian*, 25 September 2014: www.theguardian.com/music/2014/sep/25/electric-wizard-time-to-die-review

384 'Electric Wizard: "We had a fantasy we'd get busted for having satanic sex orgies"', Dom Lawson, *Guardian*, 2 June 2015: www.theguardian.com/music/2015/jun/02/electric-wizard-we-had-a-fantasy-wed-get-busted-for-having-satanic-sex-orgies

385 'Electric Wizard interview with Jus Oborn: 'Wizard Bloody Wizard', Klemen Breznikar, *It's Psychedelic Baby* magazine, 13 November 2017: www.psychedelicbabymag.com/2017/11/ electric-wizard-interview-with-jus.html

386 'Born Again', Dom Lawson, *Metal Hammer*, November 2017.

387 'Doomed For All Time', Jim Martin, *Iron Fist*, January 2018.

388 'Doom with a View', Nick Hasted, *Classic Rock*, February 2018.

389 *Classic Rock,* February 2018.

390 *Iron Fist*, January 2018.

391 *Metal Hammer*, November 2017.

392 *Iron Fist*, January 2018.

393 'In the Studio: Electric Wizard', *Metal Hammer*, October 2017.

394 *Metal Hammer*, November 2017.

395 *The Morning of the Magicians*, Louis Pauwels and Jacques Bergier, Destiny Books, 2009, p.xxvi.

396 Pauwels and Bergier, op. cit., p.385.

397 Pauwels and Bergier, op. cit., p.197.

398 Pauwels and Bergier, op. cit., pp.243–4.

399 Hardy, op. cit., p.34.

400 Pauwels and Bergier, op. cit., pp.210–13.

401 Pauwels and Bergier, op. cit., pp.218–19.

402 Pauwels and Bergier, op. cit., p.110.

403 'First nuclear detonation created "impossible" quasicrystals', Davide Castelvecchi, *Nature*, 17 May 2021: www.nature.com/articles/d41586-021-01332-0

404 *Wizard Bloody Wizard* album review, Toby Cook, *Metal Hammer*, November 2017.

405 'Spitting at Mortality with Jus Oborn', Michael Friedman Ph.D., *Psychology Today*, 23 July 2018: www.psychologytoday.com/gb/blog/brick-brick/201807/spitting-mortality-jus-oborn

406 'Alex and Maxine with band Black Widow', *Alexandrian Witchcraft*: alexandrianwitchcraft.org/alex-and-maxine-with-band-black-widow/

407 *The Shout and Other Stories*, Robert Graves, Penguin Books, 1978, p.12.

408 Graves, op. cit., p.12.

409 Graves, op. cit., p.17.

410 I came across this pithy term in Eugene Thacker's *In the Dust of this Planet: Horror of Philosophy Vol. 1*, Zero Books, 2011.

411 *The Quietus,* 31 January 2017.

412 www.hplovecraft.com/writings/texts/essays/shil.aspx

413 Hardy, op. cit., p.34.

414 *Iron Fist*, November 2016.

415 *Decibel*, February 2011.
416 Brackett, op. cit., p.77.
417 *Metal Hammer*, December 2007.
418 'Spitting at Mortality with Jus Oborn', Michael Friedman
   Ph.D., *Psychology Today*, 23 July 2018: www.psychologytoday.
   com/gb/blog/brick-brick/201807/spitting-mortality-jus-oborn

Selected works

𝔈𝔩𝔢𝔠𝔱𝔯𝔦𝔠 𝔚𝔦𝔷𝔞𝔯𝔡 discography

Electric Wizard (1994)

Demon Lung (split with Our Haunted Kingdom) (1996)

Come My Fanatics . . . (1997)

Chrono.Naut (on its own, then as a split with Orange Goblin)
     (1997)

Supercoven (1998)

Dopethrone (2000)

Let Us Prey (2002)

We Live (2004)

Witchcult Today (2007)

The House on the Borderland (split with Reverend Bizarre)
     (2008)

The Processean (2008)

Black Masses (2010)

Legalise Drugs & Murder (2012)

Time to Die (2014)

Wizard Bloody Wizard (2017)

Live Maryland Deathfest (2018)

L.S.D. (2021)

Selected listening

'6 Million Ways To Die', DJ Hype and Uncle 22 mixes (1993)

13, *Hollow* 7" (1993)

13, 'Whore' (split with Eyehategod) (1994)

13, 'Wither' (split with Grief) (1993)

13, 'Wrong' (split with Eyehategod) (1995)

Add N to (X), 'Revenge of the Black Regent' (1999)

Alice Cooper, *Love It to Death* (1971)

Amon Düül II, 'Apocalyptic Bore' (1973)

Aphex Twin, 'Come to Daddy' (1997)

The Beatles, 'Come Together' (1969)

Ludwig van Beethoven, *Moonlight Sonata* (1802)

Ludwig van Beethoven, *Symphony No. 9* (1824)

Black Flag, *My War* (1984)

Black Sabbath, *Black Sabbath* (1970)

Black Sabbath, *Master of Reality* (1971)

Black Sabbath, *Paranoid* (1970)

Black Sabbath, *Sabbath Bloody Sabbath* (1973)

Black Widow, 'Come to the Sabbat' (1970)

Blood Farmers, *Blood Farmers* (1995)

Blue Cheer, *Vincebus Eruptum* (1967)

Boogie Times Tribe, 'Dark Stranger' (1993)

Budgie, *Budgie* (1971)

Burning Witch, *Crippled Lucifer* (1999)

Carcass, *Reek Of Putrefaction* (1988)

Celtic Frost, *Morbid Tales* (1984)

Celtic Frost, *To Mega Therion* (1985)

Cough, *Still They Pray* (2016)

Cream, *Goodbye Cream* (1969)

Jason Crest, 'Black Mass' (1969)

Darkthrone, *Panzerfaust* (1995)

Darkthrone, *Transilvanian Hunger* (1994)

Dream Death, *Journey Into Mystery* (1987)

SELECTED WORKS

Emerson, Lake & Palmer, *Tarkus (1971)*

Enslaved, *Monumension* (2001)

Eternal, *Lucifer's Children* (1993)

Eyehategod, *Dopesick* (1996)

Eyehategod, *Take as Needed for Pain* (1994)

Force (pre-Iron Man), *Discography 1981-1984* (2017)

Fu Manchu, *In Search Of . . .* (1996)

Serge Gainsbourg, *Histoire de Melody Nelson* (1971)

Serge Gainsbourg and Jane Birkin, 'Je t'aime . . . moi non plus'
   (1969)

Gary Glitter, 'Satan's Daughter' (1975)

Goatsnake, *1* (1999)

Hangnail, *Ten Days Before Summer* (1999)

Hawkwind, *Sonic Attack* (1981)

Hawkwind, *Space Ritual* (1973)

Hellhammer, *Satanic Rites* (1983)

Jimi Hendrix, *Are You Experienced?* (1967)

Gustav Holst, 'Mars, the Bringer of War' (1914-17)

Iron Maiden, *The Number of the Beast* (1982)

Iron Monkey, *Iron Monkey* (1996)

Jerusalem, *Jerusalem* (1972)

Judas Priest, *Sin After Sin* (1977)

Judas Priest, *Stained Class* (1978)

Kasabian, *Empire* (2006)

King Crimson, *In the Court of the Crimson King* (1969)

Anton LaVey, *The Satanic Mass* (1968)

Led Zeppelin, *Led Zeppelin II* (1969)

Led Zeppelin, *The Song Remains the Same* (1976)

Loop, *Fade Out* (1988)

Lord of Putrefaction, *Wings Over a Black Funeral* (1990)

Macabre, *Dahmer* (2000)

Machine Head, *Burn My Eyes* (1994)

Mayhem, *Deathcrush* (1987)

Melvins, *Bullhead* (1991)

Napalm Death, *From Enslavement To Obliteration* (1988)

The Obsessed, *Lunar Womb* (1991)

The Obsessed, *The Obsessed* (1990)

Mike Oldfield, *Tubular Bells* (1973)

Pentagram, *Last Daze Here* (2001)

Pentagram, *Pentagram* (1985)

Pink Floyd, *Dark Side of the Moon* (1973)

Pink Floyd, *Meddle* (1971)

Pink Floyd, *Ummagumma* (1969)

Pod People, *Doom Saloon* (2001)

The Pretty Things, *S.F. Sorrow* (1968)

Putrefaction, *Necromantic* (1989)

Queens of the Stone Age, *Rated R* (2000)

Reverend Bizarre, *II: Crush The Insects* (2005)

Reverend Bizarre, *III: So Long Suckers* (2007)

Saint Vitus, *Born Too Late* (1986)

Saint Vitus, *Mournful Cries* (1988)

Satan's Satyrs, *Wild Beyond Belief!* (2013)

Sir Lord Baltimore, *Kingdom Come* (1970)

Slayer, *Reign in Blood* (1986)

Slayer, *Seasons in the Abyss* (1990)

Sleep, *Dopesmoker* (aka *Jerusalem*) (1999)

Solitude Aeternus, *Through the Darkest Hour* (1994)

Sons of OTIS, *Spacejumbofudge* (1996)

Sourvein, *Sourvein* (1999)

Sourvein, *Will To Mangle* (2002)

Sweet, *Sweet Fanny Adams* (1974)

T. Rex, 'Children of the Revolution' (1972)

Tyrannosaurus Rex, 'King of the Rumbling Spires' (1969)

The Stooges, *Fun House* (1970)

The Stooges, *Raw Power* (1973)

Thy Grief Eternal, *. . . on Blackened Wings* (1992)

Trouble, *Psalm 9* (1984)

Trouble, *The Skull* (1985)

Unearthly Trance, *Season of Seance, Science of Silence* (2003)

Van der Graaf Generator, 'Killer' (1970)

Various, *Drum and Bass Selection 1* (1994)

Venom, *At War with Satan* (1984)

Venom, *Possessed* (1985)

Warhorse, *As Heaven Turns to Ash . . .* (2001)

Warning, *The Strength to Dream* (1999)

The White Stripes, *Elephant* (2003)

The Who, *Quadrophenia* (1979)

Winter, *Into Darkness* (1990)

Selected reading

Codex Gigas aka *Devil's Bible* (thirteenth-century illuminated manuscript)

Form (magazine)

Key of Solomon (fourteenth/fifteenth-century grimoire)

Man, Myth & Magic (1970s magazine)

Witchcraft (1970s UK magazine)

Jillian Becker, *Hitler's Children* (1977)

Jacques Bergier and Louis Pauwels, *The Morning of the Magicians* (1960)

Robert Bloch, 'Spawn of the Dark One' (aka 'Sweet Sixteen') (1958)

Leigh Brackett, *The Long Tomorrow* (1955)

Edgar Rice Burroughs, *A Princess of Mars* (1912)

Arthur C. Clarke, *Childhood's End* (1953)

Arthur Conan Doyle, *The Hound of the Baskervilles* (1902)

Robert DeGrimston, *As It Is* (late 60s)

Steven Eisler, *The Alien World: The Complete Illustrated Guide* (1980)

Harvey Fenton and David Flint, *Ten Years of Terror: British Films of the 1970s* (2001)

J.F.C. Fuller, 'The Black Arts' (1921)

J.F.C. Fuller, *The Star in the West* (1907)

Gerald Gardner, *High Magic's Aid* (1949)

Gerald Gardner, *Witchcraft Today* (1954)

Robert Graves, 'The Shout' (1929)

Thomas Hardy, *Two on a Tower* (1882)

S.E. Hinton, *The Outsiders* (1967)

William Hope Hodgson, *The House on the Borderland* (1908)

Michel Houellebecq, *H. P. Lovecraft: Against the World, Against Life* (1991)

Robert E. Howard, 'The Mirrors of Tuzun Thune' (1929)

Robert E. Howard, 'Red Nails' (1936)

Robert E. Howard, 'A Witch Shall Be Born' (1934)

Gary Lachman, *Turn Off Your Mind* (2001)

Anton LaVey, *The Satanic Bible* (1969)

Anton LaVey, *The Satanic Rituals* (1972)

H.P. Lovecraft, 'The Dreams in the Witch House' (1933)

H.P. Lovecraft, 'The Dream-Quest of Unknown Kadath' (1943)

H.P. Lovecraft, 'The Dunwich Horror' (1929)

H.P. Lovecraft, 'The Haunter of the Dark' (1936)

H.P. Lovecraft, 'Nyarlathotep' (1920)

H.P. Lovecraft, 'The Outsider' (1926)

H.P. Lovecraft, 'The Shadow Out of Time' (1936)

H.P. Lovecraft, 'The Shadow Over Innsmouth' (1932)

H.P. Lovecraft, 'Supernatural Horror in Literature' (1927)

H.P. Lovecraft, 'The Whisperer in Darkness' (1931)

Arthur Machen, *The Great God Pan* (1894)

Arthur Machen, 'Novel of the White Powder' (1895)

David Mann and Ron Main, *Races, Chases and Crashes: A Complete Guide to Car Movies and Biker Flicks* (1994)

Carey Miller, *The World of the Unknown: Monsters* (1977)

C.L. Moore, 'Black God's Kiss' (1934)

C.L. Moore, 'Black God's Shadow' (1934)

SELECTED WORKS

C.L. Moore, 'Shambleau' (1933)

C.L. Moore, 'The Tree of Life' (1936)

Margaret Murray, *The Witch-Cult in Western Europe* (1921)

Lawrence Pazdar, M.D., *Michelle Remembers* (1980)

G.G. Pendarves, 'The Altar of Melek Taos' (1932)

Michael Pitt-Rivers, *Dorset: A Shell Guide* (1966)

Frank Reynolds, *Freewheelin Frank* (1967)

Leopold Ritter von Sacher-Masoch, *Venus In Furs* (Ger. *Venus im Pelz*) (1870)

David St. Clair, *Say You Love Satan* (1987)

Ed Sanders, *The Family* (1971)

W.G. Sebald, *The Rings of Saturn* (Ger. *Die Ringe des Saturn: Eine englische Wallfahrt*) (1995)

Alex R. Stuart, *The Devil's Rider* (1972)

Cathal Tohill and Pete Tombs, *Immoral Tales: Sex & Horror Cinema in Europe 1956–1984* (1995)

J.R.R. Tolkien, *The Hobbit* (1968 BBC dramatisation)

Alfred Watkins, *The Old Straight Track* (1925)

Robert Anton Wilson, *The Historical Illuminatus Chronicles* (1982-91)

Selected viewing

13 (aka *Eye of the Devil*), dir. J. Lee Thompson (1968)

All the Colours of the Dark (It. *Tutti i colori del buio*), dir. Sergio Martino (1972)

The Amityville Horror, dir. Stuart Rosenberg (1979)

Bad News Tour (*The Comic Strip Presents* . . . series), dir. Sandy Johnson (1983)

Beneath the Planet of the Apes, dir. Ted Post (1970)

The Blair Witch Project, dir. Daniel Myrick and Eduardo Sánchez (1999)

The Blood on Satan's Claw, dir. Piers Haggard (1971)

Bloodsucking Freaks, dir. Joel M. Reed (1976)

Caligula, dir. Tinto Brass, Giancarlo Lui, Bob Guccione (1979)

Cannibal Ferox (aka *Make Them Die Slowly*), dir. Umberto Lenzi (1981)

A Clockwork Orange, dir. Stanley Kubrick (1971)

Conan the Barbarian, dir. John Milius (1982)

The Defiance of Good, dir. Armand Weston (1975)

Deviation, dir. José Ramón Larraz Gil (1971)

Devil's Angels, dir. Daniel Haller (1967)

The Devil Rides Out (aka *The Devil's Bride*), dir. Terence Fisher (1968)

The Devil Worshippers (*20/20* series, prod. Peter W. Kunhardt and Kenneth Wooden) (1985)

Dracula, dir. Terence Fisher (1958)

Dracula A.D. 1972, dir. Alan Gibson (1972)

The Dunwich Horror, dir. Daniel Haller (1970)

The Erotic Rites of Frankenstein (Fr. *La Malediction de Frankenstein*), dir. Jess Franco (1973)

Female Vampire (aka *The Bare-Breasted Countess*), dir. Jess Franco (1973)

Flash Gordon, dir. Mike Hodges (1980)

The Great Rock 'n' Roll Swindle, dir. Julien Temple (1980)

Gummo, dir. Harmony Korine (1997)

The Hells Angels Take a Mini-Break (aka *Hells Angels London*, BBC documentary) (1973)

Hells Chosen Few, dir. David L. Hewitt (1968)

The Hills Have Eyes, dir. Wes Craven (1977)

Hooked, dir. Lasse Braun (1974)

Horror Hospital, dir. Anthony Balch (1973)

House of Whipcord, dir. Pete Walker (1974)

Janie, dir. Jack Bravman, Michael Findlay, Roberta Findlay (1970)

Last Days Here, dir. Sean Pelletier (2011)

Last House on Dead End Street (aka *The Fun House, The*

Cuckoo Clocks of Hell), dir. Roger Watkins (1977)

The Last House on the Left, dir. Wes Craven (1972)

The Last Temptation of Christ, dir. Martin Scorsese (1988)

Legend of the Witches, dir. Malcolm Leigh (1970)

The Living Dead at the Manchester Morgue (aka *Let Sleeping Corpses Lie*), dir. Jorge Grau (1974)

Lucifer's Satanic Daughter, dir. Chandler Thistle (2021)

Mad Max 2, dir. George Miller (1981)

Mark of The Devil, (Ger. *Hexen bis aufs Blut gequält*), dir. Michael Armstrong (1970)

Northville Cemetery Massacre, dir. William Dear and Thomas L. Dyke (1976)

The Nude Vampire, dir. Jean Rollin (1970)

The Outcasts (BBC *40 Minutes* series), prod. Andy Murrow (1985)

The Outsiders, dir. Francis Ford Coppola (1983)

Pink Flamingos, dir. John Waters (1972)

Pink Floyd: Live at Pompeii, dir. Adrian Maben (1972)

The Power of the Witch (BBC documentary, prod. Oliver Hunkin) (1971)

The Producers, dir. Mel Brooks (1967)

Profondo Rosso, dir. Dario Argento (1975)

Psychomania, dir. Don Sharp (1973)

Robert Fripp: New York – Wimborne (BBC *Late Night in Concert* series, prod. Iain Softley) (1985)

Requiem for a Vampire, dir. Jean Rollin (1971)

The Sadist of Notre Dame, dir. Jess Franco (1979)

The Satanic Rites of Dracula, dir. Alan Gibson (1973)

Shiver of the Vampires (Fr. *Frisson Des Vampires*), dir. Jean Rollin (1971)

The Shout, dir. Jerzy Skolimowski (1978)

Simon, King of the Witches, dir. Bruce Kessler (1971)

The Sinful Dwarf, dir. Vidal Raski (1973)

Take an Easy Ride, dir. Kenneth Rowles (1976)

The Texas Chainsaw Massacre, dir. Tobe Hooper (1974)

'To Kill a Mocking Alan' (*I'm Alan Partridge* series), dir. Dominic
  Brigstocke (1997)

Tombs of the Blind Dead, dir. Amando de Ossorio (1972)

A Town Called Bastard (aka *A Town Called Hell*), dir. Robert
  Parrish (1971)

Vampyres, dir. José Ramón Larraz Gil (1975)

Vampyros Lesbos, dir. Jess Franco (1971)

Venus In Furs, dir. Jess Franco (1969)

The Vikings, dir. Lasse Braun (1971)

Wake in Fright, dir. Ted Kotcheff (1971)

The Warriors, dir. Walter Hill (1979)

Werewolves On Wheels, dir. Michel Levesque (1971)

Witchfinder General, dir. Michael Reeves (1968)

Zombie Flesh Eaters, dir. Lucio Fulci (1979)

Zero Hour: Massacre at Columbine High, dir. David Hickman
  (2004)

Acknowledgements

Without whom: Jus Oborn and Liz Buckingham, Mark Lewis, Jake Gill, Lee Brackstone and all at White Rabbit, Matthew Hamilton, Luke Bird, Audrey, Axel and Bea.

Picture credits

Credits

White Rabbit would like to thank everyone at Orion who worked on the publication of *Come My Fanatics*.

Editor
Lee Brackstone

Copy-editor
Lucian Randall

Proofreader
Paul Baillie-Lane

Editorial Management
Georgia Goodall
Frances Rooney
Alice Graham
Jane Hughes
Claire Boyle

Audio
Paul Stark
Jake Alderson
Georgina Cutler

Contracts
Dan Herron
Ellie Bowker
Alyx Hurst

Design
Nick Shah
Steve Marking
Joanna Ridley
Helen Ewing

Finance
Nick Gibson
Jasdip Nandra
Sue Baker
Tom Costello

Inventory
Jo Jacobs
Dan Stevens

Production
Sarah Cook
Katie Horrocks

Marketing
Tom Noble

Publicity
Jenna Petts

Sales
Jen Wilson
Victoria Laws
Esther Waters
Group Sales teams across Digital, Field, International and Non-Trade

Operations
Group Sales Operations team

Rights
Rebecca Folland
Alice Cottrell
Ruth Blakemore
Ayesha Kinley
Marie Henckel

Index

INDEX

INDEX

351

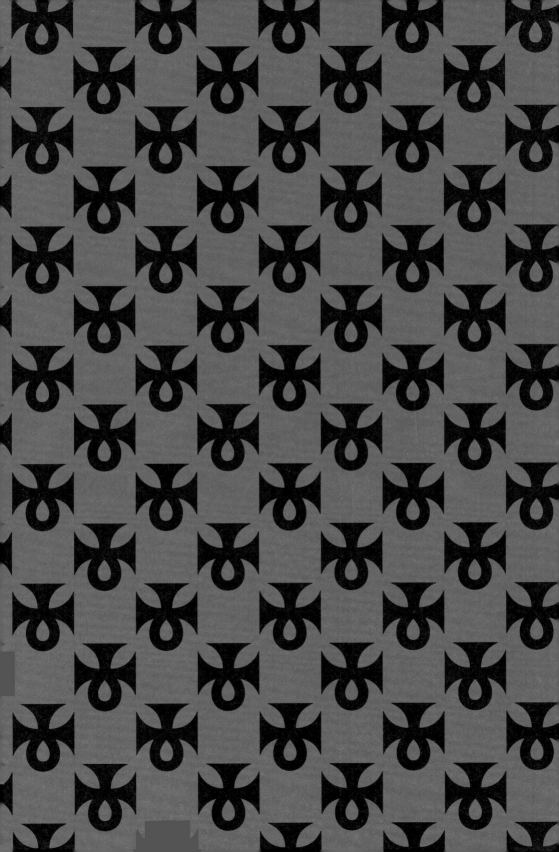